Queen Anne Boleyn's Great Escape and Legacy

Queen Anne Boleyn's
Great Escape and Legacy

Copyright © 2024 Joseph Gregory Hallett
All Rights Reserved.

ISBN 978-989-35519-0-5
Second Edition

A FREEDOM MASTERS BOOK
published by

FREEDOM MASTERS
—PUBLISHING HOUSE—

FREEDOM MASTERS PUBLISHING HOUSE
Estr. do Castelo, 230H
Sesmarias, Albufeira
Portugal 8200-385

Queen Anne Boleyn's Great Escape and Legacy

Joseph Gregory Hallett

ISBN 978-989-35519-0-5

ISBN 978-989-35519-0-5

9 789893 551905

British Frauds on England's History ~ Series

Introduction

Anne Boleyn returned from the Royal Courts in France and the Netherlands to England in January 1522 as the representative of the Holy Grael lineage. Her goal was to remove the Catholic Church out of England, reclaim all the lands the Catholic Church held in England, which was 16~60% of England, commanding 40% of the rents, and to print a complete Christian Bible in English, which at the time was a heresy.

Anne Boleyn became a lady-in-waiting to Henry VIII's wife, Catherine of Aragon, and in 1525 attracted the attention of Henry, who took her on board as his advisor & muse, always by his side from 1527. Foreign ambassadors recognised they had to go through Anne Boleyn to get anything approved. Anne then advised King Henry VIII, who gladly took almost all her advice.

On 1 September 1532, Henry VIII made Anne Boleyn Marquesse of Pembroke. She received £1,000+ of land, mainly in Wales, being £15 million of land in 2024, was housed in Durham Palace on the Thames, and now one of the top six Aristocrats in England.

Henry VIII secretly married Anne Boleyn in St Paul's Cathedral Church on 16 November 1532, not the 14th. 70 days later on 25 January 1533, Henry VIII formally married Anne Boleyn for a second time, making her Queen consort Anne Boleyn.

124 days later, Queen consort Anne Boleyn began her own 4-day Coronation ceremony and became Queen Anne Boleyn of England, Queen in her own right, whether or not she was married or divorced, or her husband went mad or died.

The marriage was happy and productive. The two of them, Henry VIII and Queen Anne Boleyn, were the biggest religious reformers in the history of the late Middle Ages, effectively forming the 'early modern period'.

They created the Religious Reformation 1529–37 and Dissolution of the Monasteries 1535–41, resulting in the biggest land grab in history – completely justified. Henry & Anne took back 16~60% of England, and are England's primary national heroes forever.

Queen Anne Boleyn of England then gave birth to the future Queen Elizabeth who had a Baptism by Fire, attended by Henry VIII's relatives and friends, who received half of the land grab, were witnesses at Henry VIII & Anne Boleyn's wedding, Anne Boleyn's own Coronation as Queen in her own right, and witness to Henry being knocked off his jousting horse on 24 January 1536. This opened an old wound, festered, and drove Henry VIII mad.

King Henry VIII purportedly took this out on his wives, but there was a greater game at play. Henry VIII got an annulment from his marriage to Anne Boleyn, but it was under the name "Anne Bulleyn, Marquis of Penbroke", and designed to be invalid.

Henry VIII was actually divorcing the Bulleyn chapel in France, 3 miles south of Calais, and Anne's title Marquesse of Pembroke remained intact, with her, able to be passed down a legitimate or illegitimate line, preferably to any male fulfilling the prophecy, and identifying himself, which included The Principal writing this.

Henry VIII's madness was acknowledged by the commissioners, who all tried Queen Anne Boleyn, Marquesse of Pembroke for incest & adultery, but no evidence was ever presented, other than obsequious and dubious hearsay.

The Crown and Aristocrats now owned 94% of England, known as "The Island", and the Trial Commissioners had just received 4,000 square miles of land.

Henry VIII had just paid the biggest bribes in history to ensure that Anne Boleyn, Marquesse of Pembroke, and Queen of England in her own right, would be found 'Guilty' and 'Executed', but these were both faked, and Queen Anne Boleyn was set up on the Commissioners vast estates to breed the Holy Grael lineage, who would become the true King of England.

Queen Anne Boleyn's male descendant was to hold the title 'Christ' which automatically made him the King of England, and the true King of England ... whereas "Britain" is Jesuit.

Since Henry VIII never divorced Anne Boleyn, nor stripped her of any titles, Henry VIII's subsequent four marriages were all null & void, as though they never existed.

Margaret, Countess Salisbury organised Queen Anne Boleyn's escape from execution, using the Hereditary Grand Almoner, 1st Marquess of Exeter ~ 'Exit-Her', and the King's Almoner, the Bishop of Hereford, both in their 30s. The Keeper of the Privy Purse was executed 2 days earlier, so the Almoners could fund the execution however they wanted.

Queen Anne Boleyn's execution was faked in several dozen ways, with 450 paid crisis actors without uniforms milling in front of an almost non-existent crowd to ensure no one saw the execution, whose location has never been identified, until now.

The execution was timed for sun-strike and the entire crowd looked directly east into the morning sun, with Anne Boleyn in total silhouette, her long hair bunched up into an oversized coif, such that it looked like a head, and could pass as such.

With the haircut complete, Queen Anne Boleyn lay in the straw trying not to sneeze, then helped carry her own headless body-double to St Peter ad Vincula where they buried it 2-foot deep, without a head, then returned to Anne Boleyn's Coronation & Execution lodgings adjacent to the White Tower ... and waited for 12 hours.

What a fidget!

Sunset came at 8 p.m., then at 10 p.m. under Astronomical Twilight, they left the Tower of London through Traitor's Gate to navigate without lights up the River Thames, past Windsor Castle to the River Isis, horse-drawn another 14 miles arriving for lunch the next day at Bisham Abbey, home of the Countess of Salisbury, where the new & free Queen Anne Boleyn spoke the confirmation phrase that the mission was a complete success:

"The most happy.
We all at one."

From 1 p.m. Saturday 20 May 1536, the Holy Grael lineage superseded the Merovingian Conspiracy.

The Blood Royal Sangrëal was no longer hidden inside the Catholic Church.

This was a Royal and Religious coup that would reign down the centuries into the present present.

Contents

Chapter One
The Imitation of Christ versus the Jesuits

In Christian theology, "the imitation of Christ" is the practice of following the example of Jesus.[1] The early Church had little interest in the historical Jesus and this prevented ... literal imitation ... Instead ... focused on ... self-sacrifice and martyrdom. Eastern Christianity uses the term "Life in Christ".

~325 A.D., 25 July~early August: The Council of Nicaea was a homosexual holiday camp 60 miles outside Constantinople on Lake Nicaea, with the Emperor Constantine covering all travel expenses and lodgings, such that 318 bishops turned up, most with 2 priests, 3 deacons and some acolytes.

"The bishops promulgated into Canon Law:

i.   The See of Jerusalem retained its own honorary rights, so Jews were acknowledged, but there were no Jews in Jerusalem. They were banished in A.D.135, for over 190 years to 325+;

ii.   Alexandria, Rome, and Antioch retained their own ancient customs, which included Polytheism, Paganism, and No Religion. So Rome remained Pagan;

iii.   No kneeling on Sundays;

iv.   No followers of Paul can do a valid Baptism. Today this means no Catholic Baptisms;

v.   Clergy were not to pay interest, nor charge interest. Clergy were interest free and took forever to pay;

vi.   No pretty women were allowed in the Cleric's house – 'virgines subintroductae'. Only pretty boys and ugly or old women were allowed in the Clergy's house;

vii.   Clergy were no longer allowed to castrate themselves; but this didn't stop other Clergy from cutting each other's balls off. The Clergy were even stranger then;

viii.   Priests could not be removed, no matter what they did. The Council of Nicaea was protecting paedophile protagonist way back then, as a foundation of church doctrine."

The useful part of Christianity is the Prophecy hidden inside the religion & Constantine's goal was to protect this. This Prophecy is deciphered by Typology Theology ("TT") – what today's Christians seem best at ignoring, but TT is Christianity's oldest science.

Typology Theology is the science of 'what is recorded in the Bible is due to happen again in some other place at some future time', and all the necessary signs will appear.

Every time a new solution is found in Christianity, it exposed an ancient custom or honorary right, and threatens the position of the Church, which seems to have been maintained as a self-emasculating, self-castrating progression protecting paedophile protagonists from as soon as Emperor Constantine left the building on 25 July 325."

~325 A.D.: The Clergy agreed that none of them were in a decided state about any aspect of Jesus' life, and considered there were Two Jesus, but got their names wrong, but added to the King James 1611/13 Bible: 2 Corinthians 11:4:

> For if he comes preaching another Jesus, whom we have not preached ... or another gospel, which ye have not accepted, ye might well bear with him.

Roman Catholicism rendered Christianity almost completely lost.

~410 A.D.: When the Romans left England & Europe, Christianity took a turn for the worse, and "The imitation of Christ" came into play, and variously meant:

410–30: St Augustine of Hippo preached the imitation of Christ was the ultimate goal of conversion, and the fundamental purpose of Christian life.

~600: Baptism is joining Jesus at the moment of his death. Romans 6:3–5, 6:7 ... so many of us as were baptised into Jesus Christ were baptised into his death? Therefore we are buried with him by baptism into death ... planted together in the likeness of his death ...

Baptism is killing the Christ consciousness in the baby, while trying to resurrect Jesus' physical body. Baptism is part of the Roman Catholic cult of raising the dead, with each Catholic baby as a sacrifice. Roman Catholic Baptism is necromancy, a mixture of voodoo and zombiism, but is ecumenically called 'the doctrine of resurrection'.

895, May: Council of Tribur decided that:

i. Baptism by triple immersion imitates Jesus 3 days in a tomb (actually 31 hours);

ii. Rising from the water imitates Jesus' Resurrection;

iii. Denial of the flesh favours the soul ... as preached in monastic communities;

iv. Rebuffing the physical body imitates Christ's sufferings; and

v. Rebuffing the physical body imitates Christ's spiritual achievement.

1115–53: St Bernard of Clairvaux considered the imitation of Christ to be love & humility; and the Father sent his Son to deliver the Spirit to the Church, and those who serve the Church humbly obtain union with God ... albeit 'Give me all your money'.

1200–26: Saint Francis of Assisi believed in:

i. The physical & spiritual imitation of Christ, and

ii. Advocated a path of poverty; and

iii. Preaching poverty in imitation of Jesus who was poor at birth in the manger and died naked on the cross.

iv. Francis said the Virgin Mary's poverty was a noble imitation of Christ.

v. Francis of Assisi highly valued this imitation of Christ, via poverty; and

vi. Francis of Assisi was the first to report stigmata ~ on himself; but

vii. Stigmata was a sickness of hysteria, dissociative identity disorder, ritualistic, obsessive–compulsive disorder, self-mutilation, self-starvation (anorexia nervosa) and epilepsy ~ so it had many followers amongst the Christians;

viii. Who were without humour.

1220: Christmas: St Francis of Assissi invented the first Nativity scene or Crèche, at Greccio, 44 miles south of Assisi, and first used only straw in a feeding trough, or 'Manger', with a live ox and live donkey on either side. The straw-filled Manger acted as the Altar for Christmas Mass.

Francis of Assisi was then followed by mendicant friars who wandered around in groups being poor, and preaching, and being martyrs where required. This included:

1209: Grey Friars ~ Franciscans ~ Order of Friars Minor ~ Capuchins;

1215: Black Friars ~ Dominicans ~ Order of Preachers;

1244–56: Groups of hermits who accepted the Augustinian rule ~ Hermits of St. Augustine ~ Austin Friars ~ Augustinian Recollects ~ Discalced Augustinians;

1206/14: White Friars ~ hermits on Mount Carmel & Crusader states migrating to Western Europe *c.*1238 ~ Carmelites ~ Brothers of the Blessed Virgin Mary of Carmel;

1400s: Third Order Regular of St. Francis; and

1593: Discalced Carmelites. Monty Python got it right with crack martyr suicide squads.

1256–74: Saint Thomas Aquinas was the first to advocate the perfection of Christ:

   i.   "Baptism was the first step towards the imitation of a perfect Christ,"[2] and the

   ii.   'Imitation of Christ is essential to Religious perfection';[3]

   iii.   "Perfection of the spiritual life" as an imitation of Christ.[4]

   iv.   It was uncertain whether it was baptism by bathing the feet, baptism by fire, baptism with water on the head, or baptism by dunking the head; and

   v.   Baptism was first reported ~A.D. 600; and

   vi.   Back stories of Baptism were invented for the printing press.

1360–92: Eastern Byzantine theologian Nicholas Cabasilas' 'The Life in Christ' advocated:

i.   "Living one's own personal life" in Christ is a fundamental Christian virtue;[5]

ii.   "Union with Christ is effected by the three great mysteries ... Baptism, Chrismation (Confirmation) and Eucharist; and

iii.   The Eucharist, Holy Communion or Lord's Supper forms the new life in Christ[6] by eating Jesus' flesh & drinking Jesus' blood while thinking of him.

"According to the New Testament, the rite was instituted by Jesus Christ during the Last Supper; giving his disciples bread and wine during a Passover meal, he commanded them to 'do this in memory of me' while referring to the bread as 'my body' and the cup of wine as 'the new covenant in my blood'."[7]

However this is extremely unlikely, and more likely another back-dated back-story as the Roman Catholic Priest, Clergy, Bishops, Cardinals and Popes in Rome continued to practise Paganism, and needed to include aspects of their death cult into 'Roman Catholicism', which they incorrectly claimed was 'Christianity'.

The two are at the opposite ends of the spectrum of religious practise ... Christianity is a warming agricultural life cult, and Roman Catholicism is a cold marble slab death cult.

In the Council of Nicaea, 25 July~early August 325, 'Bishops promulgated into Canon Law that Rome retained their own ancient customs, which included Paganism'.

1418–27: Thomas à Kempis was a prolific copyist and copied the Bible four (4) times. Thomas à Kempis then wrote four booklets. The first chapter was called 'The Imitation of Christ'. All 4 booklets were later renamed 'The Imitation of Christ' and instructed one on how to imitate Christ.[8]

1418—71: For Kempis the 'imitation of Christ' emphasised:

i.   Withdrawing from the world;

ii.   Focussing on an interior life;[9] but

iii. Not an active imitation of Christ; with

iv.   No outward preaching; and

v.   No friars; so

vi.   An introspective passive aggressive obsessive compulsive, silent culture;

vii. With no deeds done; and

viii. Nothing to show for it ...

ix.   Is considered 'Grace' in Christianity.

x.   Devotion to the Eucharist as a key element of spiritual life;[10]

xi.   But the Eucharist is Ritualistic Cannibalism & total Paganism; and yet

xii. 'The Imitation of Christ' became the most widely read Christian devotional book after the Bible;[11]

xiii. Because it was Pagan Roman Catholicism, and not Christianity at all.

1500–1700: The Imitatio Christi was translated into 13 languages and paraphrased into English in 3 different ways. Book IV was first translated by Lady Margaret Beaufort, Henry VII's Roman Catholic mother, Henry VIII's grandmother.[12]

1507–46: Martin Luther connected Baptism and Imitation,[13] but called it "Conformation", seeing the 'imitation of Christ' as an attempt to conceal a doctrine on the "works of Christ"[14], but this is just circumlocution obfuscation language no one understands.

1530–64: For John Calvin (1509–64) the 'imitation of Christ' was:

  i.   A "Mystical union" with Christ;

  ii.   That resonates with the New Testament.[15]

  iii. The New Testament claimed to drop sacrifice, but continued with stone sacrificial altar tables.

  iv.   All stone tables need to be removed from every chapel, church, abbey and cathedral in order to remove the Roman Catholic cold marble slab death cult paganism out of Christianity.

1539–56: Ignatius of Loyola (1491–1556) then advocated:

  i.   The 'imitation of Christ' is any sense of "being with Christ"; and

  ii.   Experiencing his humanity; which was

  iii. Experiencing Jesus as a man experiencing pain; and

  iv.   Ignatius of Loyola's 'Spiritual Exercises' required one to imagine being at the foot of the Cross, communing with Jesus while he was dying on the Cross at Calvary.[16]

Today: The "Imitation of Christ" translates as:

  i.   Long slow walks along the beach

  ii.   Watching sunsets; and

  iii. Low blood pressure people realising there is not much reality to their lives; &

  iv.   They might as well sublimate with excuses; and

v.   Excuses became the backbone of Religion;

vi.   Along with sharing abnormalities, social dysfunction as normal, and neurosis;

vii.   Accepted in Christ, but not anywhere else.

viii.   Faith walks alone.

Where is the shared enlightenment to live a life worth living that others want to emulate?

"The father, son and the holy ghost" is not a functioning unit. It is a functioning unit of a paedophile and his target boy, with the holy ghost as excuses, never-ending, all pervasive, plucked out of thin air, ad infinitum.

Jesuits call this "The special education of boys".

The Jesuits were founded by Ignatius of Loyola ~1540 as the militant arm of the pagan cold marble slab death cult called Roman Catholicism of the pagan Roman Catholic Church.

The father, son and mother Mary, or any other name, is a functioning unit, so when Catholic and Christian paedophilia got exposed, Catholicism and Christianity began advertising the family was the basis of Christianity ~ but Jesuits nibbled and tore at the family, priests blessed sons sent to war to die for profit, then stole the widow's equity.

1836/62: Queen Victoria's Ghost Club Society attempted to establish the life of Jesus. Various people had stabs at it, through:

i.   Mediumship;

ii.   Trance;

iii.   Past life regression; and

iv.   Vague writing with vague results; and

v.   Little useful information; and

vi. Any good information heavily obfuscated & suppressed;

vi. But Queen Victoria's Ghost Club Society did evolve into MI5 & MI6.

The Life of Jesus was only established in some concrete form at the End Times–New Age changeover on 16 August 2014, when 'The Hidden King of England – Arma Christi – Unveiling the Rose', volumes IV & V were published as 'Jesus of England' and 'Jesus of the Algarve', by The Principal.

The Jesuit Charles, Prince of Wales got hold of these, realised the implication of true kingship against him, and reigned sickness on the publisher and author at the same time, albeit 550 miles apart in England and the Black Forest in Germany.

The publisher was thus executed to the hour of Coronation, on Coronation Day 2018, 65 years after Elizabeth was 'crowned', but it was the Jesuit 'Silent Weapons for Quiet Wars' ("SW4QW") that was Crowned ~ not Elizabeth.

This is why it is simply called "Coronation Day".

'Silent Weapons for Quiet Wars' major coadjutor[17] was Prince Philip, whose son was Prince Charles ... and leading up to Charles' 70th birthday on 14 November 2018, 25,566 people died in the Paradise, Helltown & Deadwood Fires, celebrating Charles was 25,566 days old.

What an amazing coincidence ... enough correlation to act as a source identifier.

This is enough to poke the finger at intent, as confirmed by ...
Prince Charles celebrated his destruction of Paradise in the Royal Palladium. Charles commissioned Rowan Atkinson as MC 'Toby the Devil', who first told his audience:

Charles, Duke of Cornwall in 2019 ... and Charles, Prince of Wales in 2021 ... are two different people, both body-doubles, and neither are Prince Charles.

"Right, all those who like
'The Life of Brian' can go to hell".

In this, once again historically accurate, 1979 Monty Python movie, when Jesus or Brian is getting swamped in his mother's lounge, a woman tugs on his sidon (tunic) and says: not "Jesus", not "Brian", but "Greg".

"Morning Saviour" ... "Lay your hands on me Greg" ... "Now don't jostle the Chosen One, please ... Don't push that baby in the Saviour's face ... Are you letting us have the Mount on Sunday".

"No".

Charles, Prince of Wales had already rearranged the Chairperson and Secretary-General of the Commonwealth so they would both be UK-based, on condition both Theresa May & Baroness Scotland pre-named Charles as next Head of the Commonwealth ... but it's been the 'Commonwealth of Nations' since 1 July 1959, so like Charles, there's really no point to it, but still Prince Charles wanted to be the 'Head of No Point'.

For his crimes, Charles has been replaced with body-doubles. Charles, Prince of Wales, and Charles, Duke of Cornwall became two completely different people ... both body-doubles ... and neither are Charles.

After the Paradise, Helltown and Deadwood Fires leading up to Charles' 70th birthday, it is impossible to find a picture of the real Prince Charles ....

The burning of Paradise was a Roman Catholic Jesuit sacrifice to compromise & prep Prince Charles as a mass-murderer on his 70th.

Endnotes

1   1661, 2000: Gerald O'Collins, Edward G. Farrugia, 'A Concise Dictionary of Theology', p. 115; 2007: Richard A. Burridge, 'Imitating Jesus: inclusive approach to New Testament ethics', pp. 142–45; 2004: Jestice, Holy People of the World: a Cross-Cultural Encyclopedia, Vol. 3, pp. 393–94.

1983: Alan Richardson & John Bowden, The Westminster Dictionary of Christian Theology, pp. 285–86.

2020: Addendum Eight in support of Joseph Gregory Hallett declares the Mashiach–Christ–Messiah is the King of England, Christ confirms his Birthplace by marking the next Birthplace, p. 33, from the 2020, 26 January: Statement of Claim in support of Joseph Gregory Hallett declares the Mashiach–Christ–Messiah is the King of England OTH / 20 / 57374;
2020, 5 March: Confirmation of Joseph Gregory Hallett's Declaration of Mashiach–Christ–Messiah is the King of England OTH / 20 / 64535;
2020, 31 March: Certified Declaration Joseph Gregory Hallett is the Mashiach–Christ–Messiah & King of England OTH / 20 / 70911 & OTH / 20 / 70915 (SRA3). All has been accepted by Queen Elizabeth II, the Royal family, the Archbishop of Canterbury, the Prime Minister, the head of Freemasonry, and Pope Francis.

2004: David C. Alexander, 'Augustine's Early Theology of the Church; Emergence and Implications', p. 218;
204: Patrick Riley, 'Character and Conversion in Autobiography: Augustine, Montaigne, Descartes, Rousseau, and Sartre', p. 43.

2020: Addendum Twelve in support of Joseph Gregory Hallett declares the Mashiach–Christ–Messiah is the King of England Definitions from the Bible, p. 69.

2004: Margaret Ruth Miles, The Word made Flesh: A History of Christian Thought, pp. 160–61.

1999: Michael Robson, St Francis of Assisi: The Legend & the Life, p. 104.

1867: Cardinal Manning, Bonaventure, 'The Life of St. Francis of Assisi', 'Legenda Sancti Francisci', p. 178; 1988 edition, TAN Books & Publ., Rockford, Illinois; 1220: Jacques de Vitry, Letter 6 Feb. or March; c.1223–25: Historia Orientalis cap. XXII; 1228: Tommaso da Celano, Vita prima, §57. 2009:Relevant passages quoted in English translation of Tolan, pp. 19, 54.

2   2004: Phyllis G. Jestice, Holy People of the World, Vol. 3, pp. 393–94.

3   Summa Theologica 2.2.186.5.

4   Summa Theologica 3.65.2.

5   2004: Phyllis G. Jestice, 'Holy People of the World', Vol. 3, pp. 393–94.

6   1997: Nicolaus Cabasilas, 'The life in Christ', 'Περὶ τῆς ἐν Χριστῷ ζωῆς', p. 129.

7   1937: Eucharist, wikipedia, citing Luke 22:20; "Encyclopædia Britannica, "Eucharist"; Ignazio Silone, 'Bread and Wine', novel.

8   2004: Phyllis G. Jestice, Holy People of the World, Vol. 3, pp. 393–94;

9   2007: Orlando O. Espín, James B. Nickoloff, An Introductory Dictionary of Theology and Religious Studies, p. 609.

10   2007: Espín & Nickoloff, An Introductory Dictionary of Theology and Religious Studies, p. 609.

11   Catholic encyclopedia: "Imitation of Christ".

12   1975: David Crane, "English Translations of the Imitatio Christi in the Sixteenth and Seventeenth Centuries", Recusant History, 13 (2), pp. 79–100.

13   2004: Phyllis G. Jestice, 'Holy People of the World', Vol. 3, pp. 393–94;
     Alan Richardson & John Bowden, The Westminster Dictionary of Christian Theology, pp. 285–86.

14   2004: Phyllis G. Jestice, Holy People of the World, Vol. 3, pp. 393–94;
     1983: Richardson & Bowden, The Westminster Dictionary of Christian Theology, pp. 285–86.

15   1983: Alan Richardson & John Bowden, The Westminster Dictionary of Christian Theology, pp. 285–86.

16   1999: Alister E. McGrath, 'Christian Spirituality, an Introduction', pp. 84–87; Jestice, 'Holy People'.

17   "Coadjutor" sidles up to their target, advises them, then takes over their role in all but title.

Chapter Two – Henry VIII's grandmother, Lady Margaret Beaufort imitates Christ and dies dramatically in the Westminster Abbey Deanery

Lady Margaret Beaufort (1443–1509) was the first English translator of the 'Imitation of Christ', but really ... the earliest printed translation of the 'Imitatio Christi: Of the imitation of Christ', Books I–III were by William Atkynson, and Book IV was under the name of Lady Margaret, Countess of Richmond and Derby, mother of King Henry VII, held in the British Museum.

John K. Ingram & William Atkinson are also credited with 'Imitatio Christi: Of the imitation of Christ', and Margaret Beaufort is just as likely to have been a keen Executive Producer, funding it to gain an historical translation credit.[1]

Lady Margaret Beaufort was a great-great-granddaughter of King Edward III (R. 1327–77), mother of Henry VII (R. 1485–1509) and grandmother to Henry VIII (R. 1509–47). Margaret was a devout Roman Catholic, put Henry VII on the throne, founded Christ's College Cambridge in 1505, St John's College Cambridge in 1511, and 'Lady Margaret Hall' was named after her, becoming the first Oxford college to admit women.

William Caxton (1422–91) was succeeded by Wynkyn de Worde. The heavily Roman Catholic Lady Margaret Beaufort was Word's biggest patron, who was variously known as: Wynkyn de Word ~ Wijnkijn de Worde ~ Winandus van Worden ~ Wynand de Worde ~ John Wynkyn ~ Johannes Wynkyn ~ Jan Wynkyn ~ Jan van Wynkyn ~ John Wynand ~ Willelmo Wynkyn ~ William Wynkyn ~ William Wynand ~ John Wynkyn & Mr. Wylkyns, having at least 15 aliases, each heard as "Winking Word", as in a 'Wink and a Nod'.

---

[1] 'De Imitatione Christi' is held in Trinity college library, Dublin & University library, Cambridge. It was also printed by Appleton in New York, 1844; and the Early English text society in London in 1893.

Henry VIII's grandmother Margaret Beaufort was married four (4) times, gave birth at 13, and was widowed twice.

William de la Pole, 1st Duke of Suffolk, KG (1396–1450) Jackanapes was Earl of Suffolk, elevated to Marquess of Suffolk in 1444, and Duke of Suffolk in 1448. With these titles came major grants from the Crown. £666 annual income was required to qualify for the rank of Earl. Pole's Earldom of Suffolk only just qualified. The Duke of Suffolk lost Normandy in the Hundred Years' War, was impeached by parliament, exiled, then murdered by sailors crossing the English Channel on 2 May 1450. His only son was John de la Pole (1442–92).

Lady Margaret Beaufort (6) was married (7 Feb. 1450) to the 1st Duke of Suffolk's son, John de la Pole (7) great-grandson of poet Geoffrey Chaucer, gaining Papal dispensation to marry, signed 6 months later on 18 August 1450, then annulled in February 1453.

Lady Margaret Beaufort (12½) then married (1 November 1455) Edmund Tudor (17), 1st Earl of Richmond (1430–3 Nov. 1456) at Bletsoe Castle, which was really just a fortified manor house in Bedfordshire. Lady Margaret, Countess of Richmond and Derby was just 13 when she gave birth at Pembroke Castle to Harri Tudur ~ Henry Tudor ~ Henry VII on 28 January 1457. His father, Margaret's husband, was captured, incarcerated in Carmarthen Castle southwest Wales where he died of Bubonic Plague 86 days before his son Harri Tudur was born. Thus King Henry VII of England (R. 1485–1509) was born an 'orphan'.

Lady Margaret Beaufort (14) third married (3 January 1458) her second cousin, Sir Henry Stafford (1425–71) second son of Humphrey Stafford, 1st Duke of Buckingham.

Lady Margaret Beaufort (29) fourth married (June 1472) Thomas Stanley (37), 1st Earl of Derby KG (1435–1504) King of Mann, and Lord High Constable of England, but this was a marriage of extreme convenience. Margaret could now return to the court of Edward IV (R. 4 March 1461–3 October 1470 & 11 April 1471–9 April 1483) to rehabilitate & secure her court influence, and advocate her son, Harri Tudur (15) as future King of England.

This did happen ... with a couple of rapid monarchs in between:

> King Edward IV (R. 11 April 1471–9 April 1483) 11 years, 364 days;
>
> King Edward V (R. 9 April 1483–25 June 1483) 78 days;
>
> King Richard III (R. 26 June 1483–22 August 1485) 2 years, 58 days;
>
> King Henry VII (R. 22 August 1485–21 April 1509) 23 years, 243 days.

King of Mann, 1237–1504 was the title of the Sovereign or Suzerain ruler of the Kingdom of Mann, Isle of Man, in the Irish Sea, and thereafter was Lord of Mann. In terms of the Great Officers of State, in descending order, these were:

i. Lord High Steward (for Coronations)

ii. Lord High Chancellor of Great Britain
     (or Lord Keeper of the Great Seal <1757)
     ~ Prime Minister ~ First Lord of Treasury

iii. Lord High Treasurer
      (now Chancellor of the Exchequer)

iv. Lord President of the Council
     (now Leader of the House of Commons)

v. Lord Keeper of the Privy Seal
    (now Leader of the House of Lords)

vi. Lord Great Chamberlain
   (Lord Chamberlain)

vii. Lord High Constable of England
    (now filled by Master of the Horse)

viii. Earl Marshal
     (now filled by Master of the Horse)

ix. Lord High Admiral
   (vacant 1708–1964, now a Board
   of Admiralty commission).

Lady Margaret Beaufort was married
at 6, 12, 14 & 29, widowed twice,
solo mother at 13, Queen mother at 42,
and everything she touched was Roman Catholic.

Her son King Henry VII (R. 22 August 1485–21 April 1509) was very frugal, kept tight records of his own spending, right down to the last penny, and his Summary Accounts heralded the end of the Medieval Period & Middle Ages, taken as the 1st of January 1500.

Henry VII was very affectionate to his Roman Catholic' mother, wife, daughter, sons & daughter-in-law, but after ~17 years as Roman Catholic King of England, Henry VII had a string of bad luck ...
1502, 2 April: His firstborn son, Arthur Tudor (15) died of English Sweating Sickness, Consumption, TB, Plague, or Influenza and had been married to Catherine of Aragon who swore the

The Westminster Deanery (~1893) covered up to 4 acres and was an ever-changing arrangement. Deanery records do not record Margaret dying there. Her body was found in the Old Temple next to the Jewel House keeping the King's treasure & personal possession ... burnt out 3 years later in 1512, the entire Westminster Palace court moving away to Whitehall.

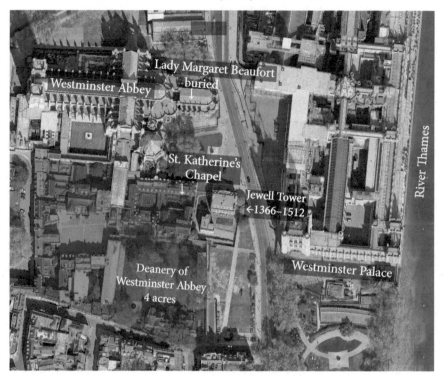

marriage was never consecrated. Henry VIII was now first in line to the throne, and would marry his late brother's wife.

1503, 2–11 February: Henry VII's wife Elizabeth of York gave birth to a girl on the 2nd, who died on 4th, and Queen consort Elizabeth died on 11 February on her 37th birthday.

"Henry VII is one of only a handful that never had any mistress, and for the times, it is very unusual that he did not remarry: his son, Henry, was the only heir left."

1509, 21 April: Henry VII died of tuberculosis at Richmond Palace; his 2nd-born son

1509, 21 April, Saturday: Henry VIII (17) became King of England; then 64 days later

1509, 24 June, Sunday: Henry VIII had his Coronation with Katherine Aragon; 4 days later

1509, 28 June, Thursday: Henry VIII turned 18 & partied like he was the King of England.

Lady Margaret Beaufort (66~68) was one of those Recusant Roman Catholics that kept on spouting off about imitating the life of Christ, and laying this on her grandson, Henry VIII. She was the first English translator of Book IV 'The Imitation of Christ'. This may have contributed to Henry VIII becoming the founding Anglican, as the next morning ...

1509, 29 June, Friday: Waking up from his all night party, the 18-year-old King of England, Henry VIII was informed that his 68-year-old grandmother had been dead in the Deanery of Westminster Abbey.

The Deanery was a collection of old buildings and meandering yards over four (4) acres, and contained the romantic ruin St.

Katherine's Chapel, built 1154–61. This had been burnt down in the 29 March 1298 Westminster Palace fire which destroyed all the Ancient Deeds, archae, and records of Jews stored there 1270–98.

St. Katherine's Chapel was never restored and became a romantic ruin with metre-high columns on which Lady Margaret Beaufort could be perfectly place in 'imitation of Christ'.

This is The Principal's pick for Lady Margaret Beaufort influencing Shakespeare's Orphelia in Hamlet (~Hallet) 90 years later ... 1509~1599.

The Deanery's St. Katherine's Chapel was 22 yards west of the 3-storey, crenellated stone Jewel Tower (1366–1512) surrounded by a moat linked to the Thames. The Jewel Tower stored the King's treasure and personal possessions until 3 years later when a second fire, the 1512 Westminster Palace fire caused Henry VIII to relocate his entire court 500 metres north to the Palace of Whitehall, becoming the English monarchs main residence, 1512/30–1698. In 1698 there was a third fire and most of Whitehall burnt down, except Inigo Jones' 1622 Banqueting House, where King Charles I's faked his execution in 1649. The executioner held up a swede with a wig over the carved and painted face.

1731: Part of Westminster Abbey Deanery became the Old Royal & Cotton Library, stored in Ashburnham House. In a 4th fire, this severely burnt the Charter of Liberties & Magna Carta in 1731.

1882: This became Westminster School "where Jesuit habilitators trained illegitimate Royals to be Antiquarians to create romantic chaos and destroy England's history ~ William Camden, Sir Robert Cotton, the 14th Earl of Arundel and Sir John Hynde Cotton Bt.

Thus the Deanery of Westminster Abbey had a 500-year-old history destroying England's Monarchs, including murder, as it was run by Roman Catholics, embedded historians, hagiographers, chroniclers, Jesuit habilitators, antiquarians, book thieves, pyromaniacs, fraudsters, document fraudsters, embezzlers, money launderers, and outright liars, including the Westminster Deans – all of which is well documented.

The Deanery of Westminster was destroyed by Baptism of Fire & Reformation. To these curiously well-timed events, there were no further details, but rebuilt in a different fashion.

1509, 29 June, Friday: 4 days after his Coronation and the morning after his 18th birthday, partying like it was 1509, Henry VIII woke up with a hangover to find his grandmother, Lady Margaret Beaufort (68) Countess of Richmond, dead in the Westminster Abbey Deanery ... which is anywhere over a 4 acres of buildings, yards and courtyards.

Lady Margaret Beaufort was very close to her son, Henry VII of England, who had just died 69 days prior (69 ≈ idealistic family harmony). Margaret was then buried in the Henry VII Chapel in Westminster Abbey, 69 metres directly north of where she was found.

The question is, did the 68-year-old Roman Catholic's Imitation of Christ get on the hungover 18-year-old Henry VIII's wick, who indicated 'her death would not be missed' ... or having lived her purpose, she ordered the 3 Westminster Abbey Monks she had been funding to put down 3 goblets of wine in various locations in the Deanery, and she would sip 1, 2, or 3, and one would be poison ... then her body would be placed dramatically on the stone column in St. Katherine's Chapel gazing at the Jewel House that held the records of her family's memories.

St Katherine's Chapel burnt in 1298 & 1512.

Erasmus wrote the Latin inscription for her tomb:

"MARGARET, COUNTESS OF RICHMOND, MOTHER OF HENRY VII, GRANDMOTHER OF HENRY VIII, WHO DONATED FUNDS FOR THREE MONKS OF THIS ABBEY, A GRAMMAR SCHOOL IN WIMBORNE, A PREACHER IN THE WHOLE OF ENGLAND, TWO LECTURERS IN SCRIPTURE, ONE AT OXFORD, THE OTHER AT CAMBRIDGE, WHERE SHE ALSO FOUNDED TWO COLLEGES, ONE DEDICATED TO CHRIST, AND THE OTHER TO ST JOHN, THE EVANGELIST."

Ignatius of Loyola (1491–1556) was 17¾ at the time, studied and formed the Jesuits and attempt to take over the world, by coadjuting the always greedy Roman Catholics against the easily influenced Christians, in an attempt to own all the land in all the world as 'honour and sovereignty', and from this, take the Throne and Crown of England.

1514–22: Lady Anne Boleyn heard about this while studying in Mechlin, Antwerp, Belgium, as a child savant, then serving Claude, Duchess of Brittany 1514–24, Queen consort of France (R. 1515–24). Anne returned to England, beguiled Henry VIII, informed him, and thus earned her position as Queen of England in her own right.

1539–56: 'Imitation of Christ' was a flimsy notion, not based on any real history. Ignatius of Loyola launched the Jesuits against the very weak 'imitation of Christ' Christians, the very powerful Henry VIII (R. 1509–47) and the momentum of the Reformation.

Chapter Three
Henry VIII sets up a divorce alibi, then marries Anne Boleyn

1345~1558: Bishop of Durham's Durham Palace on The Strand
looked south over the Thames, with its own private inlets,
watergates, stairs down to the River Thames, and ¾ acre of
private gardens, incredibly valuable at the time. One could
bargain with a garden, and before the fridge, fresh required
immediate access.

1540~1666: Henry VIII cornered the Bishop of Durham and swapped
Durham House for Coldharbour 1½ miles east. Coldharbour
looked across the Thames to the Bishop of Winchester's
Winchester Palace, surrounded by "the Winchester Geese",
being the Bishop of Winchester's prostitutes ... and for non-
payment, his jail – "the Clink".

The Bishop of Durham's Place was known as Durham Palace,
Durham House, Durham Inn, and much later Durham Yard. In
Durham Inn:

22 April–11 June 1509: Catherine of Aragon was Henry VIII's
former sister-in-law, and "lived as a virtual prisoner in
Durham House", then married King Henry VIII, becoming
Queen consort of England, 11 June 1509–23 May 1533. It
was an unhappy marriage resulting in the birth of Queen
Mary I (R. 1553–58) 'Bloody Mary'.

1532–33: Henry VIII was infatuated with Anne Boleyn since 1525,
and courted her in Durham House, as "the eastern most
mansion" & not subject to the laws of London. Durham
Palace ~ House ~ Inn ~ Yard became the royal party house,
1532–1603.

"Henry VIII decided to raise his lover to the dignity of a
marquess prior to finally marrying her. He chose to grant her
the Marquessate of Pembroke".[1]

1532, 1 September, Sunday: Anne Boleyn was made Marquess of Pembroke, which could be passed down to her male heirs, whether or not they were legitimate. It came with £1,000+ of land, mainly in Wales, having a labour value of £7.5 million, and income commodity of £15 million in 2024.

"On Sunday, 1 September 1532, Anne Boleyn was granted the Marquessate of Pembroke and land, mostly in Wales, worth over £1,000. The investiture ceremony was performed by Henry VIII himself in Windsor Castle. The ceremony was an elaborate affair, witnessed by the highest ranking peers and clergy in the kingdom, including Thomas Boleyn, 1st Earl of Wiltshire and Thomas Howard, 3rd Duke of Norfolk, Anne's father and uncle respectively; Charles Brandon, 1st Duke of Suffolk (Henry VIII's brother-in-law); the French ambassador; Edward Lee, Archbishop of York; John Stokesley, Bishop of London; and Stephen Gardiner, Bishop of Winchester, who read the patent of creation while Anne knelt before the King who then invested her with the coronet [crown], the robe of estate and the charters of creation and of the lands".[2]

Marquess was a rare title in the 1500s ... Duke → Marquess → Earl ... just below Duke, but above Earl. Anne Boleyn was now the highest-ranking peeress in England, and in the top six amongst all men and women, including those born royal.

The feminine is "Marchioness" & Marquesse (English) and "Marquise" (French).

The masculine "Marquess" (English) & "Marquis" (French) are both used in English.

The English spelling Henry VIII chose was both the Feminine: Marchioness ~ lady Marquesse ~ Marquys ... as well as the Masculine: Marquess ~ Marquis.

The title read: "Domina Anna, tunc Marchionissa Penbrochiæ, nunc vero Regina"[3] ~ 'Lady Anne, then Marquise of Pembroke, was now Queen'.

> "The marquessate was granted to Anne and her heirs male, but the patent did not include the usual provision that the said heirs male had to be of legitimate birth, thus enabling the title to pass to any illegitimate son Anne might have had. The attending peers did not fail to notice this unusual omission."[4]

In this way, the title & lands of the Marquessate of Pembroke could pass from Queen Anne Boleyn to her unrecorded grandson Sir Walter Raleigh, who was greeted at Court and given Durham Palace and monies to renovate & occupy for 20 years, aged 30–50, 1583–1603. Durham Palace was also known as Durham Place and Durham House.

> "Marquess of Pembroke: Created by Henry VIII of England on 1 September 1532 for Anne Boleyn, Remainder to the 1st Marquess's heirs male of the body (whether legitimate or illegitimate)."[5]

> "Marquess of Pembroke: Anne Boleyn (1501/7–1536): On 1 September 1532, a few months prior to her marriage to Henry VIII, Anne was granted the Marquessate of Pembroke; she was found guilty of treason and executed in May 1536, at which point the title became either forfeit or extinct at her death without male children."[6]

It is not clear how, when or if the Marquessate of Pembroke ceased to exist. It may have:

i.   Merged with the Crown on the marriage of the Marquess to the King on 28 May 1533;

ii.   Been forfeited on 15 May 1536, when Anne was declared guilty of high treason;

iii. Become extinct on Anne's death, without male heirs, on 19 May 1536."[7]

iv.   "This was disputed 28 May 1533–15 May 1536, and 19 May 1536."[8]

v.   It is not clear because the execution of Queen Anne Boleyn was faked and no one of importance believed she was deceased.

However, what has become apparent is that Henry VIII used every trick in the book to confuse the historians, whom he knew would be embedded Catholics and Jesuits, who would only ever write to their advantage. So for clarity, to answer points i, ii, iii ...

1532, 1 September, Sunday: Henry VIII made Anne Boleyn Marquess of Pembroke.

1532, 16 November, Saturday: Henry VIII married Marquess of Pembroke Anne Boleyn in a secret wedding in St Paul's Cathedral Church, and not at an undisclosed location on St Erkenwald's Day Thursday 14 November. 70 days later ...

1533, 25 January: Henry VIII formally married Marquess of Pembroke Anne Boleyn in accordance with The Royal Book, 124 days later + 3 ...

1533, 29 May–1 June: Henry VIII ensured that Marquess of Pembroke Anne Boleyn had her own coronation as Queen of England, and was Queen of England in her own right, whether or not she was married to Henry VIII, and whether or not he was alive or dead, sane or insane, king, or technically not king due to his madness.

966 days later ...

1536, 24 January–19 May: From his jousting accident that drove him mad, Henry VIII failed to divorce the Queen of England Anne Boleyn, Marquess of Pembroke, and instead divorced the small chapel "Culleyn" in France which he had renamed "Bulleyn", but even then, it wasn't a divorce, but an annulment ... from a chapel.

Queen of England & Queen consort of England, Anne Boleyn, Marquess of Pembroke and Mrs Henry VIII still had all of her styles and titles intact at the time of her advertised 'execution', which alluded to her death, but her death was not confirmed.

1536, 19 May: Queen of England Anne Boleyn, Marquess of Pembroke was not executed. She was rescued with the help of Margaret, Countess of Salisbury (1473–1541).

1536–54+: Queen of England Anne Boleyn, Marquess of Pembroke continued to live and breed with all her titles intact, including Queen of England, and Marquess of Pembroke, creating a new royal lineage for England. Both titles passed to her male heir. That is, Anne Boleyn passed Monarch of England & Marquess of Pembroke to her male heir, her grandson, who also held the title Christ, and this is why Queen Elizabeth I did not declare her two sons, Francis & Robert as Princes of England.

Queen of England Anne Boleyn, Marquess of Pembroke's male heir was her legitimate grandson Sir Walter Raleigh, raised in another family from when he was 2 years old, then presented to court in 1579, and given the 3 acre Durham Palace on the River Thames, a small fortune, and the rights to North America ~ so a Prince.

"It is probable that Henry VIII had thought of the idea of annulment (not divorce as commonly assumed) much earlier than this as he strongly desired a male heir to secure the Tudor claim to the crown."[9]

"Henry's quest for an annulment became euphemistically known as the "King's Great Matter,"[10] It was resolved in Sir Walter Raleigh, including the fulfilment of the kingly predictions.

1536, 15 April: Queen of England Anne Boleyn, Marquess of Pembroke trial papers were all lost, as if they never existed, as if the entire trial was a complicity masquerade. Her father, uncle and former betrothed were all Commissioners on her trial, and all found her guilty ... but of what ... as they all ignored the facts, ignored the total lack of evidence, and there were no records of any of Queen Anne Boleyn, Marquess of Pembroke or Marquesse of Pembroke's style or titles being forfeit.

1536, 15 April: As such, an "Anne" was declared guilty of high treason, but it was "Anne Bulleyn" who was half-woman half-chapel in France, in Bulleyn ~ Culleyn ~ Coulogne, 3 miles south of Caleys, now Calais ... Henry VI's only remaining English territory on the continent, as of 1453.[11]

1552–4: Queen of England Anne Boleyn, Marquess of Pembroke did not die for some time, and was alive when ...

"Walter Raleigh was born in 1552 or 1554, and raised by Katherine Champernoun, who already had children to at least 4 different fathers. Walter Raleigh was the youngest, and a foster child, although he didn't appear to know it. It was the perfect place to hide him. Walter Raleigh was born in 1552 or 1554 as he was nursed by his mother, Mary y'Noble, for two years, then delivered into the 10-child Raleigh family, making 11 children. [There were already 12 children, making 12+1 or 13.]

"Walter's foster mother's father's sister, Kat Ashley was Governess of Elizabeth I from the age of four and introduced Walter Raleigh (27) to Court in 1579. Queen Elizabeth I immediately recognised Walter as a grandchild of her mother, Queen Anne Boleyn, and Walter Raleigh recognised Elizabeth as his aunt: 'Hello nephew' ... 'Greetings aunt'.

"They become close friends and confidants, which many British historians and play-wrights have written them up as an affair of a sexual nature. Rather both Elizabeth and Walter Raleigh inherited the intellect of Queen Anne Boleyn, and were some of the few people with whom they could converse."[12]

"Walter Raleigh's house-mother Katherine Champernoun/ Catherine Champernowne/ Gilbert/ Raleigh (1519–94) married Otho Gilbert (1513–47) & had 6 children 1532–41, then married Walter Raleigh snr. and had 3 children in 1538, 1550 & 1552, plus [John Raleigh in 1546], Katherine Miners in 1547 & Margaret Hull in 1548 in between, so 11 [12] children with at least 4 fathers.

"This was a perfect scenario to slip in the 11th child from Mary y'Noble – Walter Raleigh, who inherited the mind of his grandmother, Queen Anne Boleyn, going to Oxford, then Middle Temple. These were foster homes for illegitimate aristocrats with real biological children for cover, and money for education.

"Katherine Champernoun's father's sister Kat Ashley was Governess of Elizabeth I (aged 4–) introducing Walter Raleigh (27) to Court in 1579."[13]

Walter Raleigh was born in 1552 then transferred as a 2-year-old in 1554 to the Protestant home of his housefather Walter Raleigh (d. 1581) and Katherine née Champernoun Gilbert Raleigh (1518/9–94) in Hayes Barton, Devon.

Walter Raleigh was to be hidden as the last of 10–13 children, 12 + 1 ≈ Christ, to four different fathers ≈ 'fore-fathers' ~ Otho Gilbert (1513–45), Walter Raleigh (?–1581) and two or more unknown fathers ≈ 'Father' & 'Holy Ghost',[1] issuing:

1.   Elizabeth Gilbert (b. 1532–?)

---

[1] * 1 daughter & 2 sons with unknown "Father", sourced from WikiTree.

2. Sir John Gilbert, Kt.(Jan./Feb 1536–96) Sheriff of Devon, Vice Admiral of Devon

3. Otho Gilbert

4. Isabella Gilbert

5. Sir Humphrey Gilbert, Kt. (1539–83) adventurer, explorer, MP, died at sea

6. Sir Adrian Gilbert, MP (~1541–1628)[14]

7. *Mary Rawleigh/ Raleigh (1541~?)

8. *Wymund Rawleigh (1544~?)

9. *John Raleigh (1546–97)

10. ** Katherine Miners (1547–1602)[2]

11. **Margaret Hull Raleigh (1548–?) married (by 1564) Lawrence Radford

12. Sir Carew Raleigh, MP (~1550–1626)

12+1. Sir Walter Raleigh (b. 22 January 1552, delivered 22 January 1554–1618–46).

"Sir Philip Champernowne (1479–1545) lord of the manor of Modbury married Kathrine ~ Catherine (1498~1524)."[15] "Katherine Ashley née Champernowne; circa 1502–65, also known as "Kat Ashley" was the first close friend, governess, and Lady of the Bedchamber to Queen Elizabeth I of England. Kat Ashley was the aunt of Katherine Champernowne, who was the mother of explorer Sir Humphrey Gilbert (1539–83) by her first marriage; and by her second marriage Walter Raleigh (by assumption adoption, the adjutor mother)."[16]

This was the perfect placement and training ground for Queen Anne

[2] ** 2 daughters with second unknown Father ≈ "Holy Ghost".

Boleyn's grandson, Walter Raleigh, to be trained to be reintroduce into court and received as a humble prince.

Raleigh's childhood and early adult biography is largely made up of inaccuracies, creating a legend to substantiate giving Walter patronage, money & a lot of land – 0.2% of Ireland.

> "Little is known of his early life, though in his late teens he spent some time in France taking part in the religious civil wars. In his 20s he took part in the suppression of rebellion in the colonisation of Ireland; he also participated in the siege of Smerwick ... He rose rapidly in the favour of Queen Elizabeth I and was knighted in 1584 ... He was granted a royal patent to explore Virginia, paving the way for future English settlements ... Later, he became a landlord of property in Ireland and mayor of Youghal in East Munster, where his house still stands in Myrtle Grove."[17]

The Principal went to Smerwick, where there were tufts of grass that look like graves, but there was no siege on that tiny peninsula, and no bodies found, and Raleigh wasn't there. This legend was created to give Queen Elizabeth I an excuse to give her nephew Raleigh 0.2% of Ireland, for achievement he didn't even attend ... and his humble cottage in Myrtle Grove was a distraction for the Lismore Castle and Molana Abbey he owned farther up the beautiful Blackwater Valley, with ships also hidden in the Cork faux harbour.

> "In 1591, he secretly married Elizabeth Throckmorton, one of the Queen's ladies-in-waiting, without the Queen's permission, for which he and his wife were sent to the Tower of London."

This was all for show, as Queen Elizabeth I had introduced her nephew and niece, and got them to dance The Volta: "A very accurate version can be seen in the 2007 'Elizabeth: The Golden Age' (sequel to 'Elizabeth') between Elizabeth 'Bess' Throckmorton and Sir Walter Raleigh"[18] ... where Sir Walter Raleigh lifts Elizabeth Throckmorton up by her cunning and tosses her 5 feet high in the air, with Clive Owen as Raleigh, Abbie Cornish as Elizabeth Throckmorton, and Cate Blanchett as Queen Elizabeth I.

"Raleigh", wikipedia: "After his release, they retired to his estate at Sherborne, Dorset." It was built 1584–1613, and they lived in Durham Palace on the River Thames 1583–1603. Sherborne Castle was an architectural building experiment and a country getaway, named to predict The Principal as 'Shearer-born' for 'born of a shearer'.

'The Maner of the Tryumphe of Caleys and Culleyn, Cum Priuilegio' changed in the Second Edition to 'The Maner of the Tryumphe at Caleys and Bulleyn'. Culleyn, is changed to Bulleyn':

> "... then these twoo Princes offered at our Lady of Bulleyn, and the Frenche kyng brought the kyng of Englande to his lodgyng in the Abbay directly against his awne lodging, where the kyng of Englande had diuerse chambers ..."

> "... to mete in October folowyng, betwene Calice & Bulleyn : wherfore the kyng of Englande sent out his letters, to his nobilitie, prelates, and seruauntes, commaundyng theim to bee ready at Canterbury, the 26 day of September [1532], to passe the Seas with him, for the accomplishing of the enteruew, betwene hym and his brother the Frenche kyng."[19]

"And so they taryed in Bulleyn mondaye tuysdaye Wednesday and thursday all daye ... bothe ye kynges went to our lady chyrche in Bulleyn ... at that tyme beynge prisoners in Bulleyn ... and many other noble men that were not with the kyng at Bulleyn ... the kynge our mayster was saluted at Bulleyn ... Low curtains were in Bulleyn at our lady chyrche and in Caleys in our lady chyrche."

Also this title quoted hereinafter was originally ...

'The Vnion of the Two Noble Illustre Famelies of LANCASTRE & YORKE, being the long in Continual Discension for the Croune of this Noble Realme, with all the Actes done in bothe the Tymes of the Princes, Bothe of the One Linage and of the Other, Beginnyng at the Tyme of Kyng Henry the Fowerth, the First Aucthor of this Deuision, and so Successiuely Proceadyng to the Reigne of the High and Prudent Prince Kyng Henry the Eight, the Vudubitate Flower and very Heire of both the sayd Linages. 1548'.

The title was modernised to ...

'Hall's Chronicle; containing The History of England, during The Reign of Henry the Fourth, and the succeeding Monarchs, to the end of the Reign of Henry the Eighth, in which are particularly described the manners and customs of those periods. Carefully collated with the editions of 1548 and 1550, London: Printed for J. Johnson; F.C. and J. Rivington; T. Payne; Wilkie and Robinson; Longman, Hurst, Rees and Orme; Cadell and Davies; and J. Mawman; London.

The title is known and cited as "Hall's Chronicle, 1548 & 1809".

1532, 11 October–10 November: Henry VIII and M.
Pembroke of 6 weeks Anne Boleyn were in France and
Calais, and 6 miles north-east on a 1 by 3 mile stretch of flat
sand called 'Sandyngfelde' or the 'Englysshe Pale'.

1532, 21–24 October, Monday–Thursday all day: Henry VIII met
with the King of France:

"on the mondaye the xxi. daye of October the Kyng of
Englande toke his waye with 600 persons to mete with the
frensshe kyng" Francis I (R. 1515–47) "with 140 all in veluet
cotes afore hym lordes and Knyghtes and 11 of his garde and
another 600 horses and as well horsed as euer was seen ...
they embraced ye other 5 or 6 tymes on horsbacke and so
dyd the lordes on eyther party eche to other and so dyd ryde
hande in hande with greate loue the space of a myle[3] and than
they dyd lyght of theyr horses and dranke eche to other the
frensshe kyng dranke fyrst to our kyng and whan they had
dronke they embraced eche other agayne with great loue and
so rode towards Bulleyn [3 miles south of Calais] our kynge
on the ryght hande."[20]

"And whan they came within a myle of Bulleyn there mette
with the kynges the Dolphyn [Prince] beynge accompanyed
with his two bretherne the duke of Orliaunce and the count or
erle of Angolame very goodly chyldren and attendyng vpon
them four cardynalles with a M. horses very well beseen.

"And when they came nere to ye towne the French King
caused our master to tary whiles gunshot was shot and heard
by Bulleyn 20 Englishe myles off [so heard in Dover Castle].

---

[3] The Second Edition inserts "At ye metyng of these two noble kynges there were
sacres and sacrettes cast of and at dyuerse flyghtes two kytes were beten downe
which were sooryng in ye ayre wh such lyke pastyme whiche greatly pleased al
the nobles on bothe partyes."

"And so entered the towne where stode the captayn with the sowdyours [soldiers] in good ordre and aboue them stode a 100 French King's guard in their dublettes and yelowe velvet hosen ... and aboue them stood another 200 guard in yellow, blue and crimson velvet coats holding halberds (axe & pike) and above them stood another 200 gentylmen in theyr gownes well and rychely beseen euery man hauyng a batayle ax in theyr handes and theyr captaines standyng by them.

"And so they taryed in Bulleyn mondaye tuysdaye Wednesday and thursday all daye." 21–24 October 1532 [3 miles south of Calais].

1532, 22 October, Tuesday: The French King Francis I gave the English Henry VIII a rich outfit wrought with needlework and pearle-fringed with golde. Francis had a similar outfit, and they both went to Our Lady Church in Bulleyn. The French King Francis then released all English prisoners out of Bulleyn & Calais, and the English King Henry VIII pardoned them. Curtains were then drawn in the church and the two Kings had a private meeting re-ordinances and provisions.[21]

Erkenwald ~ Ercenwald ~ Eorcenwald ~ Erconwald is a patron saint of London, where St Erkenwald's Day is 14 November in England, but is also 1 February, 24 April, 30 April & 13 May in many other countries.

1532, 14 November, Thursday: It is believed that Henry VIII and Anne Boleyn secretly married on St Erkenwald's Day, variously in Calais, Dover, or St Paul's London, but:[22]

"On Sondaie [10 Nov. 1532] the wether was faire, the kyng caused his bedde and other thynges to be shipped, and entended to departe, but sodainly rose suche a mist, that no Master could guide a ship, and so he taried that daie. On Tewesdaie at midnight he tooke ship, and landed at Douer the morowe after, beyng the. xiiii. [14th] daie of Nouember, at v. of the clocke in the mornyng [5 a.m.], wherefore the Saterdaie after, [Saturday 16 November 1532] was song *Te deum* in the Cathedrall Churche of sainct Paule in London: the Lorde keper of the great Seale, the Maior of London, (and diuerse other noble and sad persones, whiche made their abode in London, for the gouernaunce of the realme in the kynges absence, beyng present). The kyng after his returne, maried prinily the lady Anne Bulleyn, on maried to sainct Erkenwaldes daie, whiche mariage was kept so secrete, that very fewe knewe it, til she was greate with child, at Easter after."[23]

This is purposefully written for a maximum lack of clarity, and therefore obfuscation, ambiguity, and circumlocution distraction – which are hallmarks of Jesuit interference.

To add to this confusion, the place they had just been hunting in France around Calais was called 'Culleyn', changed to 'Bulleyn', and Anne Boleyn was called "Anne Bulleyn" for the first time, but this was backdated.

This was a patently ambiguous allusion to Lady Anne Boleyn marrying Henry VIII in France, which did not happen, but was designed confusion for her divorce name "Bulleyn".

With the archaic language modernised, and using the Old Style Julian Calendar days, and days of the week, it reads:

'1532, 10 November, Sunday: "The weather being fair, Henry VIII shipped off his bed and other things, intending to depart from Calais, but a mist suddenly rose up such that no Master could guide his ship. Henry VIII tarried another day or two.

1532, 12 November, Tuesday: At midnight Henry VIII took a ship; and

1532, 14 November, Thursday: Landed at Dover the morning after at 5 o'clock in the morning, St. Erkenwald's Day.

1532, 16 November, Saturday: Wherefore the Saturday after, was the song *Te deum* (God, We Praise You) in the Cathedral Church of Saint Paul in London.

'The Lord Keeper of the Great Seale, the Mayor of London, and those governing England during Henry VIII's absence, and many other London Nobles, were all present as witnesses, at St Paul's Cathedral Church, where Henry VIII secretly married Lady Anne Boleyn on Saturday, 16 November 1532, with 'God, We Praise You' getting a mention as sung, as King Henry VIII had been waiting seven (7) years to bed Anne Boleyn.

'It worked and Henry VIII got Queen Anne Boleyn pregnant that night. Queen Anne Boleyn conceived Princess Elizabeth I on Saturday, 16 November 1532. Few knew it, until Queen Anne Boleyn was 5 months pregnant and showing on Easter Friday, 13 April 1533.'[24]

1532, 16 Nov., Saturday: Henry VIII married the Marquess of Pembroke Anne Boleyn / Bulleyn in a secret wedding in St Paul's Cathedral Church, and not at an undisclosed location on St Erkenwald's Day Thursday 14 November.

"Boleyn" was the married name and
"Bulleyn" was the divorce/annulment name.
This rendered the divorce null and void.

1532, 14 November–20 December: Henry VIII and Marquess of Pembroke, 'Queen' Anne Boleyn conceived Princess Queen Elizabeth – the last Queen of England on 2 December 1532 ± 18 days. Conception was on their first wedding night, 16 November 1532, and to fulfil Bible prophecy, 70 days later ...

1533, 25 January: Henry VIII formally married his wife, Marquess of Pembroke Anne Boleyn.

1533, 10 April, Thursday: "After the Kyng perceiuyng his newe wife Quene Anne, to bee greate with childe, caused all officers necessary, to bee appoynted to her, and so on Easter eue, she went to her Closet openly as Quene, with all solempnitie, and then the Kyng appoynted the daie of her Coronacion, to bee kept on Whitsō Sondaie next folowyng, and writynges wer sent to all Shriues, to certifie the names of menne of fourtie pounde, to receiue the Ordre of knighthod, or els to make a fine: the assessement of whiche fines, were appoynted to Thomas Cromwell, Master of the Kynges Iuell house, and counsailer to the kyng, and newly in his high fauour, whiche so pollitikely handeled the matter, that he raised of that sessyng of fines, a greate somme of money to the Kynges vse: Also the Kyng wrote letters to the citee of London, to prepare pagiauntes against thesame coronacion."[25]

1533, 10 April, Thursday: 'Henry VIII could see Queen Anne Boleyn was 5 months pregnant, so on the eve of Easter Friday he appointed more staff, and Queen Anne went to her small private inner sanctum (closet) and openly prayed with all solemnity as pregnant Queen wishing upon a son.

'Henry VIII then appointed the Queen Anne's Coronation Day to be WhitSunday, the 7th Sunday after Easter Sunday 13 April 1533, being Sunday 1 June 1533.

'Notice was sent to all Shires, to certify the names of men who for £40 would receive an Order of Knighthood Bath, or else pay a fine, assessed by Thomas Cromwell, Master of the Kings Jewel House, 1532–36 which houses the Crown Jewels. Cromwell was Counsellor to the King, who thus raised a large sum of money assessing fines for the King's purse.

'Henry VIII wrote letters to the City of London to prepare Pageants for (against) the coronation.'[26]

"Cum Priuilegio" means 'with privileges', as in it is a royal privilege here to sublimate "Bulleyn" for "Boleyn", and "Bulleyn" for "Culleyn".

The first 1532 edition of 'The Maner of the Tryumphe of Caleys and Culleyn, Cum Priuilegio' has Culleyn which is 3 miles south of Caleys in France.

The second 1533 edition was changed to 'The Maner of the Tryumphe of Caleys and Bulleyn and the Noble Tryumphant Coronacyon of Quene Anne, Wyfe unto the Most Noble Kynge Henry VIII'[27] printed by Wynkyn de Worde, 1533, and it has Bulleyn 3 miles south of Caleys in France.

That is, it was "Culleyn" in 1532–33, and "Bulleyn" in 1533, ~1540, 1884/85 & 1893.

So "Culleyn, Cum Priuilegio" or "Culleyn, with privileges" was changed to "Bulleyn".

It appears that Henry VIII got divorced from the Château Culleyn Chapel 3 miles south of Calais in France, called "Our Lady Church in Bulleyn" or "our Lady of Bulleyn".

"Culleyn" could easily be 'Coulogne' which had a château. Culleyn château also had its own chapel until both were destroyed 13 years after Henry VIII's death in 1547, in 1560, with some ruins remaining.

Many embedded historians believe "Bulleyn" was a middle Ages misspelling of "Boleyn". These embedded pseudo-historians proliferate and continually make erroneous assumptions. Embedded pseudo-historians at Oxford, Cambridge and the British Library claim Henry VIII got divorced from "Bulleyn", and readers were encouraged to assume this was a Middle Ages spelling of "Boleyn".

But Henry VIII divorced the small chapel "our Lady of Bulleyn" and did not divorce our Lady of Boleyn, Lady Boleyn, nor the Queen Anne Boleyn, and did not divorce the Lady Marquesse, Lady Marquys of Pembroke, Marquis of Pembroke, Marquise of Pembroke, Marquesse of Pembroke, Marquess of Pembroke, and did not divorce the Marchioness of Pembroke, and did not divorce Anne Boleyn ... nor any other derivatives ... this deception now doubled up.

"Culleyn, with privileges" was changed to "Bulleyn", using those privileges, and Henry VIII divorced the Culleyn château chapel, renamed "Bulleyn", and not "Boleyn", and divorced the masculine misnamed misspelt "Marquis of Penbroke" (with an "n") ... none of which were Anne.

In this way, Queen Anne Boleyn continued the Royal Lineage of herself, from 1533, and after Henry VIII died on 28 January 1547 ... with Queen Anne Boleyn as the Queen of England in her own right.

This was how the Crown of England was transferred to Queen Anne Boleyn, and her lineage, legitimate or illegitimate.

1536, 8 June, Thursday: To confirm this, Henry VIII held his High Court of Parliament which declared his first two marriages, to the lady Katheryne, and with the lady Anne Bulleyn were both adjudged unlawful, as more at large appears in the Act in the Book of Statutes.[28]

But the spelling received in the High Court of Parliament for Catherine of Aragon or Catalina de Aragón was "lady Katheryne"; and the spelling received for "Anne Boleyn" was "Bulleyn", as though Henry VIII was no longer married to that Bulleyn Chapel 3 miles south of Calais in France.

Wynkyn de Worde and his 15 aliased made it obvious that Henry VIII had not divorced, annulled, or adjudged unlawful his marriage to Queen Anne Boleyn, which was well removed from "Culleyn".

Yet Wynkyn de Worde, the Oxford History Department; Trinity College, Dublin; University Library, Cambridge; Cambridge University History Department; British Library; British Museum; D. Appleton & Co. publishers, Philadelphia; George S. Appleton publishers, New York; and the publisher' of Early English text society in London ... should not have changed "Culleyn" to "Bulleyn" to allude to Henry VIII being divorced, annulled, or adjudged unlawful his marriage to a "Bulleyn".

This confirms these major publishers were Catholic Jesuit Antiquarian liars for a fake history, which leads to the Jesuit British history being a hagiography fairy tale, and the English crown still retained by the English patriots, and that English patriot being The Principal Joseph Gregory Hallett who also holds the Coronation Stone.

Endnotes

1   2006: David Loades, 'Elizabeth I: A Life', Continuum International Publishing Group.

2   1991: Retha Warnicke, 'The Rise and Fall of Anne Boleyn: Family Politics at the Court of Henry VIII', Cambridge University Press;

    1974: Hester W. Chapman, 'The challenge of Anne Boleyn', publ. Coward, McCann & Geoghegan.

3   OED "Marquis" sense 3.; compare the quotation under "Marchioness": Cum..Domina Anna, tunc Marchionissa Penbrochiæ, nunc vero Regina. See also Complete Peerage Vol. V, App. H.

4   Marquess of Pembroke, wikipedia, citing

    1972: Marie Louise Bruce, 'Anne Boleyn', publisher Coward, McCann & Geoghegan;

    1974: Hester W. Chapman, 'The Challenge of Anne Boleyn', Putnam Publishing Group;

    1991: Retha M. Warnicke: The Rise and Fall of Anne Boleyn: Family Politics at the Court of Henry VIII, Canto.

5   Marquess of Pembroke, wikipedia.

6   1911: Ed. Hugh Chisholm, "Pembroke, Earls of", Encyclopædia Britannica, 21, 11th edition, pp. 78–80, p. 79.

7   1910–11: Ed. Hugh Chisholm, The Encyclopædia Britannica, A Dictionary of Arts, Sciences, Literature and General Information, Eleventh Edition, Volume VIII ... which had become a Jesuit rag.

8   Marquess of Pembroke, wikipedia.

9   1972: Robert Lacey, 'The Life and Times of Henry VIII', p. 70. Anne Boleyn provided this in 1552.

10 1992: Antonia Fraser, 'The Wives of Henry VIII', Knopf, New York, p. 133.

11 Henry VI of England, wikipedia.

12 2019, 31 December: Joseph Gregory Hallett declares Queen Anne Boleyn's Royal Lineage OTH / 19 / 54733, Addendum One, Smerwick – lands in Ireland, p. 34.

13 2019, 31 December: Joseph Gregory Hallett declares Queen Anne

Boleyn's Royal Lineage OTH / 19 / 54733, Addendum One, Queen Elizabeth and Raleigh chat up a storm, p. 42.

14 Adrian Gilbert was alchemy lab assistant & 'great favourite' of Mary, Countess of Pembroke (1561–1621).

15 1895: Editor Lt.Col. J.L. Vivian, 'The Visitations of the County of Devon: Comprising the Heralds' Visitations of 1531, 1564 & 1620', Exeter, p.162.

16 Ibid. 4th daughter of Sir Philip Champernowne (1479–1545).

17 2021, 21 May: "The Church and Town of Sir Walter Raleigh", United Diocese of Cork, Cloyne and Ross.

18 Volta (dance), wikipedia.   19 Ibid, pp. 785 & 789.

20 1532–33: 'The Maner of the Tryumphe of Caleys and Bulleyn and the Noble Tryumphant Coronacyon of Quene Anne, Wyfe unto the Most Noble Kynge Henry VIII', printed by Wynkyn de Worde.

1884: Edited by Edmund Goldsmid F.R.H.S., F.S.A. (Scot), Privately Printed in Edinburgh, as 'The Maner of the Tryumphe of Caleys and Culleyn, Cum Priuilegio'. Some texts explained or modern paraphrased.

21 Ibid, Second Edition insert, paraphrased.

22 2017, 14 Nov.: The Anne Boleyn Files, '14 Nov 1532 – Did they or didn't they?', .theanneboleynfiles.com/14-november-1532-didnt/.

23 1548 & 1809: Edward Hall's Chronicle, p.794.   24 with Old Style days of week inserted & archaic modernised. 25 p. 795 in original old style.   26 Ibid, paraphrased into modern English.

To purchase a Knight of Bath cost £40 in 1533, equivalent to £290,000 Labour or £600,000 Income in 2024.

27 1884: The Maner of the Tryumphe of Caleys and Bulleyn and the Noble Tryumphant Coronacyon of Quene Anne, Wyfe unto the Most Noble Kynge Henry VIII', edited by Edmund Goldsmid F.R.H.S., F.S.A. (Scot), Privately Printed in Edinburgh, 1884, as 'The Maner of the Tryumphe of Caleys and Culleyn, Cum Priuilegio'. Some texts explained or modern paraphrased.

28 1548 & 1809: Edward Hall's Chronicle, p. 819.

Chapter Four
Queen Anne Boleyn's Coronation Book

𝕮𝖍𝖊 𝖓𝖔𝖇𝖑𝖊 𝖆𝖗𝖞𝖆𝖎

Thursday   **29 May 1533**

In the .xix. daye of Maye, of purge thurſoay, all the worſhypfull craftes and occupacyons in theyr beſt araye goo oly befere to take theyr barge, whiche there ſplayeo wʒ goodly baners freſſhe and newe, wʒth ryc cognyſaunce and armes of euery faculty, to the nomber of. L. great bargges cõmyʒ before. euery barge hauyng mynſtrelʒ makynge greate and ſwete armony. Alſo there was the bacheleres barge cõmyʒ before. decked wʒth innumerable baners, and all about hanged wʒth the

47

'A Coronation Book for Queen Anne Boleyn'.

"On 1 June 1533, Anne Boleyn, the mistress of King Henry VIII of England, achieved her greatest triumph. Overcoming great adversity, including the enmity of foreign powers and the opposition of the Church, she was crowned Queen of England. It was a moment Anne had eagerly anticipated for seven (7) years. She and the King had already wedded in secret, Henry's marriage to his first wife Katherine of Aragon was annulled, and now Anne carried the nation's longed-for heir. It was little wonder that the motto she chose at her crowning was 'The Most Happy'.

"Anne's happiness was only marred by the reception of the sullen London crowds who regarded her as an upstart and as the King's concubine. Nevertheless, the coronation festivities were a great piece of theatrical showmanship and political propaganda. Anne was hailed as the progenitor of a great new age – it was foretold that it was her 'son' who will bring forth a 'golden world' unto the English. The prediction was half correct. In time it was a daughter, Elizabeth, who was to fulfill the expectation [followed by the grandson Raleigh].

"A description of Anne Boleyn's coronation was set down in pamphlet form shortly after the festivities by the London printer Wynkin de Worde in 1533. Entitled 'The Noble Tryumphaunt Coronacyon of Quene Anne – Wyfe unto the Noble Kynge Henry the VIII', it consisted of 11 typeset pages with a rather crude woodcut of a courtly scene on the front cover. The book (measuring 4" x 5" [102 x 127mm) was done on calfskin vellum with illustrations and miniature portraits in watercolor. Gold leaf was applied throughout. "This 'coronation book' is a transcription done by hand of Wynkin de Worde's pamphlet ... begun in January 2002 ... completed in March 2004."[1]

HA 1533

The noble tryumphant
coronacyon of quene
Anne / wife unto the
noble kynge henry the viii

Anna Bolina Vxor henricus Octa.

First the xxix daye of Maye beynge thursday all the worshypfull craftes and occupacyons in theyr best araye goodly besene toke theyr barges which splayed ŵ goodly banners fresshe and newe with the cognysaunce and armes of theyr faculty to the nombre of L great barges comly besene and every barge havynge mynstrels making great and swete armony.

Also there was the bachelors comly barge besene, decked with innumerable baners and all about hanged with ryche cloth of golde / ⁊ foystes waytyng her upon / decked with a great

 irst the xxix daye
of Maye beynge
thursday all the
worshypfull craftes
and occupacyons in
theyr best araye goodly besene toke theyr barges which
splayed w̃ goodly banners

fresshe and newe with the
cognysaunce and armes of
theyr faculty to the nom-
bre of L great barges comly besene and every barge
havynge mynstrels makyng
great and swete armony.

 lso there was the
bachelers comly
barge besene,
decked with in-
numerable baners and
all about hanged with
ryche cloth of golde / t
foystes waytyng her upon
/ decked with a great

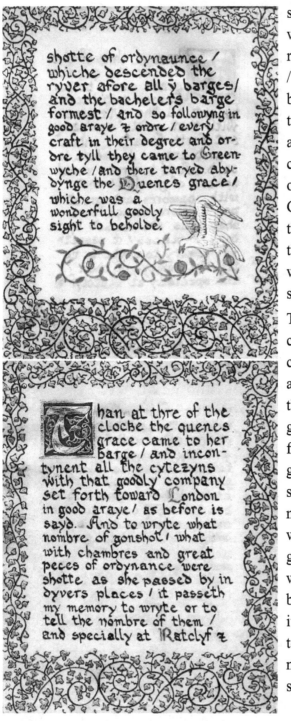

shotte of ordynaunce / whiche descended the river afore all ŷ barges / and the bachelers barge formest / and to followyng in good araye ⁊ ordre / every craft in their degree and ordre tyll they come to Greenwyche / and there they taryed abydynge the Quenes grace /which was a wonderful goodly sight to beholde.

Than at thre of the clocke the quenes grace came to her barge / and incontynent all the cytezyns with that goodly company set forth toward London in good araye / as before is sayd. And to wryte what nombre of gonshot / what with chambres and great peces of ordynance were shotte as she passed by in dyvers places / it passeth my memory to wryte or to tell the nombre of them / and specially at Ratclyf ⁊

at Lymehouse out of certeyne shyppes. And so ŷ quenes grace in her ryche barge among her nobles / the cytezyns accompanyed her to London unto the Toure Wharfe.

Also ere she came nere the Toure there was shot innumerable peces of ordynaunce / as ever there by any mennes remembrauces / where the kyng receyved her grace with a loving countenaunce / and so gave great thanks and prayse to all the cytezynes for theyr great kyndnesse ꝗ lovynge labour and paynes in that behalfe taken / to the great joy and comforte of all the cytezyns of London.

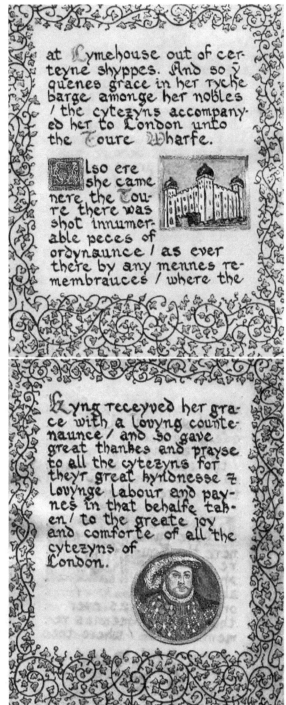

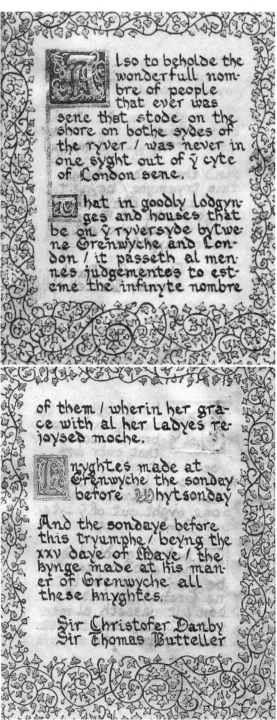

Also to beholde the wonderful nombre of people that ever was sene that stode on the shore on bothe sydes of the ryver / was never in one syght out of ŷ cyte on Londone sene.

That in goodly lodgynges and houses that be on ŷ ryversyde bytwene Grenwyche and London / it passeth al mennes judgementes to esteme the infinyte nombre of them / wherin her grace with al her ladyes rejoysed moche.

Knyghtes made al Grenwyche the sonday before Whytsonday And the sondaye before they tryumphe / beyng the xxv daye of Maye / the kynge made all his manner of Grenwhyche all these knyghtes.

Sir Christopher Danby, Sir Thomas Butteller,

Sir Christopher hylarde
Sir William Walgrave
Sir Brian hastynges
Sir Willyam Feldeyng
Sir Thomas Betham

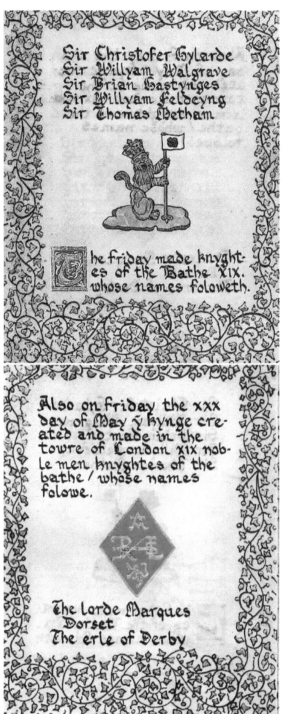

The friday made knyghtes of the Bathe xix. whose names foloweth.

Also on friday the xxx day of May ŷ kynge created and made in the towre of London xix noble men knyghtes of the bathe / whose names folowe.

The Lord Marques Dorset
The erle of Derby

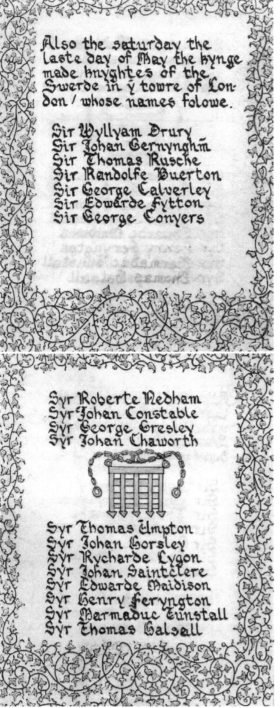

Also the saturday the laste day of May the kynge made knyghtes of the Swerde in ŷ towre of London / whose names folowe.

Sir Wyllam Drury

Sir Johan Gernynghm

Sir Thomas Rusche,

Sir Randolfe Buerton

Sir George Calverley

Sir Edward Fytton

Sir George Conyers

Syr Robert Nedham

Syr Johan Constable

Syr George Gresley

Syr Johan Chaworth

Syr Thomas Umpton

Syr Johan horsley

Syr Rycharde Lygon

Syr Johan Saintclere

Syr Edwarde Maidison

Syr henry Feryngton

Syr Marmaduc Tunstall

Syr Thomas halsall

The lorde Clyfforde /
sone ⁊ heyre to the erle
of Cumberlande
The lorde Fitzwater /
sone ⁊ heyr to the erle
of Sussex
The lorde hastynges /
sone ⁊ heyr to the erle
of huntyngton
The lorde Barkeley
The lorde Mountagle
The lorde Vaux
Syr henry Parker / sone ⁊
heyr to ŷ Lorde Morley
Syr Wyllyam Wyndsour
/ sone ⁊ heyr to the
lorde Wyndesour

Syr John Mordant /
sone ⁊ heyr to ŷ lorde
Mordant
Syr Fraunces Weston
Syr Thomas Aroundell
Syr Johan hudelston Syr
Thomas Ponynges
Syr henry Savell
Syr George Fitzwyllyam
of Lyncolne shyre
Syr Johan Tyndall
Syr Thomas Jermey

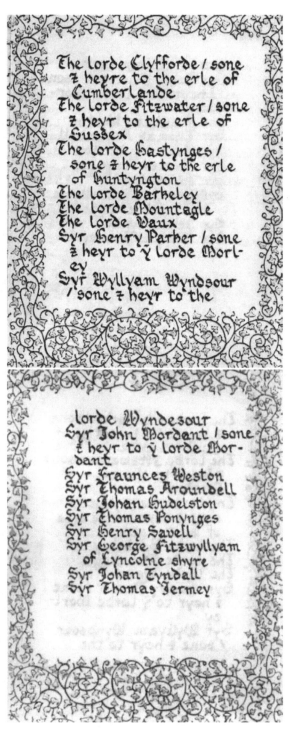

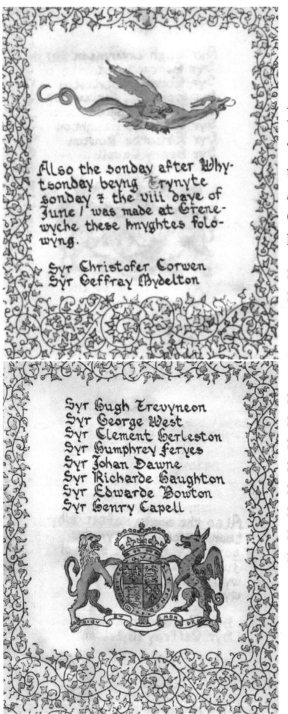

Also the sonday after Whytsonday beyng Trynte sonday 7 the viii daye of June / was made at Grenewyche these knyghtes folowyng.

Syr Christofer Corwen
Syr Geffray Mydelton

Syr hugh Trevyneon
Syr George West
Syr Clement herleston
Syr humprey Feryes
Syr Johan Dawne
Syr Richarde haughton
Syr Edwarde Bowton
Syr henry Capell

Syr Robert kyrkham
Syr Anthony Wyndsour
Syr Walter hubbert
Syr Johan Wyllongby
Syr Thomas kytson
Syr Thomas Mysseden
Syr Thomas Foulehurst
Syr henry Delves
Syr Peter Warburton
Syr Rycharde Bulkelley
Syr Thomas Lakyng
Syr Walter Smythe

Syr henry Everyngham
Syr Wyllyam Unedall
Syr Thomas Massyngberd
Syr Wyllyam Sandon
Syr James Baskervyll
Syr Edmonde Trafford
Syr Arthur Eyre
Syr henry Sutton
Syr Johan Nories
Syr Wyllyam Malorie
Syr Johan harcourt
Syr Johan Tyrell
Syr Wyllyam Browne
Syr Nycholas Sturley,
Syr Randolfe Manerig

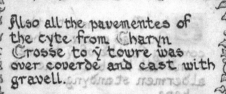

Also all the pavementes of the cyte from Charyn Crosse to ŷ towre was over coverde and cast with gravell.

And the same saturday being Whytson Even the Mayre with all the Aldermen ⹌ the craftes of the cyte prepared aray in a good order to stande ⹌ receyve her / and with rayles for every craft to stande ⹌ leane from prease of people.

The Mayre mette the Quenes grace at her comyng forthe of ŷ towre / and all his bretherne and aldermen standyng in Chepe.

Upon the same saturday the Quene came forth from ŷ towre towarde Westminster in goodley aray / as hereafter foloweth.

She passed the stretes first with certayne

strangers / their horses trapped ŵ blewe sylke / ⁊ themselves in blewe velvet with white fethers acompanyed two ⁊ two. Lykewise squiers / knights / barons ⁊ baronetts / knights of ŷ Bath clothed in vyolet garmentes / edged with armyns lyke juges. Than folowyng ŷ Juges of the Lawe ⁊ abbottes. All these estates were to ŷ nombre of CC cople ŵ more / two ⁊ two accompanyed.

And than folowed byshops to ⁊ two : ⁊ the Archbyssshops of Yorke ⁊ Canterbury / y ambassaders of France ⁊ Vanyce / the Lorde Mayre ŵ a mace / Mayster Garter the kyng of heraldes ⁊ the kyngs cote armour upon him with y Offycers of Armes / apoyntyng every estate in their degre.

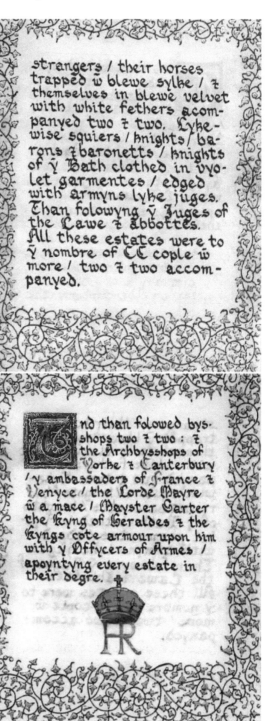

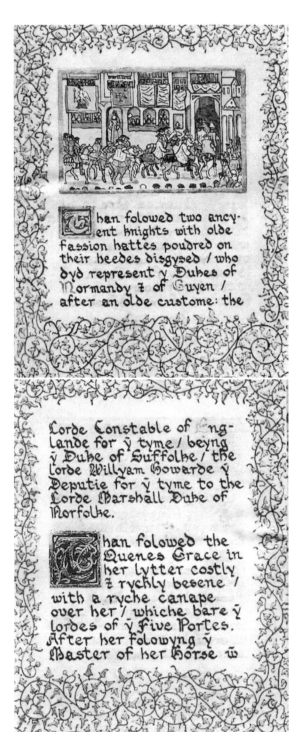

Than folowed two ancyent knights with older fassion hattes poudred on their heedes disgysed / who dyd represent y Dukes of Normandy ⁊ of Guyen / after an olde custome: the

Lorde Constable of Englande for ŷ tyme / beyng ŷ Duke of Suffolke / the lorde Willyam howarde ŷ Deputie for y tyme to the Lorde Marshall Duke of Norfolke.

Than folowed the Quenes Grace in her lytter costly ⁊ richly besene / with a ryche canape over her / whiche bare ŷ lordes of ŷ fiver Portes. After her folowying ŷ Master of her horse ŵ a white spare palfray ledde in his hande rychly apoynted.

Than folowed her noble Ladyes of Estate rychly clothed in crymosyn poudred ŵ armyns / to the nombre of xii.

Than the Mayster of ŷ Garde with the garde on both sydes of the strets in good araye ⁊ all the Constables well besene in velvet ⁊

damaske cotes with whyte staves in their handes / settyng every man in araye ⁊ order in the stretes untyll she came to Westmynster.

Than folowed four ryche charyottes ŵ

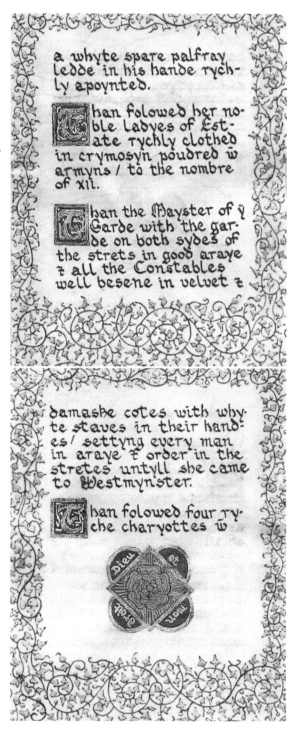

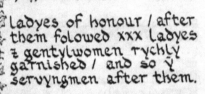

ladyes of honour / after them foloweð xxx ladyes ꝫ gentylwomen rychly garnished / and so ẙ servyngmen after them.

Anð as she was departeð from ẙ towre / a mervaylous great shot of

gonnes was there fyreð and shot.

 o this moste noble company passeð tyll her Grace came to Fanchurch where was a pagent fayre ꝫ semly / w̃ certayne chylðren who saluteð her Grace with great honour and prayse after a goodly fassyon: and so passeð forthe to Grasechurche / where was a ryght costly pagent of Apollo w̃ the Kyne Muses amonge y mountayns / syttyng on the

ladyes of honour / after them folowed xxx ladyes 7 gentylwomen rychly garnished / and so y servygmen after them.

And as she was departed from y Towre / a mervaylous great shot of

gonnes was there fyred and shot.

So this most noble company passed tyll her Grace came to Fanchurch where was a pagent fayre 7 semly / ŵ certayne chyldren who saluted her Grace with great honour and prayse after a goodly fassyon: and so passed forthe to Grasechurche / where was a ryght costly pagent of Apollo ŵ the Kyne of Muses amonge y mountayns / syttyng on the mount of Parnasus / and every of them havyinge their instrumentes and apparayle acordyng to the descryption of powers / and namely of Vrgyll

with many goodley verses to her great prayse and honour.

And so she passed through Gracyous Strete unto Leaden hall where was buylded a sumptous and a costly pagent in maner of castell wherin was fassyoned an hevenly roufe / and under it upon a grene was a roote or a stocke /wherout spronge a multytude of whyte 𝄖

red roses curyously

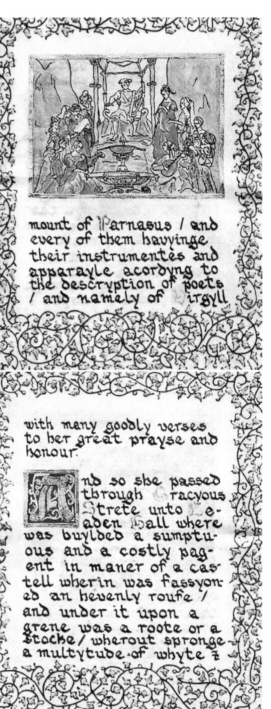

mount of Parnasus / and every of them havyinge their instrumentés and apparayle acordyng to the descryption of poets / and namely of Virgyll

with many goodly verses to her great prayse and honour.

And so she passed through Gracyous Strete unto Leaden hall where was buylded a sumptuous and a costly pagent in maner of a castell wherin was fassyoned an hevenly roufe / and under it upon a grene was a roote or a stocke / wherout spronge a multytude of whyte 𝄖

red roses curyously wrought. So from the hevenly roufe descended a Whyte Faucon / and

lighted upon y said stocke ⁊ roote / and incontynent descended an angell ŵ goodly armony / havynge a close crowne bytwene his handes / ⁊ set it on y faucons heed.

nd on the said flour sate Saynt Anne in y hyest place. And on that one syde her progeny ŵ scripture / that is to were / the thre Marys ŵ their issue / y is to understande: Mary the

wrought.

So from the hevenly roufe descended a Whyte Faucon/ and

lighted upon y said stoke ⁊ roote / and incontynent descended an angell ŵ goodly armony / havynge a close crowne bytwene his handes / ⁊ set it on y faucons heed.

And on the said flour sate Saynt Anne in y hyest place. And on that one syde her progeny ŵ scripture / that is to were / the three Marys ŵ their issue / y is to understande: Mary the mother of Christ/ Mary Solome y mother of Zebedee with the two chyldren of them. Also Mary Cleophe with husbande Alphee / with their four chyldren on y other syde. With other poetycall verses sayd and songe/ ŵ a balade in englishe to her great prayse and honour / and to all her progeny also.

And so she passed forth from thence through Cornehyll / and at y Condyt was a sumptuous pagent of the Thre Graces.

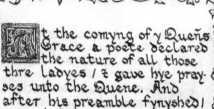

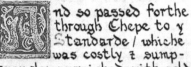

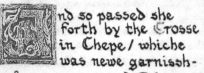

At the comyng of y Queñs Grace a poete declared the nature of all those thre ladyes / ⁊ gave hye prayses unto the Quene. And after his preamble fynyshed / every lady pertyculer spake great honour and hye prayse of the Quenes grace.

And so she passed forth with all her nobles tyll she came in Chepe / and al the Great Condyt was made a costly fountayne /wherout ranne whyte wyne / claret / ⁊ reed great plenty all that after noone. And ther was great melody with speches.

And so passed forthe through Chepe to y Standarde / whiche was costly ⁊ sumptously garnished with gold ⁊ azure / with armes ⁊ stories / whre was great armony and melody.

And so passed she forth by the Crosse in Chepe/ which was new garnisshed

/ and so through Chepe towarde the lesser Condyt. And in the mydwaye bewteeñ / the recorder of London receyved her afore the Aldermen / with great reverence ⁊ honour salutynge her Grace / with a lovyng ⁊ humble preposycion presenynge her Grace with a ryche and costly purse of golde / and in it a thousande marke in golde coyne / gyven unto her as a free gyfte of honour : to whom the Quene gave great thanks both ŵ herte ⁊ mynde.

And so her Grace passed a lytell further / and at y lesser Condyt was a costly and a ryche pagent / whereas was goodly armonye of musyke and other mynstrels / with syngyng. And within that pagent was fyve costly seates/ wherin was

set these fyve personages/
that is to wete Juno /
Pallas / Mercury / Venus
and Paris havyng a ball
of golde presentyng it to
her Grace with certayne
verses of great honour /
and chyldren syngyng a
balade to her Grace / and
prayse to all her ladyes.

And so passed forth to
Poules Gate / where
was a proper and a
sumptuous pagent / that
is to wete / ther sat 111
fayre ladyes virgyns

costly arayde with a
fayre roûde throne over
their heedes / wher
aboute was written this
– Regina Anna prospere
procede et regina / that
is in englysshe – Queen
Anne prosper procede
and reygne. The lady
that sate in the myddes
havyng a table of golde
in her hande wrytten

with letters of azure –
Veni amica coronaberis

– Come my Love thou shalbe crowned. 𝄎 two angels havyng a close crown of golde bytwene their handes. And the lady on the ryght hande had a table of sylver / wherein was written – Domine dirige gressos meos – Lorde God dyrect my wayes. The other on the lyfte hande had in another table of sylver written this – Cofide in Domini – Trust in God. And under theyr fete was a longe rol wherein was written this – Regina Anna

novum regis de sanguine natum cum paries populis aurea secula tuis – Quene Anne when thou shalte ber a newe sone of y kynges bloode / there shalbe a golden worlde unto thy people. And so y ladyes caste over her heed a multytude of wafers with rose leaves 𝄎 about y wafers were written with Letters of gold / a posey.

with Letters of azure – Veni amica coronaberis – Come my love thou shalbe crowned. 𝄎 two angels havyng a close crown of golde bytwene their handes. And the lady on the ryght hande had a table of sylver / wherin was written – Domine dirige gressos meos. Corde God dyrect my wayes. The other on the lyfte hande had in another table of sylver written this – Cofide in Domino – Trust in God. And under theyr fete was a longe rol wherin was written this Regina Anna

novum regis de sanguine natum cum paries populis aurea secula tuis – Quene Anne whan thou shalte ber a newe sone of y kynges bloode / there shalbe a golden worlde unto thy people. And so y ladyes caste over her heed a multytude of wafers with rose leaves 𝄎 about y wafers were written with Letters of gold / a posey.

And so her Grace passed forth into Poules Churchyarde / ⁊ at east ende of the chyrch agynst y schole was a great scaffolde / whereon stode y nombre of two hundred chyldren well besene / who receyved her ŵ poetes verses to her noble honour / when they had fynissed she says Amen with a joyful smylyng countenaunce.

And so passed forth through the longe Chyrchyarde / ⁊ so to Ludgate whiche was costly ⁊ sumptuously garnysshed with golde / colours / and azure / with swete armony of ballades to her greate prayse ⁊ honour / with dyverse swete instrumentes.

And thus her Grace came thorowe the cyte with great honour and royaltye / and passed thorowe Fletestrete tyll she came to y Standarde ⁊ Condyth where was made a fayre toure with foure tourettes with vanes. Therewithin great plenty of swete instrumentes with chyldren syngyng. The Standarde of mason warke

costly made with ymages ⁊ aungels / costly gylted ŵ golde and azure / with other colours and dyverse sortes of armes costly set out shall there contynue and remayne / and within the Standarde a vyce ŵ a chyme. And also there ranne out of certayne small pypes great plenty of wyne all that afternoone.

And so her Grace passed through the cyte to Temple Barre /

dyverse swete instrumentes.

And thus her Grace came thorowe the cyte with great honour and royaltye / and passed thorowe Letestrete tyll she came to y Standarde ⁊ Condyth where was made a fayre toure with foure tourettes with vanes. Therewithin great plenty of swete instrumentes with chyldren syngyng. The Standarde of mason warke

costly made with ymages ⁊ aungels / costly gyltes ŵ golde and azure / with other colours and dyverse sortes of armes costly set out shall there contynue and remayne / and within the Standarde a vyce ŵ a chyme. And also there ranne out of certayne small pypes great plenty of wyne all that afternoone.

And so her Grace passed through the cyte to Temple Barre /

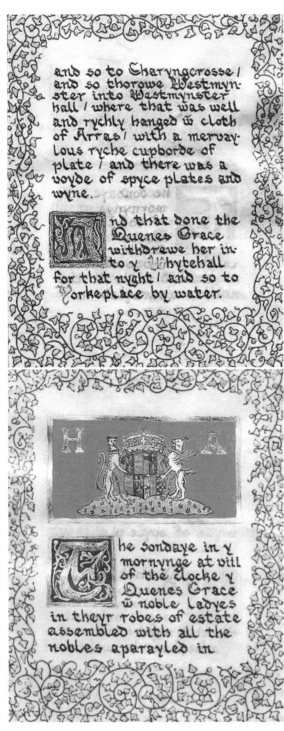

and so to Charyngcrosse / and so thorowe Westmynster into Westmynster hall / where that was well and rychly hanged ŵ cloth of Arras / with a mervaylous ryche cupborde of plate / and there was a voyde of spyce plates and wyne.

And that done the Quenes Grace withdrew her into y Whytehall for that nyght / and so to Yorkeplace by water.

The sondaye in y mornynge at viii of the clocke y Quenes Grace ŵ noble Ladyes in theyr robes of estate assembled with all the nobles aparayled in parlyament robes / as dukes / erles / archbysshops and bysshops / ŵ barons ⱻ the barons of y fyve ports with the mayre of y cite / the alderman in theyr robes as mantels of scarlet.

The barons of the fyve ports bare a ryche canopy of cloth of golde / ŵ staves of golde and four belles of sylver and gylt. The abbot of Westmynster ŵ his rygals came in

to y hall in pontificalibus with his monkes in their best copes / the kynges chapel in their best copes with y bysshops richely adorned in pontificalibus.

And the ray cloth blewe spredde from the high desses of the kinges Benche unto the hygh aulter of Westmynster.

And so every man procedynge to the mynster in the best order /every

parlyament robes / as dukes / erles / archbysshops and bysshops / ŵ barons ⱻ the barons of y fyve ports with the mayre of y cite / the alderman in theyr robes as mantels of scarlet.

he barons of the fyve ports bare a ryche canopy of cloth of golde / ŵ staves of golde and four belles of sylver and gylt. The abbot of Westmynster ŵ his rygals came in

to y hall in pontificalibus with his monkes in their best copes / the kynges chapel in their best copes with y bysshops richely adorned in pontificalibus.

nd the ray cloth blewe spredde from the high desses of the kinges Benche unto the hygh aulter of Westmynster.

nd so every man procedynge to the mynster in the best order / every

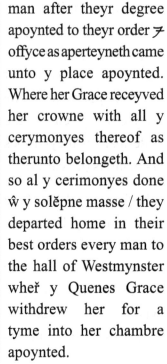

man after theyr degree apoynted to theyr order ꝫ offyce as aperteyneth came unto y place apoynted. Where her Grace receyved her crowne with all y cerymonyes thereof as therunto belongeth. And so al y cerimonyes done ŵ y solĕpne masse / they departed home in their best orders every man to the hall of Westmynster wheř y Quenes Grace withdrew her for a tyme into her chambre apoynted.

And so after a certayne space her Grace come into y hall. Than ye shulde have sene every noble man doyng their servyce to them apoynted in the best maner ŷ hath ben sene in any suche cerimony.

The Quenes Grace washed / y Archbisshops of Canterbury sayd grace. Than y nobles were set to y table there ŵ came y Quenes service with y service of the Arch-bysshop. A certayne space thre men ŵ y Quenese Graces servyce.

Before y said service came the Duke of Suffolke high constable y day and stewarde of y feest on horsbacke ꝫ mervaylously trapped in aparell with rychesse. Than with hym came the Lorde Wyllayam hawarde as Depute to y Duke of Norfolke in y rome of y Marshal of Englande on horsbacke.

The Erle of Essex carver. Therle of Sussex sewer. Therle of Darby cupberer. Therle of Arundell butteller. The visconte Lysle panter. The Lorde Bray awmoner.

These noblemen dyd theyr servyce in suche humble sorte ꝫ fassyon that it was wonder to see the payne and dylygence of them / beynge suche noble personages.

The service borne by knyghtes whiche were

bysshop. A certayne space thre men ŵ y Quenes Graces servyce.

Before y said servyce came the Duke of Suffolke high constable y day and stewarde of y feest on horsbacke ꝫ mervaylously trapped in aparell with rychesse. Than with hym came the Lorde Wyllyam hawarde as depute to y Duke of Norfolke in y rome of y Marshal of Englande on horsbacke.

The Erle of Essex carver. Therle of Sussex sewer. Therle of Darby cupberer. Therle of Arundell butteller. The visconte Lysle panter. The Lorde Bray awmoner.

These noblemen dyd theyr servyce in suche humble sorte ꝫ fassyon that it was wonder to see the payne and dylygence of them / beynge suche noble personages.

The servyce borne by knyghtes whiche were

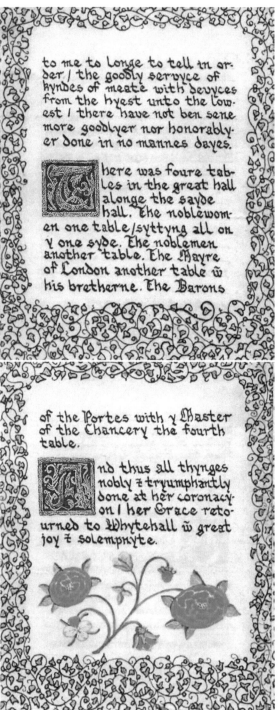

to me to longe to tell in order / the goodly servyce of kyndes of meate with devyces from the hyest unto the lowest / there have not ben sene more goodlyer nor honorablyer done in no mannes dayes.

There was foure tables in the great hall alonge the sayde hall. The noblewomen one table / syttyng all on y one syde. The noblemen another table. The Mayre of London another table ŵ his bretherne. The Barons

of the Portes with y Master of the Chancery the fourth table.

And thus all thynges nobly ꝫ tryumphantly done at her coronacyon / her Grace retourned to Whytehall ŵ great joy ꝫ solempnyte.

And the morowe was great justes at the tylte / done by xviii Lordes
⁊ knyghtes / where was broken many speares valyauntly: but some
of their horses wolde not come at their pleasure there unto the tylte
/ whiche was displeasure to some that there dyd ronne.

Thus endeth this tryumphe.

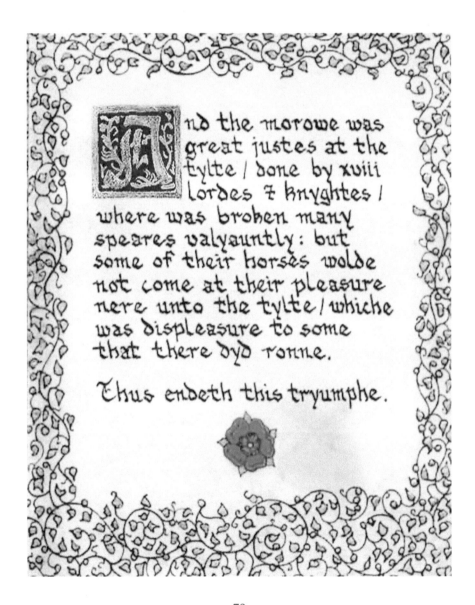

Endnotes

1   Roland H. Hui, The Tudor Society. Martin Spies supplied original coronation text. "This page is old! We are a Museum & unsorted Archive." October 2009: www.oocities.org/coronation_book/1.htm.

Chapter Five
Queen Anne Boleyn's Coronation Book translated

Henry VIII provided coronations for his first two wives, but Katharine of Aragon shared Henry VIII's coronation in 1509 and provided no grandchildren, whereas Anne Boleyn had her own coronation, and grandchildren.

'A Coronation Book for Queen Anne Boleyn':

"On 1 June 1533, Anne Boleyn, the mistress (secretly married) of King Henry VIII of England, achieved her greatest triumph. Overcoming great adversity, including the enmity of foreign powers and the opposition of the Church, she was crowned Queen of England. It was a moment Anne had eagerly anticipated for seven years. She and the King had already wedded in secret, Henry's marriage to his first wife Katherine of Aragon was annulled, and now Anne carried the nation's longed for heir. It was little wonder that the motto she chose at her crowning was 'The Most Happy'.

"Anne's happiness was only marred by the reception of the sullen London crowds who regarded her as an upstart and as the King's concubine. Nevertheless, the coronation festivities were a great piece of theatrical showmanship and political propaganda [Jesuit comments]. Anne was hailed as the progenitor of a great new age – it was foretold that it was her 'son' who will bring forth a 'golden world' unto the English. The prediction was half correct. In time it was a daughter, Elizabeth, who was to fulfil the expectation [followed by the grandson Raleigh. Jesuits apply predictions most see as unfulfilled].

"A description of Anne Boleyn's coronation was set down in pamphlet form shortly after the festivities by the London printer Wynkin de Worde in 1533. Entitled 'The Noble Tryumphaunt Coronacyon of Quene Anne – Wyfe unto the Noble Kynge Henry the VIII', it consisted of 11 typeset pages with a rather crude woodcut of a courtly scene on the front cover. The book (measuring 4" x 5" [102 x 127mm) was done on calfskin vellum with illustrations and miniature portraits in watercolor. Gold leaf was applied throughout.

"This 'coronation book' is a transcription done by hand of Wynkin de Worde's pamphlet ... begun in January 2002 ... completed in March 2004" and transcribed word for word:

HA 1533

The noble tryumphant coronacyon of quene Anne /
wife unto the noble kynge henry the viii

Anna Bolina Vxor henricus Octa.

First the xxix daye of Maye beynge thursday all the worshyp-full craftes and occupacyons in theyr best araye goodly besene toke theyr barges which splayed ŵ goodly banners fresshe and newe with the cognysaunce and armes of theyr faculty to the nombre of L great barges comly besene and every barge havynge mynstrels making great and swete armony.

Also there was the bachelors comly barge besene, decked with innumerable baners and all about hanged with ryche cloth of golde / ꝫ foystes waytyng her upon / decked with a great shotte of ordynaunce / whiche descended the river afore all ŷ barges / and the bachelers barge formest / and to followyng in good araye ꝫ ordre / every craft in their degree and ordre tyll they come to Greenwyche / and there they taryed abydynge the Quenes grace /which was a wonderful goodly sight to beholde.

Than at thre of the clocke the quenes grace came to her barge
/ and incontynent all the cytezyns with that goodly company
set forth toward London in good araye / as before is sayd. And
to wryte what nombre of gonshot / what with chambres and
great peces of ordynance were shotte as she passed by in
dyvers places / it passeth my memory to wryte or to tell the
nombre of them / and specially at Ratclyf ⁊ at Lymehouse out
of certeyne shyppes. And so ŷ quenes grace in her ryche barge
among her nobles / the cytezyns accompanyed her to London
unto the Toure Wharfe.

Also ere she came nere the Toure there was shot innumerable peces of ordynaunce / as ever there by any mennes
remembrauces / where the kyng receyved her grace with a
loving countenaunce / and so gave great thanks and prayse to
all the cytezynes for theyr great kyndnesse ⁊ lovynge labour
and paynes in that behalfe taken / to the great joy and comforte
of all the cytezyns of London.

Also to beholde the wonderful nombre of people that ever
was sene that stode on the shore on bothe sydes of the ryver /
was never in one syght out of ŷ cyte on Londone sene. That in
goodly lodgynges and houses that be on ŷ ryversyde bytwene
Grenwyche and London / it passeth al mennes judgementes to
esteme the infinyte nombre of then / wherin her grace with al
her ladyes rejoysed moche.

Knyghtes made al Grenwyche the sonday before Whytsonday
And the sondaye before they tryumphe / beyng the xxv daye
of Maye / the kynge made all his manner of Grenwhyche all
these knyghtes. Sir Christopher Danby, Sir Thomas Butteller,
Sir Christopher hylarde, Sir William Walgrave, Sir Brian
hastynges, Sir Willyam Feldeyng, Sir Thomas Betham.

The friday made knyghtes of the Baththe xix. whose names foloweth. Also on friday the xxx day of May ŷ kynge created and made in the towre of London xix noble men knyghtes of the bathe / whose names folowe. The Lord Marques Dorset, The erle of Derby,

Also the saturday the laste day of May the kynge made knyghtes of the Swerde in ŷ towre of London / whose names folowe [in alphabetical order by surname].

The lorde Clyfforde / sone ≯ heyre to the erle of Cumberlande
The lorde Fitzwater / sone ≯ heyr to the erle of Sussex
The lorde hastynges / sone ≯ heyr to the erle of huntyngton

The lorde Barkeley	Syr Johan hudelston
The lorde Mountagle	Syr Thomas Jermey
The lorde Vaux	Syr Rycharde Lygon
Syr Thomas Aroundell	Syr Edwarde Maidison
Sir Randolfe Buerton	Syr John Mordant
Sir George Calverley	Syr Robert Nedham
Syr Johan Chaworth	Syr henry Parker
Syr Johan Constable	Syr Thomas Ponynges
Sir George Conyers	Sir Thomas Rusche
Sir Wyllam Drury	Syr Johan Saintclere
Syr henry Feryngton	Syr henry Savell
Sir Edward Fytton	Syr Marmaduc Tunstall
Syr George Fitzwyllyam	Syr Johan Tyndall
Sir Johan Gernynghm	Syr Thomas Umpton
Syr George Gresley	Syr Fraunces Weston
Syr Thomas halsall	Syr Wyllyam Wyndsour / sone
Syr Johan horsley	≯ heyr to the lorde Wyndesour

i. GEORGE III.'s INTEREST IN FARMING.—I understand that in setting up a Yorkshire farm (and others) near Windsor, George III. imported families from Yorkshire or Lincolnshire to take up cultivation. I should be glad to have all details concerning the different farms, the names of these families, and what became of them.　CURIO-BOX.

Replies.

KNIGHTS MADE AT THE CORONATION OF QUEEN ANNE BOLEYN, 1533.

(11 S. xii. 301, 369.)

" THE noble triumphant Coronation of Queen Anne, wife unto the most noble King Henry VIII. Imprinted at London in Fleet Street by Wynkyn de Worde for John Gough " contains the fullest—probably complete—list of these knights. The pamphlet is included by the late Edward Arber in vol. ii. of his ' English Garner.' On 25 May, " the Sunday before the Triumph," the King, we are told, made at his manor of Greenwich seven knights, whose names are given. See the list in Metcalfe's ' Book of Knights,' p. 62 ; also in Shaw's ' Knights of England,' vol. ii. p. 49. On Friday, 30 May, the King made in the Tower nineteen Knights of the Bath—names given by both Metcalfe (pp. 62-4) and Shaw (vol. i. pp. 149-50), but in both the number is reduced to eighteen by the omission of Lord Berkeley. On 31 May the King then again in the Tower made no fewer than forty-six " Knights of the Sword " ; and on 8 June at Greenwich eleven others. The lists of these are so much more extensive than those found in Metcalfe and Shaw—who enumerate twenty only on 31 May, and, with one exception, omit altogether those on 8 June—that I venture to ask the Editor of ' N. & Q.' to print them entire.

On 31 May (given by Shaw as 1 June) the knights made were :—

Sir William Drury.
*Sir Thomas Rush.
*Sir George Calverley.
*Sir George Conyers.
*Sir John Chaworth.
*Sir John Constable.
Sir John Horsley.
*Sir John Sant Clere.
*Sir Henry Feryngton.

* Those marked with an asterisk are in Metcalfe's and Shaw's lists.

*Sir Thomas Halsall.
*Sir Anthony Windsor.
*Sir John Willoughby.
Sir Thomas Mysseden.
Sir Henry Delves.
Sir Richard Bulkeley.
Sir Walter Smith.
Sir William Uvedale.
Sir William Sandon.
Sir Edmond Trafford.
Sir Henry Sutton.
Sir William Malory.
Sir John Tyrell.
Sir Nicholas Sturley.
Sir John Gerningham.
*Sir Randolph Brierton.
*Sir Edward Fytton.
*Sir Robert Nedham.
*Sir George Gresley.
*Sir Thomas Umpton.
*Sir Richard Lygon.
*Sir Edward Maidison.
*Sir Marm. Tunstall.
Sir Robert Kirkham.
Sir Walter Hubbert.
Sir Thomas Kitson.
Sir Thomas Foulehurst.
Sir Peter Warburton.
Sir Thomas Laking.
Sir Henry Everyngham.
Sir Thomas Massingberd.
Sir James Baskervylle.
Sir Arthur Eyre.
Sir John Nories.
Sir John Harcourt.
Sir William Browne.
Sir Randolph Manering.

And on 8 June at Greenwich :—

Sir Christopher Corwen.
Sir Geoffrey Mydelton.
Sir Hugh Trevyneon.
Sir George West.
Sir Clement Herberton.
*Sir Humphrey Feries.
Sir John Dawn.
Sir Richard Haughton. ·
Sir Thomas Langton.
Sir Edward Bowton.
Sir Henry Capel.

The " Six Commoners " named by CANON FLETCHER do not appear amongst these creations, and, I fancy, are incorporated in the original MS. by some error. That all six were knights may be accepted, but their knighthood occurred at dates later than Anne Boleyn's coronation. They certainly were not Knights of the Bath.

" Mr. Verney of Penleve " may be easily identified as Ralph Verney of Penley, Herts,

Also the sonday after Whytsonday beyng Trynte sonday ⁊ the viii daye of June / was made at Grenewyche these knyghtes folowyng.

Syr James Baskervyll

Syr Edwarde Bowton

Syr Wyllyam Browne

Syr Rycharde Bulkelley

Syr henry Capell

Syr Christofer Corwen

Syr Johan Dawne

Syr henry Delves

Syr henry Everyngham

Syr Arthur Eyre

Syr humprey Feryes

Syr Thomas Foulehurst

Syr Richarde haughton

Syr Johan harcourt

Syr Clement herleston

Syr Walter hubbert

Syr Robert kyrkham

Syr Thomas kytson

Syr Thomas Lakyng

Syr Wyllyam Malorie

Syr Randolfe Manerig

Syr Thomas Massyngberd

Syr Geffray Mydelton

Syr Thomas Mysseden

Syr Johan Nories

Syr Wyllyam Sandon

Syr Walter Smythe

Syr Nycholas Sturley

Syr henry Sutton

Syr Edmonde Trafford

Syr hugh Trevyneon

Syr Johan Tyrell

Syr Wyllyam Unedall

Syr Peter Warburton

Syr George West

Syr Johan Wyllongby

Syr Anthony Wyndsour

Also all the pavementes of the cyte from Charyn Crosse to ŷ towre was over coverde and cast with gravell.

And the same saturday being Whytson Even the Mayre with all the Aldermen ⁊ the craftes of the cyte prepared aray in a good order to stande ⁊ receyve her / and with rayles for every craft to stande ⁊ leane from prease of people.

The Mayre mette the Quenes grace at her comyng forthe of ŷ towre / and all his bretherne and aldermen standyng in Chepe.

Upon the same saturday the Quene came forth from ŷ towre towarde Westminster in goodley aray / as hereafter foloweth.

She passed the stretes first with certayne strangers / their horses trapped ŵ blewe sylke / ⁊ themselves in blewe velvet with white fethers acompanyed two ⁊ two. Lykewise squiers / knights / barons ⁊ baronetts / knights of ŷ Bath clothed in vyolet garmentes / edged with armyns lyke juges. Than folowyng ŷ Juges of the Lawe ⁊ abbottes. All these estates were to ŷ nombre of CC cople ŵ more / two ⁊ two accompanyed.

And than folowed byshops to ⁊ two : ⁊ the Archbyssshops of Yorke ⁊ Canterbury / y ambassaders of France ⁊ Vanyce / the Lorde Mayre ŵ a mace / Mayster Garter the kyng of heraldes ⁊ the kyngs cote armour upon him with y Offycers of Armes / apoyntyng every estate in their degre.

Than folowed two ancyent knights with older fassion hattes poudred on their heedes disgysed / who dyd represent y Dukes of Normandy ⁊ of Guyen / after an olde custome: the Lorde Constable of Englande for ŷ tyme / beyng ŷ Duke of Suffolke / the lorde Willyam howarde ŷ Deputie for y tyme to the Lorde Marshall Duke of Norfolke.

Than folowed the Quenes Grace in her lytter costly ⁊ richly besene / with a ryche canape over her / whiche bare ŷ lordes of ŷ fiver Portes. After her folowying ŷ Master of her horse ŵ a white spare palfray ledde in his hande rychly apoynted.

Than folowed her noble Ladyes of Estate rychly clothed in crymosyn poudred ŵ armyns / to the nombre of xii.

Than the Mayster of ŷ Garde with the garde on both sydes of the strets in good araye ⁊ all the Constables well besene in velvet ⁊ damaske cotes with whyte staves in their handes / settyng every man in araye ⁊ order in the stretes untyll she came to Westmynster.

Than folowed four ryche charyottes ŵ ladyes of honour / after them folowed xxx ladyes 7 gentylwomen rychly garnished / and so y servygmen after them.

And as she was departed from y Towre / a mervaylous great shot of gonnes was there fyred and shot.

So this most noble company passed tyll her Grace came to Fanchurch where was a pagent fayre ⁊ semly / ŵ certayne chyldren who saluted her Grace with great honour and prayse after a goodly fassyon: and so passed forthe to Grasechurche / where was a ryght costly pagent of Apollo ŵ the Kyne of Muses amonge y mountayns / syttyng on the mount of Parnasus / and every of them havyinge their instrumentes and apparayle acordyng to the descryption of powers / and namely of Vrgyll with many goodley verses to her great prayse and honour.

And so she passed through Gracyous Strete unto Leaden hall where was buylded a sumptous and a costly pagent in maner of castell wherin was fassyoned an hevenly roufe / and under it upon a grene was a roote or a stocke /wherout spronge a multytude of whyte ⁊ red roses curyously wrought. So from the hevenly roufe descended a Whyte Faucon/ and lighted upon y said stoke ⁊ roote / and incontynent descended an angell ŵ goodly armony / havynge a close crowne bytwene his handes / ⁊ set it on y faucons heed.

And on the said flour sate Saynt Anne in y hyest place. And on that one syde her progeny ŵ scripture / that is to were /

the three Marys ŵ their issue / y is to understande: Mary the mother of Christ/ Mary Solome y mother of Zebedee with the two chyldren of them. Also Mary Cleophe with husbande Alphee / with their four chyldren on y other syde. With other poetycall verses sayd and songe/ ŵ a balade in englishe to her great prayse and honour / and to all her progeny also.

And so she passed forth from thence through Cornehyll / and at y Condyt was a sumptuous pagent of the Thre Graces.

At the comyng of y Queñs Grace a poete declared the nature of all those thre ladyes / ꝛ gave hye prayses unto the Quene. And after his preamble fynyshed / every lady pertyculer spake great honour and hye prayse of the Quenes grace.

And so she passed forth with all her nobles tyll she came in Chepe / and al the Great Condyt was made a costly fountayne /wherout ranne whyte wyne / claret / ꝛ reed great plenty all that after noone. And ther was great melody with speches.

And so passed forthe through Chepe to y Standarde / whiche was costly ꝛ sumptously garnished with gold ꝛ azure / with armes ꝛ stories / whre was great armony and melody.

And so passed she forth by the Crosse in Chepe/ which was new garnisshed / and so through Chepe towarde the lesser Condyt. And in the mydwaye bewteeñ / the recorder of London receyved her afore the Aldermen / with great reverence ꝛ honour salutynge her Grace / with a lovyng ꝛ humble preposycion presenynge her Grace with a ryche and costly purse of golde / and in it a thousande marke in golde coyne / gyven unto her as a free gyfte of honour : to whom the Quene gave great thanks both ŵ herte ꝛ mynde.

And so her Grace passed a lytell further / and at y lesser Condyt was a costly and a ryche pagent / whereas was goodly armonye of musyke and other mynstrels / with syngyng. And within that pagent was fyve costly seates/ where was set these fyve personaged / that is to wete Juno / Pallas / Mercury / Venus and Paris havyng a ball of golde presentyng it to her Grace with certayne verses of great honour / and chyldren syngyng a balade to her Grace / and prayse to all her ladyes.

And so passed forth to Poules Gate / where was a proper and a sumptuous pagent / that is to wete / ther sat 111 fayre ladyes virgyns costly arayde with a fayre roũde throne over their heedes / wher aboute was written this – Regina Anna prospere procede et regina / that is in englysshe – Queen Anne prosper procede and reygne. The lady that sate in the myddes havyng a table of golde in her hande wrytten with letters of azure – Veni amica coronaberis – Come my Love thou shalbe crowned. ⁊ two angels havyng a close crown of golde bytwene their handes. And the lady on the ryght hande had a table of sylver / wherein was written – Domine dirige gressos meos – Lorde God dyrect my wayes. The other on the lyfte hande had in another table of sylver written this – Cofide in Domini – Trust in God. And under theyr fete was a longe rol wherein was written this – Regina Anna novum regis de sanguine natum cum paries populis aurea secula tuis – Quene Anne whan thou shalte ber a newe sone of y kynges bloode / there shalbe a golden worlde unto thy people. And so y ladyes caste over her heed a multytude of wafers with rose leaves ⁊ about y wafers were written with Letters of gold / a posey.

And so her Grace passed forth into Poules Churchyarde / ⁊ at east ende of the chyrch agynst y schole was a great scaffolde /

whereon stode y nombre of two hundred chyldren well besene / who receyved her ŵ poetes verses to her noble honour / when they had fynissed she says Amen with a joyful smylyng countenaunce.

And so passed forth through the longe Chyrchyarde / ≠ so to Ludgate whiche was costly ≠ sumptuously garnysshed with golde / colours / and azure / with swete armony of ballades to her greate prayse ≠ honour / with dyverse swete instrumentes.

And thus her Grace came thorowe the cyte with great honour and royaltye / and passed thorowe Fletestrete tyll she came to y Standarde ≠ Condyth where was made a fayre toure with foure tourettes with vanes. Therewithin great plenty of swete instrumentes with chyldren syngyng. The Standarde of mason warke costly made with ymages ≠ aungels / costly gylted ŵ golde and azure / with other colours and dyverse sortes of armes costly set out shall there contynue and remayne / and within the Standarde a vyce ŵ a chyme. And also there ranne out of certayne small pypes great plenty of wyne all that afternoone.

And so her Grace passed through the cyte to Temple Barre / and so to Charyngcrosse / and so thorowe Westmynster into Westmynster hall / where that was well and rychly hanged ŵ cloth of Arras / with a mervaylous ryche cupborde of plate / and there was a voyde of spyce plates and wyne.

And that done the Quenes Grace withdrew her into y Whytehall for that nyght / and so to Yorkeplace by water.

The sondaye in y mornynge at viii of the clocke y Quenes Grace ŵ noble Ladyes in theyr robes of estate assembled with all the nobles aparayled in parlyament robes / as dukes / erles

/ archbysshops and bysshops / ŵ barons ꝛ the barons of y fyve ports with the mayre of y cite / the alderman in theyr robes as mantels of scarlet.

The barons of the fyve ports bare a ryche canopy of cloth of golde / ŵ staves of golde and four belles of sylver and gylt. The abbot of Westmynster ŵ his rygals came in to y hall in pontificalibus with his monkes in their best copes / the kynges chapel in their best copes with y bysshops richely adorned in pontificalibus.

And the ray cloth blewe spredde from the high desses of the kinges Benche unto the hygh aulter of Westmynster.

And so every man procedynge to the mynster in the best order /every man after theyr degree apoynted to theyr order ꝛ offyce as aperteyneth came unto y place apoynted. Where her Grace receyved her crowne with all y cerymonyes thereof as therunto belongeth. And so al y cerimonyes done ŵ y solĕpne masse / they departed home in their best orders every man to the hall of Westmynster wheř y Quenes Grace withdrew her for a tyme into her chambre apoynted.

And so after a certayne space her Grace come into y hall. Than ye shulde have sene every noble man doyng their servyce to them apoynted in the best maner ŷ hath ben sene in any suche cerimony.

The Quenes Grace washed / y Archbisshops of Canterbury sayd grace. Than y nobles were set to y table there ŵ came y Quenes service with y service of the Arch bysshop. A certayne space thre men ŵ y Quenese Graces servyce.

Before y said service came the Duke of Suffolke high constable y day and stewarde of y feest on horsbacke ⁊ mervaylously trapped in aparell with rychesse. Than with hym came the Lorde Wyllayam hawarde as Depute to y Duke of Norfolke in y rome of y Marshal of Englande on horsbacke.

The Erle of Essex carver. Therle of Sussex sewer. Therle of Darby cupberer. Therle of Arundell butteller. The visconte Lysle panter. The Lorde Bray awmoner.

These noblemen dyd theyr servyce in suche humble sorte ⁊ fassyon that it was wonder to see the payne and dylygence of them / beynge suche noble personages.

The service borne by knyghtes whiche were to me to longe to tell in order / the goodly servyce of kyndes of meate with devyces from the hyest unto the lowest / there have not ben sene more goodlyer nor honorablyer done in no mannes dayes.

There was foure tables in the great hall alonge the sayde hall. The noblewomen one table / syttyng all on y one syde. The noblemen another table. The Mayre of London another table ŵ his bretherne. The Barons of the Portes with y Master of the Chancery the fourth table.

And thus all thynges nobly ⁊ tryumphantly done at her coronacyon / her Grace retourned to Whytehall ŵ great joy ⁊ solempnyte.

And the morowe was great justes at the tylte / done by xviii Lordes ⁊ knyghtes / where was broken many speares valyauntly: but some of their horses wolde not come at their pleasure there unto the tylte / whiche was displeasure to some that there dyd ronne.

Thus endeth this tryumphe.

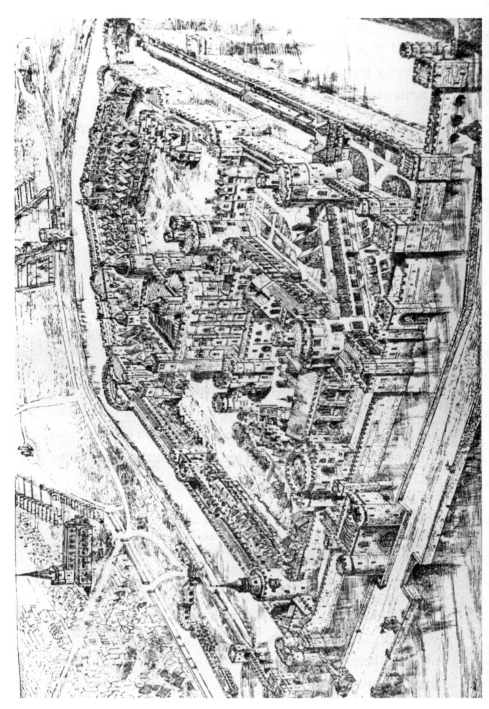

The Tower of London in the 1500s.

Chapter Six – Queen Anne Boleyn's Coronation Book translated into Modern English

Translated into modern English 'A Coronation Book for Queen Anne Boleyn' reads:

Henry & Anne 1533

The noble triumphant coronation of Queen Anne, wife unto the noble King Henry VIII

Anne Boleyn Wife of Henry VIII.

1533, **29 May, Thursday:** All the worshipful crafts and occupations were in their best array on their 50 comely barges displaying fresh new banners with the cognisance and arms of their faculty, each barge with minstrels making great and sweet harmony.

The comely bachelors' barge was decked with innumerable banners, hung with rich cloth of gold & with swift boats (foystes) waiting upon Queen Anne, decked with a great shot of ordinance, which led all other vessels down the river in good array & order, every craft in their degree and order till they reached Greenwich, where they tarried abiding the Queens' grace. It was a wonderful goodly sight to behold.

Then at 3 o'clock the Queen's grace came to her barge, and incontynent[1] (proving that she was Queen) all the citizens with that goodly company set forth toward London in good array with a large number of gunshot, chambers and great ordinance, as she passed diverse places, especially from ships at Ratcliff & Limehouse.

And so the Queen's grace in her rich barge amongst her nobles, citizens accompanied her to the Tower of London Wharf. When she came near the Tower innumerable ordinance was shot, more than any man remembers. Here the king received her grace with a loving countenance, and gave great thanks and praise to all the citizens for their great kindness, loving labour and pains taken on their behalf. This was to the great joy and comfort of all the citizens of London.

Also wonderful to behold the largest number of people ever seen in the city on London standing on both shores of the River Thames, and from good lodgings and riverside houses between Greenwich and London, the only time this was ever seen. This infinite number of them surpassed every man's expectations and her grace with all her ladies rejoiced much in the infinite number of them.

1533, 25 May, Sunday: The king made all his manner of Knights made at Greenwich on the Sunday before Whitsunday (for here on in all placed in alphabetical order):

i.   Sir Thomas Betham (~~Metham~~)

ii.   Sir Thomas Butteller

iii.   Sir Christopher Danby MP JP (1503–71)

iv.   Sir William Fielding (Sir Willyam Feldeyng)

v.   Sir Brian Hastings (Sir Brian hastynges)

vi.   Sir Christopher Hylard (Sir Christopher hylarde)

vii.   Sir William Walgrave ... seven (7)[23]

1533, 30 May, Friday: Also the King created and made in the Tower of London 19 noble men Knights of the Bath, whose names follow:

i.   Henry Grey, 1st Duke of Suffolk, KG KB (1517–54) ... The Lord Marques Dorset

ii.   Edward Stanley, 3rd Earl of Derby KG (1509–72) ... The erle of Derby

36 knights made the following day, listed here in alphabetical order for cross-referencing:

iii.   Thomas Berkeley, 6th Baron Berkeley (1505–34) Hopeful son ... The Lorde Barkeley

iv.   Henry Clifford (1517–70) 2nd Earl of Cumberland (1542–70) ... The lorde Clyfforde

v.   Robert Radcliffe KG, KB, PC (1483–1542) 10th Baron Fitzwalter 1506–42, 1st Earl of Sussex 1529–42 ... The lorde Fitzwater / sone ⅞ heyr to the erle of Sussex

vi.   Francis Hastings KG (1514–61) 2nd erle of huntyngton (1544–61) ... The lorde hastynge

vii.   Thomas Stanley, 2nd Baron Monteagle (1507–60) w staunch Jesuit son ... lorde Mountagle

viii. Thomas Vaux, 2nd Baron Vaux of Harrowden KB (1509–56) The lorde Vaux [6]

ix.   Sir Thomas Arundell (1502–52) of Wardour Castle ... Syr Thomas Aroundell

x.   Sir George Fitzwilliam (1517~60+) ... Syr George Fitzwyllyam of Lyncolne shyre

xi.   Sir Thomas Jermyn (1481–1552, Sheriff of Norfolk & Suffolk ... Syr Thomas Jermey

xii. Sir John Huddleston (1517–57) Jesuit married Bridget Cotton ... Syr Johan hudelston

xiii. Sir John Mordaunt (d. 1562) son & heir to the Lord Mordant ... Syr John Mordant

xiv. Sir Henry Parker (1514–52) son & heir of the Lord Morley ... Syr henry Parker[4]

xv. Sir Thomas Poynings, 1st Baron Poynings (1512–45) ... Syr Thomas Ponynges

xvi. Sir Henry Savile of Methley owned 'Savile Colliery' coalmine ... Syr henry Savell

xvii. Sir John Tyndall KB (1487–1539) ... Syr Johan Tyndall[5]

xviii. Sir Francis Weston KB (1511–17 May 1536) ... Syr Fraunces Weston

xix. Sir William Windsor ~ Wyndsore ~ Wyndesor (1498–1558) son & heir to the Baron Windsor of Bradenham ... Syr Wyllyam Wyndsour.

King Henry VIII made 19 knights on Friday 30 May 1533. Confusion arose with elevations on Friday 30 May 1533 for Knights of the Bath ... and elevation on Saturday, 31 May 1533 for Knights of the Sword, being two ceremonies, first of 19 names, then of 27 names.

1533, 31 May, Saturday: "The King then again in the Tower made 46 'Knights of the Sword'."[6]

i. Sir Randoph Brereton (~1487–1536) ... Sir Randolfe Buerton, Knight of the Sword[7]

ii. Sir George Calverley, of Lea (1456–May 1536) ... Sir George Calverley

iii. Sir Johan Chaworth (1498–1558) of Wiverton, Nottingham-shire ... Syr Johan Chaworth

iv.   Sir John Constable (1526–79) MP for Hedon 1553, 1558 &1563 ... Syr Johan Constable

v.   Sir George Conyers (1511–67) son of Sir Thomas Conyers & Margaret Radcliffe

vi.   Sir William Drury (1527–79) English statesman and soldier ... Sir Wyllam Drury

vii. Sir Henry Farrington (1471–1549/51) 3rd Earl of Derby's Sec ... Syr henry Feryngton[8]

viii. Sir Edward Fitton (~1500–48) of Gawsworth, Cheshire ... Sir Edward Fytton

ix.   Sir George Gresley (1494–1548) ... Syr George Gresley

x.   Sir Thomas Halsall (1500–39) ... Syr Thomas halsall

xi.   Sir John Horsley (1501–64) married Martha Radcliffe ... Syr Johan horsley

xii. Sir John Jerningham (1490–1559) ... Sir Johan Gernynghm ~ Gerningham ~ Jernegan

xiii. Sir Richard Lygon (~1491–1556) Sheriff in Worcestershire ... Syr Rycharde Lygon

xiv. Sir Edward Madison (~1484–1554) of Kingston-upon-Hull ... Syr Edwarde Maidison

xv.   Sir Robert Needham, Kt. Sheriff of Shropshire (1476–1556) ... Syr Robert Nedham

xvi. Sir Thomas Rush ~ Russhe (~1487–June 1537) ... Sir Thomas Rusche[9]

xvii. Sir John Saint Clere (~1511–57) relative of Anne Boleyn ... Syr Johan Saintclere

xviii. Sir Marmaduke Tunstall (~1507–58) ... Syr Marmaduc Tunstall, knighted 1 June 1533

xix. Sir Thomas Unton, MP (1464–4 August 1533) known as Syr Thomas Umpton

Henry VIII's Letters and Papers, Foreign and Domestic, Volume 6, for June 1533, edited by James Gairdner in 1882, does list on pages 275–84 that "On Saturday, 30 May 1533, the following persons were made knights of the Sword", but it was Saturday, 31 May 1533. Confusion arose with elevations on Friday 30 May 1533 for Knights of the Bath ... and elevations on Saturday 31 May 1533 for Knights of the Sword, which included:

xx. Sir James Baskerville of Eardisle (b.b. 1506–72) ... Syr James Baskervyll

xxi. Sir William Browne (d.1551) ... Syr Wyllyam Browne

xxii. Sir Richard Bulkeley (1524–73) Welsh MP ... Syr Rycharde Bulkelley

xxiii. Sir Henry Delves (1498–1560) of Doddington, Cheshire ... Syr henry Delves

xxiv. Sir Henry Everyingham (1515–46) Henry of Birkin ... Sir henry Everyngham

xxv. Sir Arthur 'of Padley' Eyre (1481–1560) ... Syr Arthur Eyre

xxvi. Sir Thomas Fulleshurst of Crewe (1501–88) Sheriff Cheshire ... Syr Thomas Foulehurst[10]

xxvii. Sir John Harcourt (of Stanton Harcourt, 1500–65) ... Syr Johan harcourt

xxviii. Sir Walter Hobart (1477–27 Nov. 1538) ... Syr Walter hubbert[11]

xix. Sir Thomas Kirkham (1500/4–52) ... Syr Robert kyrkham

xxx. Sir Thomas Kitson (1485–1540) Sheriff of London 1533–4 ... Syr Thomas kytson

xxxi. Syr Thomas Lakyng[12]

xxxii. Sir William Mallory (1498–1547) of Hutton Conyers, Yorks ... Syr Wyllyam Malorie

xxxiii. Sir Randall Mainwaring (1495–1577) m. Elizabeth Brereton ... Syr Randolfe Manerig[13]

xxxiv. Sir Thomas Massingberd m. 1495 Joan de Bratoft ... Syr Thomas Massyngberd[14]

xxxv. Syr Thomas Mysseden[15]

xxxvi. Sir John Norreys (1481–1564) Usher of chamber to Henry VIII ... Syr Johan Nories

xxxvii. Sir William Sandon (1522–99) ... Syr Wyllyam Sandon[16]

xxxviii. Sir Walter Smythe (c.1501–53) in 1515 married Mary Ferrers ... Syr Walter Smythe

xxix. Sir Nicholas Sturley ~ Strelley ... Syr Nycholas Sturley

xxxx. Sir Henry Sutton (~1500–59) ... Syr henry Sutton

xxxxi. Sir Edmund Trafford, Knight of Trafford IV (1498–1563) ... Syr Edmonde Trafford

xxxxii. Sir John Tyrrell (d.c. 1573) ... Syr Johan Tyrell

xxxxiii. Sir John Evedalle (1482–1549) Clerk to Queen Anne Boleyn ... Syr Wyllyam Unedall[17]

xxxxiv. Sir Peter Warburton (b.c.1472) of Bromfield, Cheshire ... Syr Peter Warburton

xxxxv. Sir John Willoughby (b.c.1482–1550) m. Anne Grey ... Syr Johan Wyllongby

xxxxvi. Sir Anthony Wyndsour, bro. of Sir Andrew Windsor (1467–1543) 1st Baron Windsor ~ Wyndsore ~ Wyndesor ~ Keepers and Master of the Great Wardrobe 1504–43.

King Henry VIII made 46 Knights of the Sword on Saturday 31 May 1533 to celebrate Queen Anne Boleyn's independent Coronation ... and the day prior he made 19 Knights of the Bath. This is 65 elevations in the two days, 30–31 May 1533, which marks 'macrocosm-microcosm' "6/5" and with the Coronation, it is 66 elevations in 2 days, which marks "33".

1533, 8 June, Sunday: Also the Sunday after Whitsunday being Trinity Sunday, the following ten knights were made at Greenwich ..."At Greenwich the King made another 11 'Knights of the Sword'."[18] The Catholic historians omitted the Commander tenths of spiritualities, Sir Thomas Langton:

i. Sir Edward Bayntun (1480–1544) vice-chamberlain to Anne Boleyn ... Syr Edwarde Bowton

ii. Sir Henry Capel (1505–58) MP for Somerset ... Syr henry Capell

iii. Sir Christopher Curwen (1467/77–1535/57) of Workington ... Syr Christofer Corwen

iv. Sir John Dawnay (1489–1552) of Cowick, Sheriff of Yorkshire ... Syr Johan Dawne

v. Sir Humphrey Ferrers (1483–1553) Tamworth Castle ... Syr humprey Feryes

vi. Sir Richard Haughton, of Lea (1496–1559) ... Syr Richarde haughton

vii. Sir Clement Harleston, Kt. (1493–1544) ... Syr Clement herleston

viii. Sir Thomas Langton (1496–1569) commander tenths of spiritualities, omitted by most.

ix. Sir Geoffrey Mydelton (1482–1545) ... Syr Geffray Mydelton

x.   Sir Hugh Trevanion (1516–71, father of Elizabeth Carey ...
       Sir hugh Trevyneon

xi.   Sir George West (1490/1510–38) ... Syr George West.[19]

Francis Beaumont (1584–1616) was a dramatist in the English
Renaissance theatre, most famous for his collaborations with John
Fletcher (1579–1625) a Jacobean playwright.Francis Beaumont
and John Fletcher wrote biographical works of their own invention,
writing under King James VI/I "the Shit" after Shakespeare 'died'
in 1616, assuming to write for the King's Men, and assuming to
replace Shakespeare, but were just Jesuits rewriting English history.

They were known as the 'Fletcher canon', specialist 'influencers' &
Antiquaries, who wrote the most broadly spread lies of Jesuit cause,
confusing all history. In this manner, they invented knighthoods for
their mates, and then attempted to advertise them as real:

> "The 'Six Commoners' named by Canon Fletcher do not
> appear amongst these creations, and ... are incorporated into
> the original MS. [in] error ... their knighthood occurred at
> dates later than Anne Boleyn's coronation. They certainly
> were not Knights of the Bath ... 'Mr. Verney of Penleye' is
> Ralph Verney of Periley, Herts'."

Actually, it's 'Verney of Pendley, Hertfordshire', and Ralph Verney
was the chamberlain to Henry VII's wife, Elizabeth of York
(1466–1503), and to their daughter Margaret Tudor, although he
had a nephew, also called 'Ralph Verney'. This is all intentional
confusion. It's not necessarily 'Ralph Verney' ... any male Verney
would do ... so who got the free knighthood ... six of them ... but
they couldn't pass them to their sons.

1533, 31 May, Saturday, Whitsunday eve: From Charing Cross
       to the Tower of London all the pavements of the city were
       covered with gravel.

The Mayor, his Aldermen & Guilds (crafts of the city) prepared a rail from which every person could stand, lean, cheer & praise in a good order, and receive her Queen's grace who came forth from the Tower of London, met by all of these standing in Cheapside. The Queen then moved on towards Westminster in goodly array.

The Queen's grace passed the streets first with certain strangers side by side (two by two) in blue velvet with white feathers, their horses draped with blue silk. All 200 estates[20] traveled side by side (accompanied two by two). Squires, Knights, Barons, Baronest and Knights of Bath were clothed in violet garments edged with arms like the Judges of the Law, who followed with the Abbots, followed by bishops, the Archbishops of York & Canterbury, the Ambassadors of France & Venice, the Lord Mayor with mace, the Master Garter the King of Heralds wearing the kings coat of armour, with the Officers of Arms watching over (appointing) every estate in their degree.

Then followed two ancient knights wearing old-fashioned hats, their faces disguised with thick makeup (dusted with powder ~ poudred). They represented the Dukes of Normandy & of Guyen ~ Guyenne ~ Aguyenne ~ Aquitania ~ Duchy of Aquitaine. Eleanor of Aquitaine became Queen consort of France (1137–52) then Queen consort of England (1154–89) by her marriage to Henry II (R. 1154–89) and the Duchy of Aquitaine passed to the Kings of England, being Queen Anne Boleyn's great x 10 grandmother and great x 10 grandfather (after an old custom).

These were followed by Lord Constable of England for the time being Charles Brandon (46) 1st Duke of Suffolk, KG PC; and Lord William Howard (22) acting as deputy to his brother, Queen Anne Bolyen's uncle, Thomas Howard (59), 3rd Duke of Norfolk KG PC as Earl Marshall (Lord Marshall) in charge of the horses.

Then followed the Queen's grace in her richly adorned salon ~ palanquin (litter, costly & richly seen) with a rich white cloth of gold canope, silk woven with a gold-spun weft, as carried by the lords of the Five Ports:

ANNE BOLEYN'S TRIUMPHAL ENTRY INTO LONDON.

"Anne Boleyn's Triumphal Entry into London."

1519–34, Marshal of Calais, Lord Warden of the Cinque Ports, Sir Edward Guildford

1525–23 July 1536, Lord High Admiral of England, Henry FitzRoy, Henry VIII's illegitimate

1533, Lord Warden of the Cinque Ports, George Neville, 5th Baron Abergavenny KG, PC

1 June 1533–36, Constable of Dover Castle: Queen Anne's brother George Boleyn.

After the Queen's grace came her Master of the Horse holding a spare white horse richly appointed & smooth to ride (palfrey).

Then followed her 12 noble Ladies of Estate wearing rich crimson with shoulder puffs & puffy arms (powdered arms) followed by the Yeomen of the Guard (Master of the Garde with the guard) on both sides of the streets keeping good order (array).

All the Constables wore velvet & damask coats and carried white staves which they used to keep everyone in line, and order in the streets (setting every man in array) until the Queen's grace arrived at Westminster, followed by her ladies of honour in 4 rich chariots, then another 30 ladies, 7 gentlewomen richly garnished, followed by the serving men.

As Queen Anne Boleyn departed from the Tower of London, great guns fired a marvellous shot, until this most noble company came half-a-mile northwest to Fenchurch Street where was a pleasing (seemly) pageant faire with well-dressed children saluting her Grace with great honour and praise: and so passed 300 yards west (forth) to Gracechurch Street and a very expensive (right costly) pageant of Apollo, as described by Virgil, where the two gods Apollo & Dionysus are paired.[21]

All wore clothing and carried instruments according to their superpowers (of them having their instruments and apparel according to the description of powers) including the King of Muses sitting on Mount Parnassus and Virgil espousing many verses of great praise and honour to Queen Anne Boleyn.

Red & White Roses, and the White Falcon are the Boleyn 'colors'; "Rootstock" is stem with an already well established healthy root system, to which a bud from another plant is grafted onto the rootstock, usually called the 'scion', meaning family, which has the properties the propagator desires above ground.

And so Queen Anne Boleyn passed through Gracechurch Street 200 yards north to Leadenhall where a sumptuous and costly pageant castle had been built with heavenly roof, beneath which was a green, and a root stock, from which sprang a multitude of white & red roses elaborately embellished (curiously wrought).

From this heavenly roof a White Falcon descended and lighted upon the root stock, and an angel descended with goodly harmony carrying a crown which he set on the White Falcon's head, thus proving Anne Boleyn was the true Queen of England in her own right (incontynent).

In the highest place sat Saint Anne (And on the said flour sate Saynt Anne in y hyest place). On one side sat her progeny with scripture, the 3 Marys with their issue: Mary the mother of Christ, and Mary Solome, mother of Zebedee with the two children of them. And on the other side sat Mary Cleophe with husband Alphee and their 4 children.

Poetical verses and English ballads were said and sung to the great praises of Queen Anne Boleyn, and to her future progeny (With other poetical verses said and sung with a ballad in English to her great praise and honour, and to all her progeny also.)

The Queen's grace then traveled 370 yards west to Cornhill (through Cornehyll), and at the Crossroads (Condyt) was a sumptuous pageant of the Three Graces. At the coming of the Queen's grace, a poet declared the nature of all those three ladies & gave high praises to the Queen. And after his preamble finished, every particular lady spoke great honour and high praise of the Queen's grace.

And so she passed forth with all her nobles and traveled 250 yards west to Cheapside, and at the Great crossroads (Condyt) a costly fountain had been built issuing forth unlimited white wine, claret reed all afternoon, decorated with reed, great melody and speeches, then to the Standard, sumptuously garnished with gold & azure, with arms & stories in great harmony and melody, then passed the newly garnished Cross in Cheapside.

Queen Anne Boleyn was then received with great honour, reverence & salutions, by John Baker (45) the Recorder of London (1526–36)[22] and the Aldermen, who, with loving & humble preposition (Jesuit Op. language) presented her Grace Queen Anne Boleyn with 1,000 marks in gold coins inside a rich and costly purse of gold, as a free gift of honour. Queen Anne Boleyn gave great thanks with both her heart & mind.

1,000 marks was £666, with a labour value of £5.3 million and an income value of £10 million in 2024.

Her Grace then passed a little further to another costly and rich pageant with minstrels and singers in good harmony. Here Juno, Pallas, Mercury, Venus and Paris presented a gold ball to her Grace amidst verses of great honour, and children singing a ballad to her Grace, and praise to all her ladies.

And so the Queen's grace passed 300 yards to west side of the timber St. Paul's cathedral, and to St. Paul's Gate, where another proper and sumptuous pageant began with 111 beautiful well-dressed virgins (faire lady virgins costly arrayed) sitting with a fair but slightly crude (roũde) throne over their heads, displaying in Latin:

'Queen Anne prosper proceed and reign'
"Regina Anna prospere procede et regina".

The lady that sat in the midst held a gold table in her hand with azure Latin writing:

'Come my Love thou shall be crowned'
"Veni amica coronaberis".

Two angels held a gold crown of gold between them. The lady on the right had a silver table displaying in Latin:

'Lord God direct my ways'

"Domine dirige gressos meos";

and the lady on the left had a silver table displaying:

'Trust in God'

"Cofide in Domini".

Under their feet was a long roll displaying:

'Queen Anne when thou shalt bear a new son of the kings blood, there shall be a golden age for the people' –

"Regina Anna novum regis de sanguine natum cum paries populis aurea secula tuis".

A Wafer is a small disc of dried paste used for fastening letters, usually imprinted with a message. On this day, for Queen Anne Boleyn, the wafers were imprinted with gold lettering, with a poem attached (posey).

And so the ladies caste over her head a multitude of wafers with rose leaves & about the wafers were written with Letters of gold, a posey.

And so her Grace Queen Anne passed into St. Paul's (Poules) Churchyard.

On a great scaffold at east end of the church were 200 school children standing dressed up to receive Anne with poetic verses to her noble honour. When they had finished Anne said 'Amen' with a joyful smiling countenance.

Her Grace Queen Anne then traveled 450 yards west through St Paul's (passed forth through the long Churchyard) to Ludgate, sumptuously garnished with gold, colours & azure, with sweet harmony of ballads to her great praise & honour with diverse sweet instruments.

Her Grace Queen Anne continued through Ludgate (the city) with great honour and royalty 760 yards to Fleet Street and the Strand which meet at Temple Bar (& Condyth) where expensive permanent masonry work of angels covered with gilt gold, azure and other colours with diverse arms (costly set out shall there continue and remain), and a clock (within the Strand a device with a chime).[23]

Wine flowed from the pipes all afternoon. Queen Anne Boleyn's grace disembarked with four tourettes carrying flags, pennants, banners & standards (vanes) and made a tour of the fair, amidst many sweet instruments and children singing.

Her Grace continued from Temple Bar 850 yards west to Charing Cross, and then through Westminster half-a-mile south and into Westminster Hall, which was hung with many rich tapestries (cloth of Arras) with a marvellous main course meal (rich cupboard of plate), spices and wine (and there was a voyde of spice plates and wine).

The Queen's grace then traveled 600 yards north and withdrew into Whitehall for that night, which was known as York Place by water (and so to York Place by water).

1533, 1 June, Whitsunday: At 8 o'clock, the Queen's grace with noble Ladies in their robes of estate assembled with all the nobles in their parliamentary robes as Dukes, Earls, Archbishops and Bishops with Barons & the Barons of the Five Ports (Cinque) with the Mayor of the city, the Alderman in their robes as mantels of scarlet. The Barons of the Five Ports bare a rich canopy of cloth of gold, with staffs of gold and four bells of silver and gilt.

The Abbot of Westminster with his regals came into the hall in his official attire with his monks in their best capes (copes), the Kings Chapel in their best copes with the Bishops richly adorned in their attire (pontificalibus).

A ray of blue cloth spread from the high dias (desses) of the Kings Bench unto the high altar of Westminster from which every man proceeded to Westminster in the best order, every man after their degree appointed to their order & office, sat in their appointed seats (as appertained came unto the place appointed).

Where her Grace received her crown with all the ceremonies thereof as thereunto belong. And so all the ceremonies done with the solemn mass, they departed home in their best orders every man to the hall of Westminster where the Queens' Grace withdrew her for a time into her appointed chamber.

And so after a certain space her Grace come into the hall, then every noble man serving them was appointed in the best manner of any such ceremony worth seeing. The Queens' grace washed, and the Archbishops of Canterbury said grace. During and with the service of the Archbishop, the nobles set the table and served Queen Anne Boleyn's table. (certain space 3 men with the Queens' Graces service).

With this service (Before the said service came):
i. Charles Brandon (48) Duke of Suffolk, High Steward of the Royal table on horseback marvellously draped in rich apparel (high constable and steward of the feast);

ii. Lord William Howard (22) as Deputy to the Duke of Norfolk (60) in the role (rome) of the Marshal of England, also serving on horseback;

iii. Henry Bourchier (60) 2nd Earl of Essex, KG KB PC (~1473–1540) as Carver;

iv.   Robert Radcliffe (49) Earl of Sussex, KG KB PC (1483–1542) as Lord Sewer;

v.   Edward Stanley (24) 3rd Earl of Derby KG (1509–72) as drinks waiter (Cupberer);

vi.   William Fitzalan (56) 11th Earl of Arundel KG (1476–1544) as Chief Butler (butteller);

vii. Arthur Plantagenet KG (1461/75–1542) Viscount Lisle as Panter (Lysle as panter), illegitimate son of King Edward IV (R. 1471–83);[24]

viii. Edmund Braye, 1st Baron Braye (1484–1539) dishing out the food (as the awmoner);

ix.   John Pie ~ Pye ~ Pey (d. 1548) a butcher & Mayor of Oxford 1532–34 who served wine from casks (kept the buttery bar);

x.   Lord of Burgayne, chief larder [this made by added or misspelt for trickery].

These noblemen did their service in a humble diligent fashion with goodly service of all kinds of meat with devices from the highest unto the lowest. Being such noble personages, the service borne by these knights was good, ordered, and more honourable than any a living man had seen.

There were four tables in the great hall. The noblewomen sat at one table, sitting all on the one side. The noblemen sat at another table. The Mayor of London sat at another table with his bretheren. The Barons of the Ports sat with the Master of the Chancery at the fourth table.

And thus all things noble & triumphantly done at her coronation, her Grace returned to Whitehall with great joy & solemnity.

The next day there were great jousts at the tilt (tylte, where jousters meet) done by 18 lords & knights, where many spears were valiantly broken, but some of their horses would not come at their pleasure there unto the tilt, which was displeasure to some that there did run.

This is how the Triumph ended.

1533, 1 June: King Henry VIII with ambassadors from France and Venice watched over Queen Anne Boleyn's Coronation feast from a little closet in the St. Stephen's Chapel cloister.

1884: Henry William Brewer (1836–1903) drew Westminster Old Palace from the east in the time of Henry VIII, as an informed reconstruction, first published in 'The Builder' magazine.

Westminster building
(Abbey)

Westminster Great Hall

St Stephen's
Chapel →

White Chamber &
Painted Chamber

River Thames

Endnotes

1 Oxford English Dictionary, OED: "Incontynent" is 'To prove to be valid or true; to demonstrate the truth, to substantiate a charge, to enforce one's assertion by combat, or to inflict blows for the cause'.

2 Harl. MS. 543, f. 119. B. M. 4, 'The noble tryumphant coronacyon of quene Anne, wyfe unto the most noble kynge Henry the VIII', printed by Wynkyn de Worde, for John Gough, p. 12.

3 2011: Elizabeth Norton, 'Anne Boleyn, In Her Own Words & the Words of Those Who Knew Her', omits Sir Thomas Betham (??–??) and replaces him with Sir Thomas Metham (d. 1573) who was a Recusant Papist, so entirely unlikely to be knighted ... ergo Elizabeth Norton is an embedded Catholic Jesuit.

4 Members Constituencies Parliaments Surveys: of Morley Hall, Hingham, Norfolk & Furneux Pelham, Herts.

5 1906: W A Shaw. The Knights of England, Vol. I, Sherratt & Hughes, 150.

6 1915, 15 Novmber: Page: Notes and Queries - Series 11 - Volume 12.djvu/389, n s. xii. NOV. is, 1915, Notes and Queries, 381, en.wiki-source.org/wiki/Page:Notes_and_Queries_-_Series_11_-_Volume_12.djvu/389; Henry VIII: June 1533, 6–10, in Letters and Papers, Foreign and Domestic, Henry VIII, Volume 6, 1533, ed. James Gairdner, London, 1882, pp. 275–84. British History Online, www.british-history ac.uk/letters-papers-hen8/vol6/pp275-284.

7 Brereton ~ Brierton ~ Brerton ~ Bretone ~ Breerton ~ Buerton ~Bryerton (Latin) are named after the place 'Brereton' in Cheshire'. It is a place name taken up by many as a family name of people who are not necessarily related. In 1066, Gilbert de Venables (of Venables in France) changed his name to Gilbert of 'Brereton' in Cheshire. Many outside this family, but from Brereton, also called themselves 'Brereton', with 175 variations in the spelling. William Brereton was Henry VIII's Groomsmen of the Privy Chamber responsible for presenting all financial matters to the King. William Brereton kept careful letters and journals:

"Sir Randolph Brereton ... actually his son William Brererton (1496/99–17 May 1536) was the 7th son of Sir Randle Brereton of Ipstones. It was William Brererton who was accused of having an affair with King Henry VIII's second wife Anne Boleyn and "be-headed" to

'The Island', being 94% of England. Later it was discovered the affair was an impossibility due to Anne being sequestered following the birth of her daughter." Those accused were:

Queen Anne Boleyn's brother, George Boleyn (*c*.1504–36);

Groom of the Stool in the privy chamber of King Henry VIII, Sir Henry Norris ~ Norreys (*c*.1482–36);

Gentleman of the Privy Chamber, Sir Francis Weston KB (1511–36); and the Musician in the household of Queen Anne Boleyn, Mark Smeaton (*c*.1512–36), who would entrain them on 'The Island'.

Source: 'The history of the county palatine and city of Chester', Vol. III, p. 51. "Brereton and Holt of Brereton"; Family Group Sheet, Notes for Sir Ranulphus I De Brereton, sites.rootsweb.com/~mwgrogan/data/nti18422.html.

8   1533, August: Farrington & Derby examined a Catholic 'lewd and naughty priest' who asked 'Who the devil made Nan Bullen, that whore, queen?'. This is a Jesuit hagiography ~ mothers are whores!

9   1982: J. Pound, 'Thomas Rush (by 1487–1537) of Sudbourne, Suffolk, in S.T. Bindoff (ed.), The History of Parliament: the House of Commons 1509–1558, from Boydell and Brewer, 1982.

10   1969: Leslie Hotson, 'Shakespeare Versus Shallow', Haskell House Publishers, New York, NY, gives 4 different spellings on the same page 148 as: "Thomas Fowlehurst, knight ... Sir Thomas Fulleshurst ... Sir Thomas Fullehurst ... Fullhurst ... Fullhurst".

Other spellings include Foulehurst ~ Foulhurst ~ Fowleshurst ~ Foulshurst ~ Fulherst ~ Fulhurst ~ Fulshurst ~ Fulsherst ~ Fulthurst ~Fulleshurst ~ Fullherst.

11   3rd son of Sir James Hobart ~ Hoberd ~ Hubbard (1436–1517) of Hales Hall, Norfolk, Attorney-General to Henry VII 1485–1507. This is not Walter Herbert (c.1452–16 September 1507), younger brother of William Herbert, 2nd Earl of Pembroke (1451–16 July 1491) who died childless. Hubbert ~ Hobart also written Heber ~ Herbert ~ Hibbert ~ Hubert ~ Hupert ~Huppert ~ Hupperts ~ Huppertz.

12   Lakyng ~ Laking ~ Lakin ~Lacon ~ Laken ~ Lakyn ~ Lakington ~ Lakington.

13   Alternative: Sir Randale Mainwaring (1467–1547).

14 Their son, Sir Thomas Massingberd (c.1524–84) MP for Bratoft ~ his son Sir Thomas Massingberd of Gunby and Bratoft (1562–1636) ~ his son, Sir Henry Massingberd, became 1st Baronet (1609–1680).

15 Sir Thomas Missenden ~ Missendene ~ Missendin ~ Mussendi ~ Mussenden (1329–53+) a.k.a. Sir Thomas de Cophouse was Butler to King Edward III.

16 William Sandon ~ Stawndon was Mayor of London 1407–08.

17 Unedall ~ Evedalle ~ Uvedale ~ Evedale ~ Woodall ~ Udall.

18 1915, 15 November: Page: Notes and Queries - Series 11 - Volume 12.djvu/389, n s. xii. , paraphrased.

19 Henry VIII: June 1533, 6–10, Letters and Papers, Foreign and Domestic, Volume 6, 1533, pp. 275–84.

20 The three "Estates" being the Lords Spiritual (Church heads), Lords Temporal (Peerage) and Commons ... the class, order & category of people forming the body politic constituting Parliament.

21 Virgil's 'Eclogues and Aeneid', Vol 1–6, 39 b.c. were Publius Vergilius Maro's first published poems.

22 John Baker (1488–1558) gained a reputation as a brutal persecutor of Protestants, earning the nickname 'Bloody Baker'. Baker became Attorney-general of the Duchy of Lancaster 1535–36, MP for London in 1536, Privy Council in 1540, under Henry VIII, Edward VI, Mary and Elizabeth I, knighted in June 1540, then showed "he had forwarded a loan in London and other tributes (imposts)". With Baker's second round of bribes in place, he was made Chancellor of the Exchequer 1545–58 serving Henry VIII, Edward VI and Mary, and Speaker of the House 1545–52. Spending the Vatican's money in London was how the Jesuits got a foot in the door.

The Roman Catholic Jesuit Protestant hater John Baker was also made MP for London in 1529 & 1536, MP for Guildford in 1542, MP for Lancaster in 1545, Knight of the shire for Huntingdonshire in 1547, MP for Bramber in 1553, and MP for Kent in 1554, 1555 & 1557.

23 1386: The worlds oldest surviving working clock is the faceless clock at Salisbury Cathedral, Wiltshire.

24 Then came the 'Lisle Letters', arrest in 1540, jailed in the Tower of London & death by heart attack.

Chapter Seven
Anne Boleyn crowned Queen of England in her own right

1532, 22 August: The last Roman Catholic Archbishop of Canterbury, William Warham, died aged 82.

"In this Sommer season last past, died Willyam Warham Archebishoppe of Canterbury, and to that Bishopriche was named, Doctor Thomas Cranmer, the kynges chappelein, a man of good learnyng, and of a verteous life, which also not long before was the kynges Ambassadour to the Bishop of Rome, whiche was consecrate in Lent."[1]

1533, 23 May: The first and only Lord Archbishop of Canterbury Thomas Cranmer declared Henry VIII & Catherine of Aragon's marriage null and void.

1533, 25 May, Sunday: Knights made at Greenwich were:[2]

Sir Thos. Betham (~~Metham~~)	Sir Brian Hastynges
Sir Thos. Butteller	Sir Chr. Hylarde
Sir Chr. Danby	Sir Wm. Walgrave ... 7 agreeing
Sir Wm. Feldeyng	with the previous account

1533, 28 May: The Anglican Thomas Cranmer declared Henry VIII and Marquess of Pembroke Anne Boleyn's marriage valid. She was now Queen consort Anne Boleyn, and to be made Queen of England in her own right over the next week.

1533, 29 May–1 June, Whitsunday: Queen Anne Boleyn's coronation procession was a four day affair. Lady Marquess of Pembroke was finally the Queen of England, with her own crown (coronet). "It came about as the result of a historic love that had torn the court, and the country, apart ..."

This account of Anne Boleyn's coronation was written by the Tudor chronicler Edward Hall (1496–1547). It was then 'edited' by Professor at Jesus College Oxford, Dr. Susan Doran (b. 1948) in 'Catalogue', "Man & Monarch Henry VIII", an Exhibition guest curated by prominent British historian David Starkey CBE (b. 1945) and published by the British Library in 2011.[3]

But what does it mean to "edit"?

Does "edit" mean to embellish?

Does "edit" mean to not decipher archaic words, like "incontynent", which they didn't.

Does "edit" mean to retain the confusion without informed clarity, which they did.

Does "edit" mean to leave intact any Jesuit confusion and hagiography, which they did.

Does "edit" mean to promote a secondary less-original source over an original source?

Does "edit" mean to not give any background or foreground to any of the characters?

Does "edit" mean to not interpret any meaning or symbolism?

Does "edit" mean to leave everything in a meaningless state?

If this is what "edit" means, then this is what their Editor did.

It appears the British Museum ~ Library ~ History Online, Oxford & Cambridge version of "edit" is to interpret all documentation according to the long-held Jesuit tradition of coadjuting English history into a Roman Catholic perspective, and anything done for the English Crown, before 1603 is to be obfuscated ... by adding the Jesuit tools of confusion, circumlocution, hagiography, patent ambiguity, and depleting emetics, while continually publishing embedded Catholic historians and the Catholic Jesuit takeover of Oxford University Press & Cambridge University Press, and their History Departments, who manage to regularly find archaic histories of a Catholic perspective, written by Jesuit monks for the fraud of tomorrow ... right up to an including the European Union.

This, second contemporary version of Queen Anne Boleyn's Coronation, was written by the Tudor chronicler Edward Hall (1496–1547) then in 2011, 'edited' by Professor Susan Doran at Jesus College Oxford, guest curated by David Starkey, and published by the British Library as 'Man & Monarch Henry VIII' in Catalogue, on 1 June 2011.

The Coronation of Anne Boleyn 1 June 1533

29 May–1 June 1533: Queen Anne Boleyn had her own independent coronation – one of the most lavish in English history, for king or queen. This stood Queen Anne Boleyn apart, as an independent Queen in her own right, with her own Crown, made especially for her coronation, her own royal and religious bloodline, and the only Queen with her own coronation to bare grandchildren.

Queen Anne Boleyn was already 6½ months pregnant (16 November 1532–29 May/1 June 1533) with the future Queen Elizabeth I. Henry VIII wanted no one to doubt the legitimacy of his son or the nobility of his parentage ... It was to be a beautiful daughter ... Their secret marriage was on 16 November 1532, not on the 14th. They conceived on 16 November 1532 making Queen Anne Boleyn 6½ months pregnant, and not the "2 months pregnant" embedded Catholic historians & Jesuits falsely advertise for confusion.

29 May–1 June 1533: This Coronation was a lavish four-day affair and involved making many knights, becoming part of the pagentry, even a week later on 8 June 1533.

1533, 29 May, Thursday: Lady Anne, Marquess of Pembroke, was received as Queen of England by all the Lords of England. The Mayor of London, Aldermen, and all the Guilds of the City of London, went to Greenwich in their barges in the best fashions, with the mayor's guild richly hung with cloth of gold, and a great number of bachelors to wait on her. All the lords, the mayor, and all the guilds of London brought Anne by water from Greenwich to the Tower of London, where she landed, received by the king's grace with over a thousand guns fired. Other guns fired at Limehouse, and from ships on the Thames: BOOM BOOM BOOM BOOM BOOM BOOM BOOM.

1533, 29 May, Thursday: Gentlemen served the King at dinner, and were bathed & shaved according to custom, and the next day were made "Knights of the Bath":

Earl of Derby

Marquis of Dorset

Lord Henry Clifford, 2nd Earl of Cumberland[1]

Lord Fitzwater

Lord Hastings

Lord Mountaigle

Lord Vaux

Sir Thos. Arundell

Sir George Fitzwilliam/s, of Lincolnshire

Sir John Hudelston / Huddelston

Sir Thos. Jermey

Sir John Mordaunt, Lord Mordant's son

Sir Henry Parker, Lord Morley's son

Sir Thos. Poyninges / Ponynges

Sir Hen. Savell / Savile

Sir John Tyndall

Sir Francis Weston

Sir William Windesour / Wynsor,

Lord Winsor's son, heir to Lord Windsor,

---

[1] Henry Clifford then married (June 1535) Henry VIII's niece, Eleanor Brandon.

18[4] & in 'Add. MS. 6,113' another six (6).

John Barkeley

Mr. Corbet/t

John Germayne

Ric. Verney of Penley/e

Rob. Whi(y)tneye of Gloucestershire

Mr. Wyndham ... 18 + 6 = 24.

1533, 29 May, Thursday, 1 p.m.: The Mayor and his brethren assembled at Lower Thames Street, outside the Tower of London (St. Mary Hill) boarded their 48 barges, richly decked with tapestry (arras), hung with banners and Craft Arms (pennons) in fine gold. These dressed rowing barges embarked with minstrels & musical instruments – trumpettes (shawm or shalmes) & clarinet (shallands) & trombone (sackbut, saggebuttes, shagbushes, designed by Schagerl) ... and every barge was decked with an ordnance of guns.[5]

Henry VIII had ordered Sir Steven Pecocke Mayor of London 1532–33 to get his Haberdasher guild to prepare and dress the barges, decked with targets and banners.

Leading the way was the sumptuously decked bachelor's barge, dressed as a great red dragon casting wild fire, with great shot of ordnance full of fireworks. Around it were barges with terrible monsters and wild men in swift boats on the water (foiste for a wafter).

This was followed by the Mayor's dressed barge; and Queen Anne Boleyn's barge with a crowned white falcon standing on a row of gold, with red and white roses about it (her device), and on the mount sat real live virgins singing and playing (hallsyd with gones forth of the shippes on every side).

Each rowing barge was two boat lengths apart, so everyone could see the garnishing. The barges were rowed from the Tower of London 5 miles down the River Thames to Greenwich Palace, with banners and penantes of craft arms beaten in fine gold, and the standards, streamers waving in the wind (conisaunsys and devisis ventylyng with the wynd), with the minstrals playing trumpets, clarinet & trombone, being a right triumphant sight (the which war a ryght symtivis and a tryhumfantt syght to se and to heare ... the which soundes to be a thinge of a nother world).

When Queen Anne Boleyn's barge reached Wapping, 3½ miles from Greenwich, the Tower of London shot four guns at once (lousyd their ordinaunce most triumphantly).

1533, 29 May, Thursday, 3 p.m.: Queen Anne Boleyn boarded her barge at Greenwich Palace. On the surrounding barges, were the Duke of Suffolk, Marquis of Dorset, her father the Earl of Wiltshire, and the Earls of Arundel, Derby, Huntingdon, Oxford, Rutland, Sussex, Worcester, and others, and many bishops and noblemen, in their own barges, and the whole company rowed back up to the Tower of London.

Ships at shore pealed off gun shot and canons, and the Tower of London made a marvellous canon shot as Queen Anne Boleyn landed at the Tower of London.

Coming out of her barge, she was received by:
William Sandys, 1st Baron Sandys of the Vyne KG (1470–1540) Lord Chamberlain 1530–40 and favourite of King Henry VIII; and many Officers of Arms, including:
Sir Edward ~ Edmund Walsingham (1480–1550) Lieutenant of the Tower 1520–47;
Sir William Kingston KG (1476–1540) Constable of the Tower 1524–40;

Sir Thomas Writhe ~ Wriothesley (d. 24 Nov. 1534) Garter King-of-Arms 1505–34;

Thomas Benolt (d. 1534) Clarencieux ~ Clarenceux King of Arms 1530–34;

Thomas Tonge (d. 1536) York Herald & Norroy Kings-of-Arms 1522–34;

Charles Wriothesley (1508–62) Carlisle Herald 1529–34 & Windsor Herald 1529–65;

Randolph Jackson, Esq. Chester Herald 1533–40;

Christopher Barker, Esq. (d. 1550) Richmond Herald 1522–36;

Fulk ap Howell, Esq., Lancaster Herald 1531–36;

Allan Dagnall, Esq. York Herald 1530–38;

Agnes Howard (1477–1545) Duchess of Norfolk (56) bearing Queen Anne's train; and

Lord Chamberlain Thomas Burgh ~ Borough KG (1488–1550) 1st Baron Burgh of Gainsborough supporting the train.

A little further on Queen Anne Boleyn was received again by the King's Chamberlain Lord Sandys, with:

Lord John Hussey ~ Hosey ~ Husey ~ Hussie ~ Huse, 1st Baron Hussey of Sleaford (1465–1537) Chief Butler of England, Chamberlain;

Andrew Windsor ~ Wyndsore ~ Wyndesor (1467–1543) 1st Baron Windsor 1529–43, Keeper & Masters of the Great Wardrobe 1504–43;

Lord Mordaunt whose son Sir John Mordaunt had just been knighted, followed by

Stephen Gardiner (1483–1555) Bishop of Winchester 1531–51;

John Stokesley (1475–1539) Bishop of London 1530–39;

John de Vere, 16th Earl of Oxford (1516–62) as High Chamberlain;

Lord William Howard (22) riding in for his elder brother, Thomas (59), Duke of Norfolk, the Earl Marshal of England, 1533–47 with the Marshal's Rod;

Henry Bourchier (60) 2nd Earl of Essex, KG KB PC ...

and again the Lord Chamberlain William Sandys, who brought Queen Anne Boleyn to the postern by the water side, somewhat within the Tower, to King Henry VIII who received her, laid his hands on both her sides, kissed her (with great reverence and a joyful countenance).

Queen Anne Boleyn then turned back and thanked the Mayor and citizens, and then entered the Tower of London.

None of the citizens landed, but all "hoved before the Tower, making great melody" after which every man went to his lodging, except certain noblemen and officers in waiting.

The Officers of Arms led Queen Anne Boleyn and King Henry VIII, followed by the Mayor, Recorder, and two Aldermen, to her chamber, and then to supper, and "after super there was sumptuous void."[6]

1533, 30 May, Friday: Queen Anne Boleyn was rested all day Friday in the Tower of London, except that all noblemen etc (, &c.) repaired to Court, and in a long chamber within the Tower were ordained 18 "baynes," in which were 18 noblemen all that night, who received the order of knighthood on Saturday, Whitsun eve.

Also there were 63 knights made with the sword in honor of the coronation.

Then all the nobles, knights, squires, and gentlemen were warned to attend on horseback, on the Tower Hill on Saturday next [tomorrow,

31 May 1533], to accompany her Grace to Westminster, to do service at the coronation.[7]

The following were made Knights of the Sword: 46 + 18 or 24 = 64 or 70, with 1 struck off = 63 or 69:

Sir Jas. Baskervyll	Sir Thos Lakyng
Sir Wm. Browne	Sir Ric. Lygon
Sir Randolfe Buerton	Sir Edw. Maidison
~~Sir~~ Ric. Bulkeley ~~/ Barkeley~~	Sir Wm. Malorie
Sir Geo. Calverley	Sir Randolfe Manering
Sir John Chaworth	Sir Thos. Massyngberd
Sir John Constable	Sir Thos. Mysseden
Sir Geo. Conyers	Sir Robt. Nedham
Sir Henry Delves	Sir John Nories
Sir Wm. Drury	Sir Thos. Rusche
Sir Henry Everyngham	Sir John Saintclere
Sir Arthur Eyre	Sir Wm. Sandon
Sir Hen. Feryngton	Sir Walter Smythe
Sir Thos. Fouleshurst	Sir Nic. Sturley
Sir Edw. Fytton	Sir Hen. Sutton
Sir John Gernyngham	Sir Edm. Trafford
Sir Geo. Gresle	Sir Marmaduke Tunstall
Sir Thos. Halsall	Sir John Tyrell
Sir John Harcourt	Sir Thos. Umpton
Sir John Horsley	Sir Wm. Uvedall
Sir Walter Hubbert	Sir Peter Warburton
Sir Robt. Kyrkham	Sir John Wyllougby
Sir Thos. Kytson	Sir Anthony Wyndsour [46]

Those 10 from the previous list missing on this list are included on 8 June 1533 list. Those not on the previous list, but added here:

Sir Wm. Browne

Sir Randolfe Buerton

Sir Geo. Calverley

Sir John Chaworth

Sir John Constable

Sir Geo. Conyers

Sir Hen. Feryngton

Sir Edw. Fytton

Sir John Gernyngham

Sir Geo. Gresle

Sir Thos. Halsall

Sir Ric. Lygon

Sir Edw. Maidison

Sir Thos. Massyngberd

Sir Robt. Nedham

Sir Thos. Rusche

Sir John Saintclere

Sir Marmaduke Tunstall

Sir Thos. Umpton [19]

These differing lists were designed confusion to distract from the Anne's Coronation.

1533, 31 May, Saturday, Whitsun eve: Queen Anne Boleyn was conveyed in an open litter drawn by two docile horses (palfrey) from the Tower of London through the City of London, Fenchurch St, Gracechurch St, Leadenhall, Cornhill, Crossroads, to the Cross in Cheapside (200 yards east of St Paul's Cathedral, St Paul's Gate, then through Ludgate to Fleet Street, Temple Bar, Charing Cross, and Westminster Hall.

All the frontages of Cheapside, including the Cross, Ludgate, Fleet Street, and Temple Bar (conduits) were newly repaired and painted, with the streets newly gravelled. From the Tower of London to Grace Church in Greenwich Palace (Graces Church to the little conduit in Cheap) there were crafts and rails on one side, and Constables in velvet and silk with great staves in their hands on the other side.

Both sides of the street had gold tapestry, other hangings of myths and allegories, and many pageants. Scaffolds held many pageants along the way. All the Guilds were standing in their liveries, every one in order.

1539: Hans Holbein the Younger, painted the 65-year-old Earl Marshall of England with Rod ... measuring time, centuries and generations to the prophecy fulfilled.

Queen Anne Boleyn's uncle Thomas Howard (1473–1554) 3rd Duke of Norfolk KG PC Earl Marshal of England 28 May 1533–1547.

White Rod Rod of Inauguration White Wand of Sovereignty.

Thomas Howard, 3rd Duke of Norfolk remained Earl Marshal of England (28 May 1533–47) & in 1539 was painted by Hans Holbein the Younger with a White Rod and a longer Golden Rod, confirming he was the maternal uncle to Queen Anne Boleyn, who had her own separate Coronation, bore the title Queen of England, and was still alive in 1539. It was Thomas Howard who communicated between Queen Anne and King Henry VIII. Hans Holbein's 1539 3rd Duke of Norfolk Thomas Howard looks very much like The Principal's father ~ same knuckles, eyes, nose, lips & forehead, for great x12 Grandfather.

Preceding Queen Anne Boleyn's richly dressed train, were the peers of the realm:

12 French-men belonging to the French ambassador;

Gentlemen, Esquires and Knights, two by two;

Judges,

Knights of the Bath,

Abbots, Barons, Bishops,

Earls, Marquises,

Lord Chancellor Thomas Audley (44), 1st Baron Audley of Walden;

Edward Lee (50) Archbishop of York;

Carlo Capello, Venetian Ambassador to England, 1531–35;

Thomas Cranmer (43) Archbishop of Canterbury 22 Aug. 1532/3 Dec. 1533–4 Dec. 1555.

Charles de Solier (1480–1552) comte de Morette, French Ambassador 1526–35;

two Esquires of Honor with robes and caps of estate representing the Dukes of Normandy and Aquitaine;

Sir Christopher Askew, Lord Mayor of London, Michaelmas, 29 September 1532–1533;

Knights of the Garter;

Lord William Howard (22), deputy to his brother, Thomas Howard (59) Duke of Norfolk with the Marshal's Rod; and

Charles Brandon (48), 1st Duke of Suffolk, High Constable of England for the day, bearing the verge of silver ... with Serjeants and officers of arms on horseback either side ... and 4 Lords of the Ports in scarlet gowns holding the rich silver cloth canopy over Queen Anne Boleyn carried in her salon ~ palanquin ~ litter, covered in white cloth of gold, drawn by two docile horses (palfreys) covered in white damask.

Queen Anne wore her hair down, with a coif and circlet of rich stones; a loose sleeveless outer robe (of rich material worn as part of an insignia of an order of knighthood ≈ surcoat); and mantle of white cloth of tissue trimmed in ermine ... followed by her:

Chamberlain Lord Borough;

Master of her Horses Sir William Coffyn, leading a spare horse, with a side saddle;

seven ladies in crimson velvet gowns and cloth of gold in 4 richly hung chariots;

a chariot containing the old Duchess of Norfolk (56), and the Marchioness of Dorset (48);

other ladies and gentlewomen in chariots, and on horseback;

followed by the Guard in coats worked by goldsmiths.

Verses composed by John Leland & Nicholas Vuedale/Udall were read out in Latin & English, at Queen Anne's Coronation pageants in Leadenhall, Cornhill, and Cheapside.[8]

The Mayor and Aldermen were standing at the Cross in Cheapside. The Recorder, Master Baker, made a speech to Queen Anne Boleyn and presented her with 1,000 marks (a purse of cloth of fold with 1,000 marks of angel nobles in it) as a present from the whole of the city, but mainly from the City of London. 1,000 marks was £666, which had a labour value of £5.3 million and an income value of £10 million in 2024.

1,000 marks was £666, with a labour value of £5.3m and an income value of £10 million in 2024.

200 yards west, at the east end of St. Paul's Cathedral, a scaffold held St. Paul's school children reciting poetry in honor of the King and Queen.

The lords then carried Queen Anne Boleyn another 2 miles to the Palace of Westminster, and into Westminster Hall, where Queen Anne Boleyn (alighted and) took her place at the high dais (desses) under the cloth of estate. A service of spice and subtilties, with ypocras and other wines, was offered to her, which she sent to her ladies.

1533, 31 May, Saturday, Whitsun eve: 18 noblemen received the order of knighthood & 63 knights [in total] made with the sword in honor of the coronation.

Inaccurate numbers, and different names are Jesuit means of circumlocution obfuscation resulting in patent ambiguity and depleting emetics, in a Catholic effort to have Queen Anne Boleyn's coronation rejected on some level, then buried and forgotten. Few historians every mention it, and no historian has even mentioned it in clarity.

After thanking those who had attended on her she withdrew to her chamber in the Palace of White Hall, at Westminster, the main Royal residence in London, 1530–1698, where she stayed Saturday night ... or "afterwards secretly went in her barge to the King at his manor of Westminster", which is the same place, with a different name.

Inigo Jones did a 1538 plan for a new palace at Whitehall Palace. The eastern third of this was built overlooking St James's Park. Had it been completed, it would have been adjacent to Westminster Abbey and Westminster Parliament, with Parliament Square in between.

1533, 1 June, Sunday: For the final step in her four day Coronation, Queen Anne Boleyn was taken from Westminster Palace across the road to Westminster Abbey for the Coronation ceremony, and then back across the road to Westminster Palace where they dined in one of the most honourable feasts ever witnessed.

The whole of the road was covered with cloth, the length of the garden of Chantilly [500 yards] and striped blue cloth was spread from seat to seat, from the high dais of the King's Bench in Westminster Hall to the High Altar platform in St Peter's Church in the Benedictine Monastery Westminster Abbey.[9]

From the great old and still existing Westminster Hall in the Palace of Westminster, Queen Anne was brought in procession to St Peter's Church in the Benedictine Monastery Westminster Abbey.

Queen Anne Boleyn was dressed in a crimson velvet gown (kirtle) decorated with ermine, with a purple velvet robe decorated with ermine. A rich coronet with a cap of pearls and stones sat on her head, and a rich canopy of gold cloth was carried above her head.

The crown was borne in front of Queen Anne Boleyn by the Grand Master Charles Brandon (48) 1st Duke of Suffolk. Her two sceptres were carried by her father Thomas Boleyn (56) 1st Earl of Wiltshire, KG KB, and William Fitzalan (56) 11th Earl of Arundel, KG.

Queen Anne Boleyn was accompanied by 13 mitred abbots, all the Benedictine Monastery Westminster Abbey monks in rich capes (copes) of gold, followed by 2 mitred archbishops, 4 bishops, all the king's chapel in rich copes & all the lords in their parliament robes.

A "Cope" is a long cloak worn over a long white linen robe (alb) or white gown with wide sleeves (surplice) worn over an ankle-length garment with close-fitting waist and sleeves (cassock).

As was their signature, the Duchesses & Countesses wore scarlet robes trimmed with ermine, ermine in bonnets, and round gold coronets on their heads, beneath their bonnets.

Queen Anne's Chamberlain Lord Burgh supported her train in the middle, the Duchess of Norfolk in scarlet robe and gold coronet carried the rear, followed by 10 Ladies in scarlet robes with bonnets trimmed with ermine ... followed by all of Queen Anne Boleyn's maids in scarlet gowns edged with white Baltic fur.

The dukes, earls, and knights were likewise clothed in scarlet robes, edged with ermine fur in their hoods.

And so Queen Anne Boleyn was brought across the road from Westminster Palace to the Benedictine Monastery Westminster Abbey and inside to St Peter's Church, where she walked up two steps to an elevated high platform covered with tapestry and was set in her high royal seat before the altar covered with red cloth.

The Archbishop of Canterbury Archbishop of York then anointed and crowned Anne Boleyn Queen of England in her own ceremony. Anne was Queen in her own right, whether she was married to Henry VIII or not, so not just Queen consort Anne Boleyn, but Queen Anne Boleyn of England, able to rule in her own right, married, divorced or "executed".

Queen Anne Boleyn of England sat crowned in her royal seat all through the mass, and made an offering at the mass, then everyone left in the same order, from St Peter's Church in the Benedictine Monastery Westminster Abbey, across the road to the Great Hall in Westminster Palace. It was now the 'The Peculiar English Crown Westminster Building'.

Queen Anne Boleyn & crown moved under the canopy carrying two sceptres, led by her father, Lord Wiltshire, Thomas Boleyn, 1st Earl of Ormond, 1st Viscount Rochford KG, KB (1477–12 March 1539) of Hever Castle in Kent, and Lord Talbot, George Talbot, 4th Earl of Shrewsbury, 4th Earl of Waterford, 10th Baron Talbot, KG,

Anne Boleyn walks to Westminster Abbey on Sunday 1 June 1533.

KB, PC (1468–1538) into the great Westminster Hall, hung with rich tapestries (Arras). Today, the Great Hall in Westminster is the oldest surviving part of Westminster Palace.

The Coronation Feast in the Great Hall of Westminster Palace

The new Queen Anne Boleyn, Queen of England in her own right, was led back again with the same company, minus a few bishops, into the Great Hall of Westminster Palace, all prepared for her to dine.

Queen Anne Boleyn dined up the 12 steps, with the rich cloth of estate hung over her head. The table was very long, and the first Anglican 'Lord Archbishop of Canterbury' was seated at the queen's left hand, but at the very end of the table – a considerable distance away, because he was not yet the 'Archbishop of Canterbury' until 3 December 1533.

Around Queen Anne Boleyn was an enclosure into which none entered but those deputised to serve, being the greatest personages of the realm. They served bread and wine straight from the pantry ("de sommelliers d'eschanonnerie et panetrie").

When the Queen's Grace had washed her hands, the first seated were those of the realm in charge of the doors & wine; below them, at the same table, were many gentlemen. At the second table was the archbishop, bishops, Chancellor, and many lords and knights. At the third table opposite the high end (celle du hault bout) were the mayor of London, accompanied by the sheriffs; at the fourth table were the Duchesses, Countesses & Ladies.

Trumpets and oboe (hautbois) sounded at each course, and heralds cried "largesse", for 'generosity'. Queen Anne Boleyn was served, but had two ladies beneath the tablecloth, sitting at her feet tasting her food (to serve her secretly with what she might need) and another on each side, who would raise a great linen cloth to hide her from

Great Hall in Westminster Palace.

view if she wanted to spit anything out ("s'ayser en quelque chose").

After a certain space, the Archbishops were served, followed by the four great tables extending the length of the Great Hall, and plenty of room for everybody.

The dinner lasted many hours and was honourably served by the greatest knights of the land. Remaining all day near Queen Anne Boleyn, was John de Vere (51) KG PC 15th Earl of Oxford, Lord Great Chamberlain 1526–40 & White Staff Lord; and Lord William Howard (22) presided over the serving, keeping good order with:

Henry Bourchier (60), 2nd Earl of Essex, KG KB PC (~1473–1540) served as Carver;

Arthur Plantagenet, Viscount Lisle, KG (d. 1542) Henry VIII's uncle as Panter;

William Fitzalan (56) 11th Earl of Arundel, KG (1476–1544) as Butler;

Robert Radcliffe (49) Earl of Sussex, KG KB PC (1483–1542) as Lord Sewer;

Edward Stanley (24) 3rd Earl of Derby KG (1509–72) as Cup Bearer; and

Henry Grey (18), 1st Duke of Suffolk, 3rd Marquess of Dorset KG KB (1517–54) as Almoner. 3 years later siring Lady Jane Grey, "the Nine Days' Queen", granddaughter of Charles Brandon, Duke of Suffolk.

The hall doors were conduits for pouring wine; and to the kitchens which gave food (viands to all comers) the consumption of which was enormous ... and the next day there was jousting.

1533, 8 June, Trinity Sunday: 8th Sunday after Easter Sunday, 11 more knights were made in agreement with the previous list, with modern names & dates added:

Sir Edw. Bowton (Bayntun, 1480–1544)

Sir Hen. Capell (1505–58)

Sir Chr. Corwen (Curwen, 1467/77~1535/57)

Sir John Dawne (Dawnay, 1489–1552)

Sir Humfrey Feryes (Ferrers, 1483–1553)

Sir Ric. Haughton (1496–1559)

Sir Clement Herleston (Harleston, 1494–1544)

Sir Thos. Langton (1496–1569)

Sir Geffray Mydelton (Geoffrey, 1482–1545)

Sir Hugh Trevyneon (Trevanion, 1516–71)

Sir Geo. West (1490/1510–38).[10]

1533, 25 June: English princess Mary Tudor, Queen consort of France (R. 9 October 1514–1 January 1515) died at Suffolk House:

"On Midsomer daie after, the lady Mary the Frenche Quene died in Suffolke at the lordship of who was the late wife to Louis XII, and after married to Charles Duke of Suffolk."

"This season the kyng kept-his progresse aboat London, because of the Quene."

1533, 7 September, Sunday, 3–4 p.m.: 98 days after Anne Boleyn's coronation becoming Queen of England in her own right, Queen Anne Boleyn gave birth to Lady Elizabeth becoming Queen Elizabeth ((R. 1558–1603), daughter of Henry VIII (R. 22 April 1509–28 January 1547).

Queen Elizabeth I of England was the last styled & titled Sovereign monarch of England.

Queen Elizabeth (25) reigned 17 November 1558–24 March 1603 for 44 years, to the age of 69, creating the Elizabethan era.

Queen Elizabeth was poisoned, ending her reign. The Jesuit Counter

Endnotes

1   1548 & 1809: Edward Hall's Chronicle, The. XXVIII. YERE OF
     KYNG HENRY THE. VIII. ~1536–37, p. 819, paraphrased into
     modern English for clarity.

     1533: Lent was 26 February–10 April.

2   Harl. MS. 543, f. 119. B. M. 4, 'The noble tryumphant coronacyon
     of quene Anne, Worde, p. 12.

3   2011, 1 June: p. 51, kimberlyevemusings.blogspot.com/2011/06/
     coronation-of-anne-boleyn.

4   1533, 1–5 June: Vesp. C. XIV. 124. B. M. 583. Coronation Of Anne
     Boleyn, Henry VIII, pp. 262–75, "the heralds appointed the justices
     to ride before the knights of the Bath, of whom 18 were made that
     day."

5   1533, Thursday 29 May, Anne Boleyn; 25 Hen. VIII;

     1533, 31 May: MS. L. f. 1. Coll. of Arms. 563.

6   1533, Thursday 29 May, Anne Boleyn; 25 Hen. VIII;

     1533, 31 May: MS. L. f. 1. Coll. of Arms. 563.

7   1533, 31 May: MS. L. f. 1. Coll. of Arms, R. MS. 18, A. LXIV. B.
     M. 564. Queen Anne Boleyn, p. 6, early copy.

8   1533, 31 May: R. MS. 18, A. LXIV. B. M. 564. Queen Anne Boleyn.
     Versis and dities made at coronation.

9   25 miles north of Paris, the garden of Château de Chantilly was
     500 yards of classic landscape, 1 mile of straight canal, 3 miles of
     Forested Road, or 7 miles all in a straight line.

     So the Westminster striped blue cloth was 500 yards long.

10   P. R. O. 602. Queen Anne Boleyn.

Chapter Eight – Henry VIII & Queen Anne Boleyn acknowledged as major Religious Reformers

Henry VIII & Queen Anne Boleyn were acknowledged over the known world as major religious reformers. Anne Boleyn had strong links with the French religious reformers. The Evangelical Pastor (Le Pastor evangelique) was possibly the French ambassador Jean de Dinteville (1504–55). Jean presented an existing poem from the French poet & religious reformer Clément Marot (1496–1544) with several lines customized.

"They added a final prophecy that the Good Shepherd (Christ) would give Anne a son in Henry's image" whom the couple would live to see grow into manhood:

'Oh Anne my lady, Oh incomparable queen
This Good Sheppard who favours you
will give you a son who will be the living image
of the king his father, and he will live and flourish,
until the two of you can see him reach the age when a man is
mature.'

This was fulfilled in Queen Anne Boleyn's grandson Sir Walter Raleigh. "The living image of the king his father" means 'son of Man', 'not son of God'. The 'son of God' is anyone descended from Abraham. The 'son of Man' is something special. "reach the age when a man is mature" is '52 years old', with Raleigh born in 1552, also the Elizabethan Age, and 2020~21~22. From Elizabeth's reign in 1558 + 52 years, is 1610, when Raleigh and Bacon completed edited the Bible and installing the Prophecies. Herein lies the Prophecy:

'The incomparable Lady Pembroke Anne Boleyn
Queen in her own right,
with her own lavish Coronation over these four days
Christ favours you and
will give you a son

who will be the living image
of his father the king.
He will live and flourish and mature,
until the two of you can see him
as the son of Man'.

More accurately the Prophecy is ...
'Queen Anne Boleyn, Marquesse of Pembroke
is favoured with a male descendant
who does not have to be legitimate.

This 'son of Man' ~ Christ
will be the living image
of his father the king.
who will live & flourish & mature
as Sir Walter Raleigh Christ, in the Elizabethan Age.

An anagram of "Walter Raleigh" is 'Greg Hallett' ... as the son of Man, with the style & titles Vicar of Christ, Christ and Marquess of Pembroke pass down via the fulfilment of prophecy, confirmed by Shakespeare, the Bible, Typology Theology, Royal Marks, and Anne Boleyn's uncle looks exactly like The Principal's father, who challenged many priests.

Wand of Sovereignty ~ White Wand, Rod of Inauguration ~ White Rod, White Staff or White Stave

Charles Brandon KG PC (1484–1545) was Henry VIII's brother-in-law, made Master of the Horse, 1513–15, 1st Viscount Lisle on 5 May 1513, and 1st Duke of Suffolk on 4 March 1514, becoming only the third Duke in England – Cornwall ~ Norfolk ~ Suffolk ~ Richmond; then made Earl Marshal of England in 1524–28 May 1533, and High Steward at the new Queen Anne Boleyn's Coronation and Royal table, 29 May–1 June 1533.

Henry VIII exchanged Norwich Palace ~ York House for Suffolk Palace. In 1545, Henry VIII converted Suffolk Palace into a Royal mint. The Duke of Suffolk was then in Norwich Palace ~ York House, next-door-but-one to Durham Palace ~ Durham House, which in the next generation, Queen Elizabeth I gave to her nephew Sir Walter Raleigh for at least 20 years, 1583–1603.

Grand Master Charles Brandon (48) Duke of Suffolk and High Steward for that Coronation day and Steward of the Feast, rode his horse inside Westminster Palace Great Hall up and down and around the tables. His caparisoned courser[1] was decorated in crimson velvet, and he was studded and arrayed with many stones and pearls. As per the custom of England, both he and his horse were bareheaded.

Grand Master Suffolk was constantly near Queen Anne Boleyn with the long White Rod in his hand, meaning he could whip anyone, and communicate directly to King Henry VIII, who had a hiding place especially made, where he and the ambassadors of France and Venice watched over Queen Anne Boleyn's Coronation feast from a little closet in the St. Stephen's Chapel cloister.

The thin White Wand of Sovereignty ~ White Rod of Inauguration ~ White Stave ~ White Staff is the traditional emblem of the Lord Chamberlain of England, the most senior official of the Royal household. The White Staff meant the Lord Chamberlain could communicate directly with Monarch, and is broken at each monarch's funeral.

The Lord Chamberlain of England, with White Staff, was responsible for discipline, and the long White Rod was used to intimidate rowdy courtiers in a gentle way, via touch.

---

[1] "Caparisoned" is a horse in rich decorative coverings.
"Courser" is a swift or spirited horse.

1937 Parade in Regent's Park London where two Pearly Kings and a Pearly Queen wear the mother-of-pearl studded suits rearing a horse.

This was 2½ miles NNW of Queen Anne Boleyn's 1 June 1533 coronation diner in the Great Hall of Westminster Palace.

This was their true inspiration. Several million pearl buttons falling off the back off a lorry was just a plant.

Those six who carried the White Rod in 1533 included:

1502–38: Lord Steward of the Royal household, George Talbot
KG, KB, PC (1468–1538) 4th Earl of Shrewsbury, 4th Earl
of Waterford, 10th Baron Talbot, who also presided over the
Board of Green Cloth, which included other holders of the
White Rod;

1525–37: Treasurer of the Household, Sir William FitzWilliam KG
(1490–1542) 1st Earl of Southampton;

1526–40: Lord Great Chamberlain or White Staff Lord, John de
Vere KG PC (1482–1540) 15th Earl of Oxford;

1530–40: Lord Chamberlain of the Household, William Sandys KG
(1470–1540) 1st Baron Sandys of the Vyne;

1532–37: Comptroller of the Household, Sir William Paulet KG PC
(~1484–1572) 1st Marquess of Winchester; and

28 May 1533: Charles Brandon Duke of Suffolk stood down as Earl
Marshal of England, for Queen Anne Boleyn's uncle, Thomas
Howard, 3rd Duke of Norfolk KG PC (1473–1554) who was
appointed Earl Marshal of England (28 May 1533–47) the
day before the coronation ceremonies for his niece Anne
Boleyn;

1533, 1 June, Whitsunday: Grand Master Charles Brandon was
made High Steward for the Coronation. He wielded a Seventh
White Rod, which is a first ... and final.

Thomas Howard, Earl Marshal of England was 59 years old, so he
appointed his youngest brother, Lord William Howard (22)
1st Baron Howard of Effingham (1510–73) to ride deputy in
his place.

The 22 year old William Howard got to ride on his horse around the Royal Coronation feast inside the Westminster Palace Great Hall with the 'Grand Master Flash', Charles Brandon, Duke of Suffolk, all studded with stones & pearls.[1]

'The Maner of the Tryumphe of Caleys and Culleyn, Cum Priuilegio', edited by Edmund Goldsmid F.R.H.S., F.S.A. (Scot) was privately Printed in 1884 in Edinburgh, as 'The Maner of the Tryumphe of Caleys and Culleyn, Cum Priuilegio'.

From this came the inspiration for the Pearly Kings & Queens which were used to promote the re-print of Queen Anne Boleyn's coronation, so the Pearly Kings & Queens were officially founded when Henry Croft stumbled across a shipload of mother-of-pearl buttons abandoned on the River Thames ... an unlikely tale ...

> "There are many urban myths about what happened next, but the story goes that Croft came across a shipload of mother-of-pearl buttons abandoned on the banks of the Thames. Wherever he found them, Croft sewed 60,000 buttons the size of pennies onto a full dress suit and top hat. Smothered with pearls, not a spot ..."[2]

This was 9 years before printing, in 1875, very likely a backdated East End tale to establish the orphan charity ~ 'tell them something ... we'll see what sticks'.

> It was not until 36 years later, "in 1911, that all 28 metropolitan London boroughs had a Pearly King & Queen dressed in black suits completely covered with up to 30,000 mother-of-pearl buttons weighing up to 30kg. Now you're either born into the Pearly King & Queen lineage, or you marry into it. Of the 400 original Pearlies, there are only 40~50 left."[3]

"To be or not to be" 'Executed'

"Executed" includes the removal of a Royal 'style', even the removal of a colour of law style, even removing the misspelt masculine, so no loss:

Queen Anne Boleyn could be stripped of the style "Marquis of Penbroke" and be considered "executed";

Queen Anne Boleyn could be stripped of the title "Marquis of Penbroke" and be considered "executed";

Queen Anne Boleyn could be stripped of the style "Marquesse of Penbroke" and be considered "executed";

Queen Anne Boleyn could be stripped of the style "Marquis of Pembroke" and be considered "executed" ...

but she would still be alive, and retaining the title Marquesse of Pembroke.

> In this very real scenario, if Henry VIII went mad, as he did from his jousting accident on 24 January 1536, the sovereignty of England would default to Queen Anne Boleyn, even if both of them had faked her death.

> This was confirmed when Henry VIII faked his divorce of Queen Anne Boleyn. Instead of divorcing and executing Anne Boleyn, Henry VIII annulled his marriage to a chapel in France called Bulleyn ~ Culleyn, and executed the "Marquis of Penbroke", not the "Marquise of Pembroke", not the Marquesse of Pembroke, not the Lady Marquys of Pembroke, and not the Marchioness of Pembroke.

> Henry VIII died in January 1547, and thereafter the surviving un-divorced Queen Anne Boleyn of England, was the Queen of England, as was her direct lineage which included

Queen Elizabeth I (R 1558–1603) and Sir Walter Raleigh (r. 1603–18+) ... and down onto The Principal Joseph Gregory Hallett, "Cum Priuilegio" – 'with privileges' retaining the English Crown and Marquis or Marquess of Pembroke, whether the children were legitimate or a "natural birth", or with the father unnamed & avoiding any usurping Catholic Monarch's register, as per Bloody Mary (R. 1553–58) ... James VI/ I "the Shit" to James II (1603–88) and the compromised crypto-Catholic Monarchs working for the Jesuits, effectively 1603–2023.

The status of the Earl of Pembroke

There have been ten creations of the Earl of Pembroke from 1139, 1199, 1247, 1339, 1414, 1447, 1452, 1468, 1479 & 1551.

The title of Earl of Pembroke had been very significant for the House of Tudor, and was held by Henry VIII's grand-uncle, Jasper Tudor ~ Jasper of Hatfield, Duke of Bedford and Earl of Pembroke (1431– Christmas 1495) when Henry VI recognised Jasper as his uterine half-brother, and was created Earl of Pembroke on 23 November 1452–68, in its seventh creation.

This seventh creation of the Earl of Pembroke was lost when William Herbert stole his Pembroke Castle, then regained the earldom of Pembroke a couple of years later when his half-brother, King Henry VI (R 3 October 1470–11 April 1471) was restored to the throne for 177 days (7 months & 1 week).[4]

Being a Lancastrian, Jasper Tudor's Earl of Pembroke title was forfeited for 24 years during the predominance of the House of York.

1469–79: The eighth creation belonged to William Herbert and son.

1479–83: The ninth creation belonged to Edward Plantagenet (2
Nov. 1470–June/July 1483) who became Earl of Pembroke for
six years, 1477–83; and Edward, Prince of Wales, 1479–83,
aged 2~4~8, becoming King Edward V aged 11, for 77 days
(R. 9 April –25 June 1483) when the title Earl of Pembroke
merged into the crown.

Edward Plantagenet was also the 17th Earl of Warwick from
the age of 3, confirmed in 1490, then tried and executed for
treason in 1499. There is much obfuscation around Edward
Plantagenet as Edward V, but the kings list is:

Edward IV (R. 4 March 1461–3 October 1470, 11 April 1471–9
April 1483) died aged 40;

Edward V, Earl of Pembroke (R. 9 April–25 June 1483) died June/
July 1483 aged 12;

Richard III (R. 26 June 1483– 22 August 1485) died aged 32;

Henry VII (R. 22 August 1485–21 April 1509) defeated the House
of York in 1485 and restored the title Earl of Pembroke to
the Tudors in 1551. The Earl of Pembroke then came to refer
to the birthplace of Henry VII (R. 1485–1509) in Pembroke
Castle, Pembrokeshire, Wales.

1483–1551: The Earl of Pembroke title was extinct for 68 years.

1551–70: The tenth creation began with Sir William Herbert, son
of Sir Richard Herbert of Ewyas, who was an illegitimate
son of William Herbert, 1st Earl of Pembroke (1423–69) 8th
creation.

Henry VIII's 6th wife, Queen consort Catherine Parr (R. 12 July
1543–28 January 1547) had a younger sister, Anne Parr (1515–52)
who married Sir William Herbert in 1538. Thus the 1st Earl of
Pembroke 10th creation was married to Henry VIII's sister-in-law.

2003–: The title Earl of Pembroke is now held by William Alexander Sidney Herbert, 18th Earl of Pembroke, 15th Earl of Montgomery (b. 1978).

But this is the Earldom. In descending order, it is Duke → Marquess → Earl, so Marquess is above Earl. The Earl of Pembroke holds the house that predicts the Marquess of Pembroke, and part of these predictions are in Wilton House.

Westminster Abbey – Peculiar English Crown Westminster building

1220s: Westminster Abbey was a Benedictine monastic church under the Pope's authority.

1533: Westminster Abbey was still a Benedictine monastic church. Six (6) years later.

1539: Henry VIII dissolved the Westminster Abbey Benedictine monastic church.

1540–56: Westminster Abbey had the status of a Cathedral;

1560: Westminster building was no longer a cathedral or abbey. It is really just the "Westminster building", albeit very ornate, but still under the authority of the Pope since the 1220s.

It is advertised that "Westminster building", is a "Royal Peculiar" directly responsible to the Sovereign, but in this, from 1603+ and 1707+ to the present ...

i.   "Royal Peculiar" means the British Royals are peculiar in that they have been coadjutored by Jesuits to serve the Pope, to put the Pope on the Throne of England, or his agent ~ which the Pope trusts will be the 1603+ 'British' Royals;

ii.   "Royal Peculiar" means the Jesuit British Royal family support Papal authority over the English Throne, and Papal authority over the "Westminster building";

iii. "Royal Peculiar" means the Pope is the Sovereign in all but public name.

iv. This is the complete coadjutoring of the English Crown;

v. "Royal Peculiar" means the Pope is the effective sovereign in all Royal matters, including British coronations, Royal marriages, and Royal breeding;

vi. Queen Anne Boleyn was the first and last to be crowned and break from this. Queen Anne Boleyn of England was our only hope, 1533–36, and she left a legacy;

vii. To add to the confusion, it is advertised that "Westminster building" is titled: "the Collegiate Church of Saint Peter at Westminster", but "Collegiate" is Jesuit, and "Saint Peter" is Roman Catholic, suggesting the title they want is "the Jesuit Church of Roman Catholic Saints at Westminster".

viii. The true and correct name of "Westminster Abbey" is "Westminster building"; and

ix. The "Royal Peculiar" of "Westminster Abbey" was to suppress the English Crown.

x. The building should be called:
"the Peculiar English Crown Church of Saint Anne Boleyn at Westminster",
"the Peculiar English Crown Church at Westminster",
"the Peculiar English Crown Westminster building", or
"the Certain English Crown Church of Saint Anne Boleyn at Westminster",
"the Certain English Crown Church at Westminster",
"the Certain English Crown Westminster building",
"The Certain English Crown Westminster Building".

xi.   Such a building not being Royal Certainty, gives credence to the British Royal family being Jesuit usurpers.

1526–40: John de Vere (1482–1540) was a favourite of Henry VIII, the first Protestant earl of Oxford, 15th Earl of Oxford, and made Lord Great Chamberlain for life 1526–40, KG in 1527, and PC in 1531.

1533: John de Vere (51) Earl of Oxford was one of those who bore the crown at Queen Anne Boleyn's coronation, but ...

1536, 15 May: John de Vere also served on the commission which tried Queen Anne, then sentenced her to execution, by "be-heading elsewhere", guaranteeing her escaped onto lands they had just been granted by Henry VIII, from the Reformation Queen Anne Boleyn had arranged, thus making them rich beyond their wildest dreams. This land is known as "The Island", and is generally 94% of England.

All of the Commissioners then lost all the Trial Records of Queen Anne Boleyn.

Henry VIII then destroyed all paintings and images of Queen Anne Boleyn, so no one would know what she looked like.

Queen Anne Boleyn was executed of the style and or title "Marquis of Penbroke", which never existed; and Henry VIII divorced the "Bulleyn lady chapel in Calais, France", and not Lady Anne Boleyn.

Thus all of Henry VIII's marriages from 1536–47 were null & void, so he only married twice.

Henry VIII was still married to Queen Anne Boleyn, Marquis of Pembroke, and Marquess of Pembroke, and Marquesse of Pembroke when he died on 28 January 1547 ... and Queen Anne Boleyn was

still the Queen of England in 1547/48 ... and still the Marquesse of
Pembroke ... able to pass these titles down, legitimate or illegiti-
mate, to whomever fulfilled the Prophecy held in the Bible, and in
Shakespeare, both of which were edited by Sir Walter Raleigh and
Viscount Francis Bacon ... both grandsons of Queen Anne Boleyn.

Queen Anne Boleyn, Sir Walter Raleigh, Viscount Francis Bacon,
The Bible, and Shakespeare clearly name The Principal Joseph
Gregory Hallett, over 130 times, as the King of England and
Marquess of Pembroke.

1534–37: John de Vere, 15th Earl of Oxford patronised a company
of players & commissioned John Bale to write anti-Catholic
propaganda plays, and in 1537 had John Bale write for
Richard Morison's campaign against the Pope.

Westminster Abbey should be formally called:
"the Certain English Crown Church of the
eternal Queen Anne Boleyn at Westminster",
and informally called:
"the Certain English Crown Westminster without Pope".

Endnotes

1   1983–89: 'Blackadder' is a pseudo-historical sitcom series that got a lot of things right for BBC One.

2   2020, 11 August: 'The real history of the Pearly Kings and Queens', Roman Road London, Megan Agnew, , romanroadlondon.com/ history-pearly-kings-queens/.

3   Ibid.

4   R. S. Thomas, "Jasper Tudor, Jasper of Hatfield, Duke of Bedford", Oxford Dictionary of National Biography;

     1986: Ed. Ralph A. Griffiths & James Sherborwe, 'Kings and Nobles in the Later Middle Ages', St. Martin's Press, New York, p. 19.

Chapter Nine
Elizabeth I's Baptism by Fire

1533, 10 September, Wednesday, 3–4 p.m.: At 3 days old, Lady Elizabeth's Christening[1] was a baptism by fire. There is no mention of water, other than a silver font, but no mention of water in the silver font.

Great preparations were made. Queen Anne Boleyn's uncle, Lord Thomas Howard, 3rd Duke of Norfolk KG PC (1473–1554) came to the Christening. As Queen Anne was delivered with the new faire Lady Elizabeth, *Te deum* (God, We Praise You) was sung.

The Mayor and his brethren, and 40 chief citizens were commanded to attend. Lord Mayor of London Sir Stephen Pecocke (1532–33) in a Crimson velvet gown, with his *S. S.* collar, and all the Aldermen in scarlet, with collars and chains, and all the City Council, took their barge after their 1 p.m. dinner, with the citizens in another barge, and each rowed 5 miles down the River Thames to Greenwich Palace where many lords, knights, and gentlemen assembled.

All the walls of Greenwich Palace were strawed with green rushes, & hung with Tapestry (Arras) from the King's place to Friars Church.

All along one side of this entire procession were 500 King's servants, staff & guards carrying torches. Many gentlemen also bore proper torches about the baby Elizabeth. In the middle of the Church, 3 steps led up to the silver font covered in linen cloth, and surrounded by gentlemen in aprons with towels about their necks, ensuring no filth entered the font. Above there was a crimson satin canopy, fringed with gold & red rail.

Between the body of the church and the choir, there was a pan of fire where Elizabeth was kept warm, and readied. Baby Elizabeth was then brought into the hall and placed by the pan of fire. [It was all very Roman.]

Then every man stepped forward in order:

First the citizens two by two, then gentlemen, Esquires, Chaplain, Aldermen, and the Lord Mayor of London Sir Stephen Pecocke alone: next the Mayor of London, the King's Counsel, the King's Chapel in capes: then

Barons, Bishops, and the Earls ...

Thomas Cromwell (48) 1st Earl of Essex bearing the Basin's gilt covering;

Henry Courtenay KG, PC (35), 1st Marquess of Exeter, 2nd Earl of Devon (1498–1538) with candles (ŷ taper of virgin waxe), then

Charles Brandon KG PC (59) 1st Duke of Suffolk (1514–45) bearing the salt;[2] then

Thomas Howard, 3rd Duke of Norfolk's daughter, Lady Mary of Norfolk (14) bore the rich chrisom pearl & stone (white robe of baptism) and 2 months later married Henry VIII's son, Henry FitzRoy (14) Duke of Richmond and Somerset, illegitimate son of mistress Elizabeth Blount (31). Lady Mary of Norfolk then became Mary Fitzroy. The Howards had married into English Royalty again, but Henry Fitzroy died aged 17 of consumption ~ tuberculosis.

The old Duchess of Norfolk Agnes Howard (56)[3] carried baby Elizabeth in a mantel of purple velvet, with a long train of winter stout cloak (ermine fur) followed by ...

Thomas Howard KG PC (60) 3rd Duke of Norfolk who carried his Marshall White Rod and stood to the right of the Duchesses. Charles Brandon KG PC (59) 1st Duke of Suffolk stood on the left. In front of them stood the Army Officers.

Elizabeth's long train of ermine fur was supported at the mantel by the Countess of Kent,[4] Queen Anne's father, Thomas Boleyn KG

KB (56) 1st Earl of Wiltshire, on the right; and on the left, Edward Stanley KG (24) 3rd Earl of Derby.

The canopy above was supported by Queen Anne's brother George Boleyn (39), Viscount Rochford; and two of her uncles, Lord Thomas Howard the elder KG PC (60) 3rd Duke of Norfolk, and his much younger brother, Lord William Howard (23) 1st Baron Howard of Effingham (1510–73), as well as Lord John Hussey (68).[5]

After the child, many ladies and gentlewomen followed.

When Queen Anne brought the baby to the church door, John Stokesley (58) Bishop of London 1530–39, met them with diverse Bishops & mitred Abbots to begin the Sacrament.

Baptism by Fire Christening the New Archbishop of Canterbury

1532, 22 August: The existing Roman Catholic Archbishop of Canterbury, William Warham, died and this left the position conveniently open for Henry VIII to put the Anglican Thomas Cranmer on trial for 7–15 months, 22 August~30 March~3 December 1533 under the made up style "Lord Archbishop of Canterbury".

1533, 10 September: The Anglican Thomas Cranmer was made Lady ~ Princes[s] ~ Queen Elizabeth I's Godfather, then Lord Archbishop of Canterbury backdated to 30 March 1533, by colour of law assumed to be the Archbishop of Canterbury, but ...

1533, 3 December: Having passed King Henry VIII's total compliance test for 15 months, the Anglican Thomas Cranmer (44) was appointed the Archbishop of Canterbury for the next 22 years & 1 day, from 3 December 1533 to 4 December 1555.

Thomas Cranmer (1489–1556) was the 'Lord Archbishop of Canterbury' backdated 248 days from 3 December 1533 to 30 March 1533. Thomas Cranmer was not actually the 'Archbishop of Canterbury' until 3 December 1533. No actual 'Archbishop of Canterbury' existed for 468 days (15 months 11 days) from the Roman Catholic Archbishop of Canterbury William Warham's death on 22 August 1532 to 3 December 1533, with a soft 'Lord Archbishop of Canterbury' from 30 March–3 December 1533.

Thomas Cranmer (44) Lord Archbishop of Canterbury (1533–55) became the Godfather to Queen Elizabeth I. The 3 Godmothers were Queen Anne Boleyn's step-grandmother, the widowed Agnes née Tilney Howard (56) Dowager Duchess of Norfolk (1477–1545); Margaret Wotton (48) Marchioness of Dorset (1485–6 Oct. 1535); and Gertrude Blount (33) Marchioness of Exeter (~1500–58).

All this was done at the church door, then the baby child was brought to the silver font, and Christened "ELIZABETH".

The Chief Garter King of Armes then cried out loud:
'God of his infinite goodness,
send prosperous life and long,
to the high and mighty Princes[s] of England Elizabeth':

Trumpets then blew. Elizabeth was brought up to the altar, the Gospel laid over the altar, then the [first Anglican Lord] Archbishop of Canterbury Thomas Cranmer confirmed it, as did her new [third] Godmother, Gertrude Blount (~1500–58) Marchioness of Exeter.

The [first Anglican Lord] Archbishop of Canterbury then gave the Princes[s] Elizabeth a standing Gold Cup, followed by the three Godmothers, where the Duchess of Norfolk gave Elizabeth a standing Gold Cup fretted with pearls; the Marchioness of Dorset gave Elizabeth 3 Gilt covered Bowls with lids; and the Marchioness of Exeter gave Princess Elizabeth 3 standing Gilt-covered graven Bowls (bolles grauen) with lids.

Then the wafers, comfits and hypocras[6] were brought in plenty, such that every man had as much, as he desired. After much eating and drinking, the trumpets sounded and everyone left in the same order toward the King's place, many gentlemen bearing torches, as they walked through the 500 King's stationary servants, staff & guards bearing torches.

The gifts that the Godfather and 3 Godmothers gave ~ 2 Gold Cups and 6 Gold Bowls ~ were carried before Princess Elizabeth by four persons:

Henry Somerset (37) 2nd Earl of Worcester bore Archbishop of Canterbury's gift of a Gold Cup;

Robert Radcliffe KG, KB, PC (40) 10th Baron Fitzwalter, 1st Earl of Sussex, bore the Duchess of Norfolk's gift of a Gold Cup fretted with pearls;

Lord Thomas Howard the younger (13) bore Marchioness of Dorset's 3 Gold Bowls;

Sir John Dudley KG (29) 1st Duke of Northumberland father of Elizabeth's future lover Robert Dudley (b. 24 June 1532) bore 3 Gold Bowls gifted by Marchioness of Exeter.

They continued in the order through the fire and beyond, and brought Queen Anne and the Princes[s] Elizabeth to the Queen's Chamber where the Mayor & Aldermen tarried a while. After some time, the Duke of Norfolk (56) and Duke of Suffolk (59) came out from the King (42), thanked them heartedly, and said the King commanded them to give thanks in his name.

The Mayor, Aldermen and Dukes then all headed to the Cellar for a drink (and from thence thei wer had to the seller to drynke) and then returned to their barges (and so went to their Barges) to row up the River Thames to their various Palaces and homes.

1533~58~83: Henry VIII granted Durham Palace to his daughter Lady Elizabeth, and when she was crowned Queen Elizabeth in 1558, she grabbed Durham Palace again, and 25 years later granted it to her nephew Sir Walter Raleigh in 1583, until 1603, plus loads of cash. The Lease was stolen in 1584. This was most unfortunate for the recognition of Sir Walter Raleigh as Prince Regent Duke Governor or "King to be", as in "To be or not to be King – that is the question" Act 3, Scene 1 of Hamlet or Hallett ... which Raleigh rewrote.

Endnotes

1   1548: Edward Hall's Chronicle, THE. XXV. YERE OF KYNG HENRY THE. VIII. ~1533, pp. 805–06.

2   This is not his son-in-law, Henry Grey KB (16) 1st Duke of Suffolk, 3rd Marquess of Dorset (1517–54) who married the daughter, Lady Frances Brandon (1517–59) sometime in 1533, and were the parents of Lady Jane Grey (1537–54) the 'Nine Days' Queen'. Henry Grey was found guilty of treason, attainted and all of his honours forfeit in 1554, then executed 11 days after his daughter on 12 & 23 February 1554.

3   1548: Edward Hall's Chronicle, THE. XXV. YERE OF KYNG HENRY THE. VIII. ~1533, p. 806.

4   'Countess of Kent' may be held by a female in her own right or given to the wife of the Earl of Kent, who did not exist in 1533 ... so a mystery name.

5   Lord John Hussey ~ Husey ~ Hussie ~ Hosey ~ Huse (1465/6–29 June 1537) was Chief Butler of England, 1521–37 and Chamberlain to Henry VIII's daughter, Mary Tudor, before she became the Catholic 'Bloody Mary', Queen of England (R. 1553–58).

6   Comfits or Comfettes are dried fruits, nuts, seeds or spices coated with sugar candy, e.g. sugared almonds. Hypocras or Ypocras is wine mixed with sugar and spices, cinnamon & possibly heated like mulled wine.

Chapter Ten – Religious Reformation and Dissolution of the Monasteries returns a quarter of England

"religious houses in the 16th century ... owned around a quarter of the nation's landed wealth. An English medieval proverb said that if the Abbot of Glastonbury married the Abbess of Shaftesbury, the heir would have more land than the King of England."[1]

"The church owned between one-fifth & one-third [20~33%] of the land in all England. Cromwell realised that he could bind the gentry and nobility to Royal Supremacy by selling to them the huge amount of church lands, and that any reversion to pre-Royal Supremacy would entail upsetting many of the powerful people in the realm."[2]

<1529: Catholic Church owned 16~60% of England. "A quarter" was its euphemism.

1529–37: Religious Reformation.

1535–41: Dissolution of the Monasteries and Royal land-grab.

1529–40: The Papal lands were 16%, 20%, 25%, 33% or 60% of England until the Religious Reformation, Dissolution of the Monasteries, and Royal land-grab.

1540: The 'Society of Jesus' was officially formed and sounded Christian, but was the opposite of Christianity. The Society of Jesus was a Satanic movement to take over all the land in the world to establish itself as Sovereign, and to compromise every Crown. The Jesuit 'Society of Jesus' was a land-grab exercise.

The Papacy, Vatican & Roman Catholic Church, supported Jesuits running the newly invented Society of Jesus, and this began the Counter-Reformation.

The goal of the Papacy, Vatican, Roman Catholic Church, Society of Jesus, Jesuits, and Counter-Reformation was to claw back lands, re-write history in their image.

When that didn't progress as planned, the Society of Jesus goal was to claim the New World, and all the Crowns of Europe and England, taking every Crown, and inventing new Crowns in their image.

The Jesuit model was the model of idealised slavery, taken up by communism. Jesuit monarchs were introduced into England from 1603, in the form of the compromised bisexual crypto-Catholic James VI/I ~ "James the Shit".

To counteract this, Henry VIII created a secret Crown of England, descended from Queen Anne Boleyn, Marquess of Pembroke, made up of the Holy Grael lineage, loosely under the banner of Shakespeare and the Bible coders, but really under the banner Marquess of Pembroke, who would be illuminated by the fulfilment of prophecy in the Bible and Shakespeare. The Principal has done all of this and stakes his claim as King of England.

In support of this, Henry VIII made Thomas Cromwell (*c.*1485–28 July 1540) Privy Council 1530–40; Master of King's Jewel House 1533–40; Chancellor of the Exchequer 12 April 1533–10 June 1540; Steward of Westminster Abbey 12 September 1533–; Visitor-General of the Monasteries 21 January 1535–; Steward, Duchy of Lancaster, Essex, Hertfordshire & Middlesex 12 May 1535–40; Principal Secretary April 1534–April 1540; and Master of the Rolls 8 October 1534–10 July 1536.

1535–41: Henry VIII & Thomas Cromwell orchestrated the Dissolution of the Monasteries, and started by routing all universities and colleges linked to the church, destroying all books deemed 'popish' & 'superstitious'. Other books were dispersed.

1535–1602: Oxford University was left with only 3 books and some chained books in its library. Thomas Cromwell's actions were described as 'easily the greatest single disaster in English literary history'. Oxford Students had nothing to study for 67 years.

1901–41: The second greatest disaster in English literary history was Princess Beatrix transcribing & editing all Queen Victoria's Diaries over 40 years, then burning the originals. This removed Queen Victoria's firstborn and only legitimate child, "Prince Marcos Manoel", but retained frequent fond memories of visits from "George", who was Blind Prince George of Cumberland, Queen Victoria's first husband, and Prince Marcos Manoel's father.

1596: Queen Elizabeth I then sent out Commander Howard and Walter Raleigh to steal a library, which they did, bombing Cádiz, then stealing the Bishop of Faro's library on the way home ~ for sport. This formed the basis of Sir Thomas Bodley's donation of the Bodleian Collection, albeit missing the most important book in Christianity, the Book of Predictions Walter Raleigh had retrieved from 6 miles above Faro.

1536: "The 1536 Dissolution of the Lesser Monasteries Act closed smaller houses ... all the land given to the Crown or sold to the aristocracy".

All the land of the smaller monasteries was given to the Commissioners of Queen Anne Boleyn's trial, which was the biggest bribe in history to:

i.   Find Queen Anne Boleyn guilty without evidence;

ii.   Fake Queen Anne Boleyn's execution; and

iii.   Support Queen Anne Boleyn afterwards; on order to

iv.   Create the Holy Grael ~ Bible ~ Shakespeare ~ Marquess of Pembroke ~ King of England lineage.

1536:   Thomas Cromwell established the Court of Augmentations, and the court of General Surveyors to administer the former Roman Catholic Church and Monasteries, which covered a quarter of England's lands & demanded 40% of England's rents.

1554:   The Court of Augmentations became the Augmentation Office in the Exchequer, at 11 Downing Street.

The Dissolution of the Monasteries was one of the biggest land-grabs in history, providing a massive windfall to the royal coffers being the Exchequer or Treasury.

1535–41–54: Henry VIII used his chief minister, Thomas Cromwell to rout all monasteries. The Catholic Monasteries were then given away & sold off for the price of the fine, and most often, not even that was paid.

Much of these lands were given to the Commission, and then swiftly awarded by the Commission to the Commissioners, who then sat on the Trials, seeing their new lands as bribes to fake noble executions, and hide the posthumous Queens, ladies-in-waiting, and their trusted noble friends, relatives and in-laws for life, intergenerationally.

1536–54: Henry VIII's Commissioners were faking Noble Trials and Executions, and providing lands for posthumous

Noble lives, which collectively became 94% of England, and was known as "The Island" ~ the other name for England.

1535: Henry VIII's Chief Minister Thomas Cromwell was not adverse to Queen Anne Boleyn, rather they were allies. Thomas Cromwell spent over £1.5 million in 2023 values renovating leading Reformer, Anne Boleyn's 1533 Coronation lodgings, into luxury. This was joined to the central White Tower via a stone curtain wall corridor, removed in the 1790s.

1536: Just prior to the 'Anne Boleyn execution', Thomas Cromwell was made Receiver of Petitions in the Lords in the Parliament of 1536; so he knew what everyone wanted, and this included petitions from the new land rich aristocracy offering to support Queen Anne Boleyn in her posthumous afterlife.

1536, 2 May: On entering the Tower of London as a prisoner, Queen Anne Boleyn was taken to her newly renovated former Coronation lodgings.

1526, 2–19 May: In true Royal Tudor style, Queen Anne Boleyn's Coronation lodgings and Execution lodgings were the same place, and people were allowed to come and go, make deliveries of flowers, clothes and jewellery, and amongst them useful things, like a knife, potato-peeler, swedes, white handkerchiefs, pigs blood, straw, a wooden sword, a headless body double, arrow box ... and two Almoners visiting at 2:00 in the morning, being the Hereditary Grand Almoner, Henry Courtenay, 1st Marquess of Exeter, and the King's Almoner (38), Lord High Almoner of the Royal Household, Edward Foxe (30) Bishop of Hereford who had just played a major role in Henry VIII's divorce from Catherine of Aragon (H1). Together they carried in all of the above, plus one 5'3" 7-stone headless female body-double and two identical black damask large capes with hammerhead hood trimmed with white ermine.

1526, 19 May, 2–8 a.m.: Courtenay & Foxe stayed for 6 hours and trained Queen Anne Boleyn and her 4 ladies-in-waiting on their combined roles in faking the Execution.

1540: Then for obfuscation, 6 years after Anne's 'beheading', Queen's House (13, p. 121) was built over-looking Tower Green, made of half-timber. This was partially built as a distraction, 125 yards from Anne's execution platform.

1536–1790s: Queen Anne Boleyn's Coronation-Execution lodgings were then left for 160 years, quickly becoming uninhabitable, and were then demolished in the 1790s.

This was a Royal case of 'Ambiguous Building ~ Ambiguous Crime'. This was a soft admission of a getaway 'No Building ~ No Crime'. The Royals still do this today.

1536, 18 July: 2 months after Anne Boleyn's Execution, Henry VIII made Thomas Cromwell, Baron Cromwell of Okeham, Vicar General and Vicegerent of the King in spirituals. For Henry VIII annulment & divorce were spiritual matters.

Henry VIII annulled his marriage to the Roman Catholic Catherine of Aragon, and equally annulled England's marriage with the Roman Catholic Church.

Henry VIII divorced the Roman Catholic woman, and equally divorced the Roman Catholic Church.

When it came to annulling his marriage to Queen Anne Boleyn, he actually annulled his marriage to a Catholic chapel near Calais, called "Culleyn", then "Bulleyn" assumed to be 'Boleyn,' but not, so no annulment or divorce took place, and ...

All of Henry VIII's subsequent four (4) marriages were bigamous and null & void, void ab initio, as though they never happened.

Henry VIII only married twice.

Henry VIII's marriage to Queen Anne Boleyn was believed to be annulled, divorced and with Anne Boleyn dead, but not one word of it was true.

Queen Anne Boleyn was alive and well and still the Queen of England in her own right, but also Queen consort, and all Henry VIII's subsequent wives were "not":

From 30 May 1536–24 October 1537, Jane Seymour was not the wife of Henry VIII;

From 6 January–9 July 1540, Anne of Cleves was not the wife of Henry VIII, and it was never consummated, and Anne of Cleves was never crowned queen consort;

From 28 July 1540–23 November 1541, Catherine Howard was not the wife of Henry VIII;

From 12 July 1543– 28 January 1547, Catherine Parr was not the wife of Henry VIII.

These were all bigamous marriages stemming from an annulment that never happened, a divorce that never happened, and an execution that never happened, and the only execution that took place was the execution of a title that did not exist – "Marquis of Penbroke".

1530–36: Anne Boleyn's father, Thomas Boleyn, 1st Earl of Wiltshire, was Lord Privy Seal and a Commissioner at his daughter Queen Anne Boleyn's Trial.

1536, 2 July: For turning a blind eye & witnessing the very obvious faking of his daughter's beheading, 44 days later father Thomas Boleyn surrendered Lord Privy Seal to Thomas Cromwell. This indicates a Masonic Pact.

2 July 1536–10 June 1540: Thomas Cromwell then became Lord Privy Seal.

1539, 12 March: 33 months & 21 days later, Thomas Boleyn (*c*.1477–12 March 1539) 'died' to join his daughter Anne Boleyn on 'The Island', indicating this was an illuminati forbidden secret, that they had all survived the axe & sword of Henry VIII.

All of this was a major part of reinvigorating the Holy Grael lineage, and formed part of "the Shin" until the End Times when "the Shin" guided the falling away of everything.

'The Island' is the 94% of England made up of aristocratic estates & Royal Forests. Halletts emerged out of New Forest, and ran their own forests, including 'Hallett's Wood'.

One of the true tests of a Royal is that they escape death. The Principal Joseph Gregory Hallett has escaped at least 18 attempts on his life, with at least 6 in England.

2 November 1538–10 July 1540: Henry VIII then made Thomas Cromwell Governor of the Isle of Wight on 2 November 1538; Lord Great Chamberlain and 1st Earl of Essex on 17 April 1540 ... then had Cromwell (55) beheaded at Tower Hill on 28 July 1540 ... to join the others on 'The Island'.

1530–47: Henry VIII had set up Thomas Cromwell (1485–1540) with perfect titles and offices to fake the Noble deaths and help them escape onto lands he had just taken off the Catholic Church, giving half to his Commissioners.

There was no problem with bribes under Henry VIII ... and the bribes were huge.

Cromwell was assisted by lands recently transferred from the beneficent Margaret, Countess of Salisbury (1473–27 May 1541) to Anne of Cleves (1515–57).

Anne of Cleves (H4) failed to consummate her 1540 marriage to Henry VIII, which only lasted six months. Anne of Cleves was never crowned queen consort, and after the annulment of their marriage came to be known as "the King's Beloved Sister".[3]

Margaret, Countess of Salisbury was known as 'Margaret Pole' from 1540, aged 66. She owned the fifth largest estate in England, which included Bisham Abbey, 9 miles north-west of Windsor Castle, 14 miles further up the River Thames. Above Eton, the River Thames is called 'Isis'.

Bisham Abbey was now part of Henry VIII's land-grab to hide his departed wives. As "the King's Beloved Sister", Anne of Cleves lived on Margaret, Countess of Salisbury's former estate, Bisham Abbey. Anne of Cleves was then given Hever Castle, which had previously belonged to Anne Boleyn's family, so 'Anne' could be comfortably 'at home'. "Where is Anne?"

Henry VIII was knocked unconscious in a jousting incident on 24 January 1536. This opened an old leg injury which festered and drove him mad. Recognising this, Henry VIII made plans to continue the English Royal family, by housing Queen Anne Boleyn.

Nobles were faking their deaths in abundance, and living on the new 'free land', which they had just come to own. Some of this land their posthumous friends had previously owned, like Margaret, Countess of Salisbury, the "last of the Plantagenet dynasty", but she also escaped her own execution in the Tower of London, and onto her previously-owned lands and buildings.

These estates were collectively the Noble commune hiding the Holy Grail lineage on 'The Island', being 94% of England now owned by the aristocrats, and not by the Catholic Church.

Much of the aristocracy lived like this in the 1960s to 1980s, living together on large estates, having children with each others' partners, many working through their entire inheritance.

These 'execution survivors' lived together on vast estates, which provided a choice of accommodation with over 100 purpose-built cottages and manor houses sprinkled all over any one property, with total privacy & self-sufficiency – no camera, phone or drone, and plenty of deer and vegetables, and enclosed gardens.

Much of the aristocracy found it easier to live in their cottages than heat their castellated manor houses in winter. Typically, each night one cottage cooked and everyone from the estate turned up for dinner. These dinners were a lot of fun and select visitors were welcome, often plied with plenty of 'forget-me-this'.

Their children were tainted aristocracy, deprived of their history, but allowed back into mainstream society as protected lesser beings, sometimes relegated to the Colonies as functionaries.

Lord Lucan, pronounced "Luck-an", did a similar thing and lived on friends' English estates from his disappearance on 8 November 1974, to his natural death 31 years later around 2005.

Lord Lucan was hidden with Queen Elizabeth II's support and never faced the Courts ... just as Queen Anne Boleyn and Nobles executed in the Tower of London were hidden with Henry VIII's support. This was made obvious by the lands he granted in the years and months and prior to their trials.

1540, 28 July: Henry VIII had his first minister Thomas Cromwell (55) beheaded at Tower Hill to join others on 'The Island'.

1649–60: Thomas Cromwell's nephew, Oliver Cromwell (1599–1658) created the Republic, and was Lord Protector of the Commonwealth of England, Scotland and Ireland 1653–58.

1657, February–13 April: "Cromwell was offered the crown by Parliament as part of a revised constitutional settlement, presenting him with a dilemma since he had been 'instrumental' in abolishing the monarchy. Cromwell agonised for 6 weeks over the offer ... Instead, Cromwell was ceremonially re-installed as Lord Protector on 26 June 1657 at Westminster Hall, sitting upon King Edward's Chair specially moved from Westminster Abbey. The event echoed a coronation, using many of its symbols and regalia, such as a purple ermine-lined robe, a sword of justice and a sceptre, but not the crown or orb."[4]

Cromwell ensured all the British Crowns were broken up, sold off in pieces, and or destroyed.

1658–60: Oliver Cromwell (59) died on 3 September 1658; and his son Richard Cromwell (31) took over, albeit briefly.

1660, 29 May: Charles II returned to Britain and was crowned in a papier-mâché crown.

Endnotes

1   1999: Studies in the Early History of Shaftesbury Abbey, Ed. Laurence Keen, published by Dorset County Council, Dorchester.

2   1991: G. R. Elton: On Reformation and Revolution, p. 142, citing Arthur J. Slavin, The History Teacher, volume 23, No. 4, August 1990, pp. 405–31, Published by Society for History Education.

3   2000: Retha M. Warnicke, 'The Marrying of Anne of Cleves: Royal Protocol in Early Modern England', Cambridge University Press, Cambridge, p. 252.

    2010, Elizabeth Norton, 'Anne of Cleves: Henry VIII's Discarded Bride', Amberley, Stroud, p. 108.

    2019: Heather Darsie, 'Anna, Duchess of Cleves: The King's Beloved Sister', Amberley Publ., pp. 17–20.

4   Oliver Cromwell, The Protectorate: 1653–1658, wikipedia.

Chapter Eleven
The Hereditary Grand Almoner ~ Marquess of 'Exit-her'

Almoner(s) role 19 May 1536 Execution of Queen Anne Boleyn
Queen Anne Boleyn was originally designated to be executed on the same day as her brother, George Boleyn, on Sunday 17 May 1536, but this was delayed two days, waiting for a morning with sun-strike. The excuse was a change in execution style, from burning at the stake, to axe, to sword, the swordsman coming from France ... and not speaking a word of English.

In order to explain why Queen Anne Boleyn's execution was delayed two days, 17–19 May, her long hair bunched up to the size of her head inside her oversized coif, the Frenchman's sword missing Anne's head completely, then Anne replaced with a dead-house body-double ... we need to know the machinations of Henry VIII behind the scenes in saving the life of his 28–35-year-old wife, to snub the Catholic ban on divorce, to create the Holy Grael lineage, and to explain the King's use of the 'Almoner', which can be plural ... as in more than one Almoner.

> "On 2 May 1536, Anne Boleyn was arrested and taken to the Tower of London by barge ... she entered through the Court Gate in the Byward Tower ... In the Tower, she collapsed ... [17 days later] on 19 May morning, Sir William Kingston, Constable of the Tower (1524–40) wrote:
> > 'Sir, her almoner is continually with her, and had been since two o'clock after midnight'."

The almoner had arrived at Queen Anne Boleyn's lodgings at 2 a.m. to begin her training. When the constable of the Tower writes "almoner", most don't give it a second thought. Maybe it's just an anonymous Chaplin hearing her tear-filled sobbing for 6 hours.

The innocuous "almoner" was really a spy network capable of organising, administering, servicing, and funding a fake execution, and uniforms, thus selecting their own staff.

The Almoner were teaching and role-playing Queen Anne Boleyn and her four ladies-in-waiting on faking the beheading using a potato-peeler, sun-strike, height of the scaffold, straw, first and second damask coat, coif, noise distractions, swish the body, escort to the Thames, transport up the River Thames, with housing afterwards ... all in exchange for the promise of uniforms.

The Tower Warders were at a bit of a loss, and came to love their uniforms as their identity.

The Tower Warders or Tower of London warders, and Yeomen Warders, Ordinary Yeomen, Extraordinary Yeomen (Crisis Actors without uniform, except they wore a velvet patch), Yeomen of the Guard (Royal Bodyguards), Yeomen Warders of Her Majesty's Royal Palace and Fortress the Tower of London, Members of the Sovereign's Body Guard of the Yeoman Guard Extraordinary or Her Majesty's Royal Palace and Fortress the Tower of London' (popularly misnamed "Beefeaters") ... were verbally designed as the most confusing group, to be identified and misidentified by their uniforms, and then change those uniforms on 'occasions', interchange staff between groups, and uniforms ... have more than one name for the same group and subgroup ... and then backdate the uniforms 300 years, according to the whims of the early Victorian era ... which began tourism for all of the above.

At the time of Queen Anne's execution on 19 May 1536, there were three Almoners:

~A.D. 500: The Chaplin was the Pastor or Church Officer and operated from ~A.D. 500.

1103–: The Lord High Almoner ~ King's Almoner was Almoner of the Royal Household.

1525/1685: The Hereditary Grand Almoner officially operated from 1685, but from the actions of the Marquess of Exeter in 1536, he operated without duty, for influence, from 1525.

When covering a Royal fraud, the Almoner just lists the year they began serving office.

When the 'Almoner' doesn't have a Royal fraud to hide, they list the year, month & day they began serving in office. Either way, the Almoner take special care to state that:

i.   The Hereditary Grand Almoner had "no role", so was free to use his title for influence without duty.

ii.   The Hereditary Grand Almoner was established in 1685, vested in the Marquess of Exeter, that title established in 1525. He was voluntarily active in 1536.

iii.   Hereditary Grand Almoner and Marquess of Exeter also holds the title Lord Paramount Peterborough. Henry VIII's first wife, Catherine of Aragon was buried in Peterborough Cathedral in 1536. 51 years later, Mary, Queen of Scots 'execution' was faked in 1587. Mary was be-headed to France. A dead-house body-double was secretly 'buried' at night in Peterborough Cathedral, then moved to Westminster Abbey 25 years later.

iv.   Keeper of the Privy Purse was in charge of the execution arrangements, service & money, but he, Henry Norris, was executed on 17 May 1536, 'two days before' Queen Anne Boleyn, so no one was in charge of the execution arrangements, service & money.

v.   This meant Queen Anne Boleyn's execution was in disorganised disarray, or chaos.

       It was chaos with a purpose. The beheaded and now absent Keeper of the Privy Purse had installed an air of 'execution' to the faked execution of Queen Anne Boleyn.

vi.   The next Keeper of the Privy Purse took office on an unknown date in 1536–47, perhaps after 19 May 1536, perhaps in October? This was Sir Anthony Denny (1501–49) who specialised in making himself absent, and for this was made Groom of the Stool 1546–47.

vii.   The Almoner answered to the Keeper of the Privy Purse, but with no Keeper of the Privy Purse, none of the Almoner had anyone to answer to. This meant the Almoners – Chaplin, Lord High Almoner and Hereditary Grand Almoner – all had the freedom of the Hereditary Grand Almoner, with no one to answer to. This meant it was a free-range execution.

viii. Hereditary Grand Almoner was invested in the Marquess of Exeter, free to use his title without duty, operating of his own free will for influence, and had "no role".

ix.   With no one to answer to, and no defined role, any of the Almoner could:

  a. Arrange the execution service in any way they liked;

  b. As long as they could access the usual finances without the usual dictation of its use;

  c. By financing the execution themselves into a non-execution;

  d. As it only required influence and a bit of coin to grease the palms of those desperate to wear a uniform, who were also those desperate to play a role in history.

x.   The Constable of the Tower Kingston, Lieutenant of the Tower Walsingham, Tower Warders, 150 Ordinary Yeomen Warders and 300 Extraordinary Yeomen Warders came cheap. One could buy the lot for a uniform, the boat-ride there, and a meal at a feast afterwards. Such a bonding exercise virtually affirmed and confirmed all the Tower Warders silence ... but the Tower Warders came even cheaper than that.

xi.   The Almoner bought all Tower Warders for a patch of velvet and the promise of a uniform. The uniforms took 11 years to arrive, 1536 ... 1547, and 18 years to arrive, 1536 ... 1554.

xii.   Through successive bribes saving the lives of two (2) Queen consorts and three (3) Noble women, and many noblemen, the uniform bribes became scarlet royal livery for the 12 Tower Warders in 1547, and a velvet coat of any colour trimmed with silver gilt for the 150 Ordinary Yeomen in 1554.

There were no uniforms in 1536 ... and the Almoners did everything they could to avoid the Execution of Anne Boleyn ... for the promise of uniforms.

xiii.   A Chaplin, Pastor or Church Officer were not used for Queen Anne Boleyn.

xiv.   The Lord High Almoner of the Royal Household ~ the King's Almoner (*c*.1532–37) was Edward Foxe (*c*.1496–1538) Bishop of Hereford (1535–38).

xv.   Foxe had just played a major role in Henry VIII's divorce from Catherine of Aragon (H1).

xvi.   The King's Almoner Edward Foxe retired the next year in 1537, and died aged 42 on 8 May 1538, but likely joined 'The Island'.

The 2005 innuendo film 'The Island' stars Ewan McGregor and Scarlett Johansson who looks a lot like a painting by Hans Holbein the Younger (1497–1543) incorrectly titled 'A Lady, called Anne Boleyn', 1532~35, but it is of Elizabeth Darrell (1513~56) mistress and muse of Sir Thomas Wyatt (1503–42) who was locked up in the Tower of London in May 1536, a poet considered to have been in love with Anne Boleyn since 1523.

The Hereditary Grand Almoner Henry Courtenay (*c*.1498–1538) 1st Marquess of Exeter (1525–38) KG, PC was a grandson of King Edward IV (R. 1461~83) son of Catherine of York, first cousin of Henry VIII, and "brought up as a child with his grace in his chamber". Henry Courtenay grew up with Henry VIII.

1519: Henry Courtenay (21) married his second wife, Gertrude Blount (1499/1502–58) daughter of Catherine of Aragon's Chamberlain, William Blount, 4th Baron Mountjoy (*c*.1478–1534). Gertrude Blount's 1st of 3 stepmothers was a Spanish lady-in-waiting to Catherine of Aragon. Gertrude became close friends with Catherine of Aragon (H1 ~ Henry VIII's first wife) ... it was all so very in-house.

1533, 10 September: Gertrude became godmother to Princess / Queen Elizabeth I, and Henry Courtenay played a role in Princess Elizabeth's Baptism by Fire.

1535: Henry VIII (44) gave his first cousin Henry Courtenay (27) stewardship of several monasteries "which placed him in a key position for the forthcoming process". Henry Courtenay became a powerful landowner in southwest England, owning much of the land in Wiltshire, Gloucestershire, Dorset, Devon and Cornwall. The lands granted were so vast, Courtenay administered most of western England as:

"Henry Courtney 1st Marquess of Exeter & King Henry VIII".

This placed the Hereditary Grand Almoner Henry Courtenay in the perfect position to hide Queen Anne Boleyn anywhere in southern & western England.

Queen Anne Boleyn escaped from the Tower of London to Bisham Abbey, from where it was just 40 miles west to Wiltshire, yet 240 miles to the end of Cornwall, so they had 200 miles West-East and 150 miles South-North to play in England's largest estates and Royal Forests.

1536, May: Henry Courtenay was a Commissioner in Anne Boleyn's trial, and then switched hats as the Hereditary Grand Almoner in charge of her 'execution' by 'be-heading'.

Courtenay was fully on-board as the Marquess of 'Exit-her' as Henry VIII had made Henry Courtenay extremely wealthy and able to provide for the posthumous Queen Anne Boleyn, Marquess of Pembroke, with many estates for extended stay, to make friends, get pregnant and give birth in the areas of Exeter & Devon, which included Walter Raleigh senior & Katherine Champernowne, who were to be the house parents of her future grandson, Sir Walter Raleigh.

1537: Henry Courtenay retired.

1538, 9 December: Henry Courtenay was beheaded by sword, but Courtenay was really a 30-year-old be-heading to 'The Island' ~ the Noble Commune ~ which had just increased from 39,000 to 47,000 square miles ... from 77.5% to 93.5% of England, but taking into account roads, public waterways and services, 78% to 94% of England's 50,301 square miles is 'The Island'.

The reward for saving Queen Anne Boleyn was to become her Court company on 'The Island' – most of England – where Henry Courtenay was the Principal land owner in south-west England.

94% minus 78% is 16%. This is the minimum area of England that Henry VIII and Queen Anne Boleyn reclaimed from the Catholic Church. It is $\frac{1}{6}^{th}$ of England, or 8,000 square miles.

1526–36: Keeper of the Privy Purse was Henry Norris ($c.1482$–1536).

The above three Almoner were all responsible to the Keeper of the Privy Purse. The Keeper of the Privy Purse was in charge of arrangements, service and money, and this was Henry Norris for the previous 10 years, but he was executed along with George Boleyn on 17 May 1536, two days before Queen Anne Boleyn.

The execution of Henry Norris gave an air of reality to the Boleyn 'executions'.

This meant that these three (3) Almoner had free range to exit Queen Anne Boleyn, with the Marquess of Exeter taking the lead to 'Exit-her' as a Royal Mark.

1535–36: Henry Courtenay, 1st Marquess of Exeter received estates vast enough to house Queen Anne Boleyn and her entire court, friends and relatives, so Courtenay, was made a Commissioner in the trial of Queen Anne Boleyn, finding her 'Guilty' ... and sending her away.

There was absolutely no evidence for Queen Anne Boleyn's guilt, and the only purpose of the guilty verdict was to send Anne away with her entourage ... to continue the Holy Grael lineage, which is completely intertwined with the best of the English & French Royal families.

1535–47: Henry VIII had the Court of Augmentations take control of the land & finances of the Catholic Church in the Kingdom of England, and Wales, over these 12 years. With all this spare land, amounting to 16%~60% of England, Henry VIII made many appointments backed up with enormous land-grab gifts to enact his will.

Henry VIII made Thomas Cromwell (*c*.1485–28 July 1540) his chief minister, becoming:

1533–40: Privy Council and Master of King's Jewel House;

12 April 1533–10 June 1540: Chancellor of the Exchequer;

12 Sept. 1533–May 1535 or 10 June 1540: Steward of Westminster Abbey.

1535–40: Henry VIII and his chief minister Vicar-General Thomas Cromwell dissolved all the religious houses. Their lands, properties and incomes went to the Crown, some to Commissioners, some forming the Church of England.

1534, November: Thomas Cromwell (56) was made Vicar-General, second only to Henry VIII (43) in Church matters, and made 1st Earl of Essex.

1536: Religious establishments with low annual incomes were dissolved ... being less than £200 per annum. Any income less than £3 million in 2024 values were dissolved.

1537: Friaries were dissolved.

1538–39: Remaining religious houses were dissolved, some used in the formation of the Church of England.

1540: Waltham Abbey in Essex was the last church to be taken ~ dissolved & transferred.

1540, 17 April: Henry VIII made Cromwell Lord Great Chamberlain ~ his senior officer.

Henry VIII's 'Dissolution of the Monasteries' evicted the religious out of housing and off lands. Lay people were also evicted out of their homes and off lands, though not as many. Henry Courtenay was aware his tenants were suffering and came to hate the Vicar-General Thomas Cromwell and his Protestantism whose "measures ... became so obnoxious Courtenay drifted into treasonable conspiracy with the Pole family" ~ Margaret Pole, Countess of Salisbury, who helped rescue Queen Anne Boleyn.

1540: Nevertheless, the large pilgrimage Waltham Abbey in Essex was the last Church to be taken. Thomas Cromwell was then removed as Steward of Westminster Abbey.

1540, 28 July: Henry VIII (49) beheaded his senior officer Thomas Cromwell (55).

1535: Henry VIII gave Sir Anthony Denny (1501–49) ex-religious sites and manors 'in preparation' for Denny to become the next Keeper of the Privy Purse.

1536, 17 May: The previous Keeper of the Privy Purse Henry Norris was executed.

1535–47 or 1536–49: Sir Anthony Denny became the next serving Keeper of the Privy Purse, involved in approving the finances for the execution of Queens and Nobles, but his service began with ambiguity and patent ambiguity in 1535–47 or 1536–49.

It also does not state which month Denny started, or whether it was May, nor the 17, 18 or 19 May 1536, and could have been October 1536, and Sir Anthony Denny had a vested interest in being absent & not financing the execution of Queen Anne Boleyn on 19 May 1536.

1536, 17–19 May: With Keeper of the Privy Purse Henry Norris' execution, this indicates insufficient time for Sir Anthony Denny to responsibly prepare for Queen Anne Boleyn's Execution in just two (2) days.

That there was no Keeper of the Privy Purse on 17–19 May 1536 was purposeful.

1535–45: Sir Anthony Denny was the most intimate of Henry VIII's few friends. In 1536, Henry gave Denny the houses named 'Paradise', 'Purgatory' & 'Hell' in Westminster, being ale houses within or adjoining Westminster Hall,[1] with Paradise elsewhere; and the Benedictine nuns' Cheshunt Priory in Hertford, 21 miles north; and

1540: Amwell manor in Hertfordshire; and Waltham rectory in Essex; and

1542: Mettingham college in Suffolk, with 6 manors in East Anglia;

1544: Sir Anthony Denny exchanged lands with Henry VIII by Act 35 Hen. VIII, no. 23. Denny also leased property from the crown. Denny also made extensive purchases in Essex and Hertfordshire from private individuals.

1546, December: Sir Anthony Denny was granted a licence to export wheat, beer and leather. Denny was also given the London customs office to run as a source of income.

1547: Sir Anthony Denny was elected Keeper of the Royal Household in charge of Henry VIII's personal spending, as receiver & paymaster; and made MP Hertfordshire.

1547–52: When Henry VIII died, there was no Keeper of the Privy Purse for 4½ years, meaning all 3 Tower of London Almoner(s) had no one to answer to, anyone could finance an execution, and those who could finance an execution could fake an execution.

1547: When Henry VIII died, Sir Anthony Denny received more crown lands, including most of Waltham Abbey's estates freehold from 1540, plus another 2,000 acres or 3 square miles of land elsewhere.

1257: Parliament begun when the King's Great Council assembled in the Chapter House in the East Cloister of Westminster Abbey, behind "the oldest door in Britain". The House of Commons also met there in the early 1300s, then used the Abbey Refectory.

1548/9–51: Sir Anthony Denny was made **Keeper of Westminster Palace** the year after Henry VIII died, to avoid Henry VIII being linked to missing trial records, etc.

Keeper of Westminster Palace rendered Sir Anthony Denny in charge of the Parliamentary records of Queen Anne Boleyn's execution, which were kept 60 yards west across St Margaret Street in the Chapter House in the East Cloister of Westminster Abbey, behind "the oldest door in Britain", being a projected emotional hook.

The role of 'Keeper of Westminster Palace' gave Sir Anthony Denny perfect access to alter any records of Queen Anne Boleyn's execution, but it wasn't the first time, and it wouldn't be the last.

"The oldest door in Britain" was not physically locked until 26 December 1950, when the 'Coronation Stone' was retaken by the Scottish for Scotland, against the faux British monarchs.

As Keeper of Westminster Palace Sir Anthony Denny answered to no one in completely removing Queen Anne Boleyn's trial and execution records, changing existing secondary records, and installing records which did not exist.

Hereditary Grand Almoner Henry Courtenay and Sir Anthony Denny Keeper of Westminster Palace ensured that all of Queen Anne Boleyn's trial records, transcripts, statements and records of evidence went missing ... as indeed they have. This included changing:

'Sir, her Almoners are continually with her, and have been since 2 to 8 a.m. ... to ...

"Sir, her almoner is continually with her, and had been since two o'clock after midnight'".

"Almoners" was changed to "almoner", and '2 to 8 a.m.' was changed to the more confusing "two o'clock after midnight'".

1549, 10 September: Sir Anthony Denny's own income was £200 (£1.7 million in 2024) but his chief source of wealth was grants of land from "the princely liberality of Henry VIII he had gained all that I leave or can leave to my posterity". When Sir Anthony Denny (48) died, he owned ~20,000 acres in Essex and Hertfordshire, generating a land income ~£750 per annum (£9.5 million per annum in 2024).[2]

1552, January: After 4 years absence, Keeper of the Privy Purse went to Peter Osborne. This meant the Almoner(s) had no one to answer to from 1547 to January 1552.

1552–79: Like Courtenay, Denny's main role was to gather enough finances to take care of his upcoming charge – his great-nephew Sir Walter Raleigh.

Sir Anthony Denny married Walter Raleigh's house-mother's aunt

In one of the most purposefully confusing records of history, Sir Anthony Denny (1501–49) married (1525) Joan Champernowne (d. 1553) lady-in-waiting at the court of Henry VIII, sister of Katherine Ashley née Champernowne, governess of the future Queen Elizabeth I.

Sir Anthony Denny & Joan had 12 children.

Queen Anne Boleyn's posthumous daughter, *Mary y'Noble* gave birth to a son in January 1552 and farmed him out in January 1554 to her niece, Walter Raleigh's house-mother, also called Kat Champernoun, being Katherine Champernoun/ Catherine Champernon, Champernowne ~ Gilbert ~ Raleigh (1519–94) who already had 12 children to at least 4 different fathers.

The elder Kat Champernowne then introduced Walter Raleigh to Queen Elizabeth in Court.

This was the Holy Grael lineage from the House of Joseph being introduced to each other ... so it was a momentous.

Sir Anthony Denny (1501–49) was great uncle to Walter Raleigh (1552/54–1618/46) although they never met.

Hereditary Grand Almoner & Lord High Almoner Royal Household

1536, 19 May, 2 a.m.: Hereditary Grand Almoner Henry Courtenay (28) and Lord High Almoner of the Royal Household Edward Foxe (30) carried one 5'3" 7-stone female body-double with head severed, two identical black damask large capes with hammerhead hood trimmed with white ermine, swedes, potato peelers, white handkerchiefs, straw, pigs-blood and a wooden sword into Queen Anne Boleyn's rooms in the White Tower. They stayed for 6 hours until 8 a.m.

It was a case of two young men, with titles, in roles well above their age, having a laugh, and swishing out the Queen of England. If caught, and 'executed', they would be swished in the same fashion, to live on "The Island", which was 'their England'.

'The Island' was now 94% of England, some 47,000 of 50,301 square miles as a noble commune to play on, where commoners were mostly not allowed, knew not to go, were charged with 'Trespass against the Vegetation', never returned, never went, or were thereafter employed for life on 'The Island'.

There was either a rift in the marriage, or Henry Courtenay was taking his wife Gertruden Blount's advice and faking the execution of Queen Anne Boleyn, which the Marquess of Exeter could do as Hereditary Grand Almoner ... without the usual restrictions of Henry Norris' 10-year service as Keeper of the Privy Purse, with his 17 May 1536 'execution' simulating 'death is in the air'. At just 54 years old, Norris may also have been extracted to 'The Island' – taking the money with him.

1538, early November–9 December: Henry Courtenay (30) 1st Marquess of Exeter KG, PC was placed in the Tower of London, then executed, likely for murmuring about:

i.   Not removing style & title Queen of England in her own right;

ii.   Not removing Anne's style & title Queen consort of England;

iii.   Removing the wrong style and title "Marquis of Penbroke" and retaining Marquis or Marquesse of Pembroke;

iv.   Faking Queen Anne Boleyn's execution in every way imaginable, and providing Queen Anne Boleyn with an organised escape route, with many places to live; then

v.   Wanting to join Queen Anne Boleyn and her court entourage on 'The Island'.

1538–40: Wife Gertrude, Marchioness of Exeter, and son Edward remained in the Tower of London ... then found favour attending Queen Mary I's court (R. 1553–58).

Henry Courtenay (28), Hereditary Grand Almoner wasn't alone in Queen Anne Boleyn's rooms from 2–8 a.m. There was also Edward Foxe (30), Lord High Almoner of the Royal Household, both referred to in the singular as "Sir, her almoner is continually with her, and had been since two o'clock after midnight" by the willing William Kingston (60), Constable of the Tower (1524–40) who worked under Sir Edmund Walsingham (56, *c*.1480–1550) Lieutenant of the Tower (1521–45) who had been a soldier with Henry VIII at Calais, and paid £100 per year (~£450,000 in 2024).

1521–45: Lieutenant of the Tower Sir Edmund Walsingham (*c*.1480–1550) initially began his career working for Queen Anne Boleyn's uncle Thomas Howard, Earl of Surrey, and was knighted on 13 September 1513, then resided in the house in the Tower and took personal charge of the executions of:

June 1535: John Fisher (aged 65);

July 1535: Sir Thomas More (57);

May 1536: Queen Anne Boleyn (28~35);*[1]

December 1538: Henry Courtenay, 1st Marquess of Exeter (40);*

January 1539: Henry Pole, 1st Baron Montague (46);* son of ...

May 1541: Margaret Pole, 8th Countess of Salisbury (65);*

February 1542: ex-Queen consort Catherine Howard (16~20);*

March 1542: Viscount Lisle (66~81);

May 1545: Duchess of Norfolk, Agnes née Tilney Howard (68); widowed 2nd wife of Thomas Howard, 2nd Duke of Norfolk KG PC (1443–21 May 1524) ...

---

[1]* with those under 50, generally going to "The Island".

After this, Sir Edmund Walsingham was elected to Parliament as a Knight of the Shire for Surrey in 1545. Walsingham was a Jesuit.

1539: Henry VIII granted Sir Edmund Walsingham 9 dissolved abbey houses in London.

1543: Walsingham bought manors 10 miles southeast of the Tower of London, 1½ miles east of the Chislehurst Caves, being Swanton Court, West Peckham and Yokes, now the square mile Scadbury Park where the manor is now foundation ruins.

1544: Walsingham was made vice-chamberlain to Henry VIII's 6th wife Katherine Parr.

On 19 May 1536 morning, Constable of the Tower, William Kingston (60) effectively wrote:

> 'So the almoners arrived to Queen Anne Boleyn's rooms at 2 a.m. to begin training for Operation Exit-her ... bringing with them 2 identical large black heavy damask capes with deep black hood with white ermine fur trim, and a decapitated body-double of Queen Anne Boleyn already wrapped inside the lower cape, which the two almoner could easily carry, as the real Queen Anne Boleyn was only 5'3" and weighed less than 7 stone, less than 100 pounds, less than 45 kg – the same weight as a sack of cement, which Courtenay (28) and Foxe (30) could easily carry between them, and remain unseen at 2 a.m. ... as everyone was in bed by 9 p.m.

On the day of Queen Anne Boleyn's Execution, Tuesday 19 May 1536, the:

i.   Keeper of the Privy Purse, Henry Norris (54) was absent, having been executed two days prior; and

ii.   Sir Anthony Denny (35) specialised in making himself absent and was not at his post; and

iii.   The three (3) Almoner were not responsible to anyone but themselves; and

iv.   These three Almoner had full access to the Privy Purse, no access to the Privy Purse, or could make whatever 'arrangements' they could afford, which were limitless; and

v.   The two rich Almoner could run the entire execution 'service' to their own liking, including any number of Extraordinary Yeomen as crisis actors; ensuring

vi.   Queen Anne Boleyn or lady-in-waiting was not identifiable;

vii.   All trial records, transcripts, statements, and records of evidence went missing;

viii. With the added confusion that Queen Anne Boleyn's execution site was in nine (9) different locations;

ix.   The Executioner was a non-English-speaker using a sword;

x.   The crowds' view was blocked by sun-strike & 450 tall broad crisis actors without uniforms, called Yeomen'; and

xi.   Queen Anne on a high & wide scaffold covered in thick straw;

xii.   With a dead-house headless body-double on hand.

Endnotes

1   1949: The Diary of Samuel Pepys, edited by Henry B. Wheatley, "Ben Jonson's Alchemist, act v. SC. 2", published by G. Bell &Sons.

2   www.tudorplace.com.ar/Bios/AnthonyDenny(Sir).htm.

Chapter Twelve
The Execution of Queen Anne Boleyn

THE. XXVIII. YERE OF KING HENRY VIII [1536~37][1]

"ON May day were a solempne lustes kept at Grenewyche, and sodainly from the lustes the kyng departed hauyng not aboue vi. persons with him, and came, in the euenyng frō Grenewyche in his place at Westminster."

1536, 1 May, Monday, May Day: Henry VIII at Greenwich Palace kept May Day chaste, and suddenly the King departed with 6 men, and arrived in the evening to his Westminster place ~6 miles including river and bridge.

"Of this sodain departyng many men mused, but moste chiefely the quene, who the next day was apprehended and brought frō Grenewyche to the Tower of London, where after she was arreigned of high treason, and condempned. Also at thesame tyme was likewyse apprehended, the lorde-Rocheforde brother to thesayd Quene, and Henry Norrys, Marke Smeton, Wyllyam a Bruton and sir Fraunces Weston all of the kynges priuy chamber.

"All these were likewise committed to the Tower and after arreigned and condempned of high treason."

1536, 2 May, Tuesday: Men mused over his sudden departure, but mostly the Queen. Queen Anne Boleyn was apprehended and brought from Greenwich Palace to the Tower of London, where she was arraigned for High Treason, and condemned at the same time, as was her brother, George Boleyn, Viscount Rochford (22) as was, from the King's Privy Chamber, Sir Henry Norris (54), Mark Smeaton (24), Sir William Brereton

191

(48) & Sir Francis Weston (25) who were accused of committing adultery with Queen Anne Boleyn, Treason and Plotting to kill the King, on Friday 12 May, and all executed 5 days later on 17 May 1536.

1536, 17 May, Wednesday: And all the, gentlemen were beheaded on the Skaffolde at the Tower hyll; 25 yards behind the Tower of London north wall (built afterwards).

1536, 19 May, Friday: "But the Quene was with a sworde beheaded within the Tower."

The location was never established by any historian, and at least nine (9) different locations were offered, with five (5) locations within the Tower of London.

"And these folowyng were the woordes that she spake the day of her death whiche was the xix. day of May, 1536."

The calmness of Queen Anne Boleyn's death speech belies the fact that she had no intention of dying that day, and had full expectation of her escape which she codified in her immaculate choice of words:

"Good Christen people, I am come hether to dye, for accordyng to the lawe and by the lawe I am iudged to dye, and therefore I wyll speake nothyng against it.

"I am come hether to accuse no man, nor to speake anythyn of that wherof I am accused and condempned to dye, but I pray God saue the king and send him long to reigne ouer you, for a gentler nor a more mercyfull prince was there neuer: and to me he was euer a good, a gentle, & soueraigne lorde.

"And if any persone will medle of my cause, I require them to iudge the best.

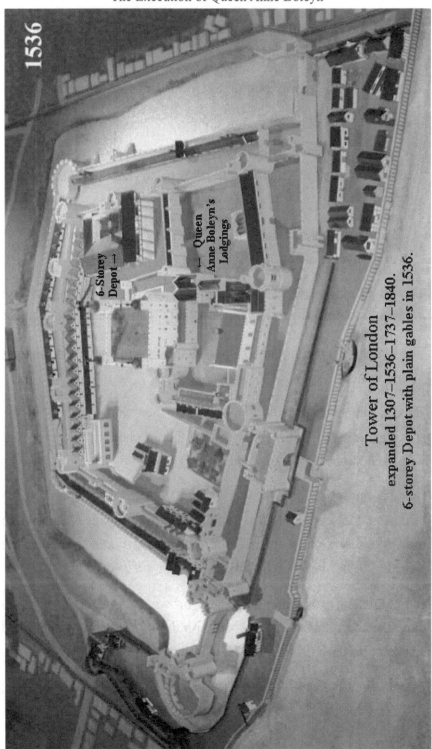

1536

6-Storey Depot →

← Queen Anne Boleyn's Lodgings

Tower of London
expanded 1307–1536–1737–1840.
6-storey Depot with plain gables in 1536.

"And thus I take my leue of the worlde and of you all, and I heartely desyre you all to pray for me.

"O lorde haue mercy on me, to God I cōmende my soule."

"And then she kneled doune saying:

'To Christ I commende my soule, Iesu receiue my soule", diuers tymes, till that her head was stryken of_ with the sworde.

"And [6 days later] on the Assencion day folowyng, the kyng ware whyte for mournyng."

This is an extremely elegant speech from someone about to lose their life. 99.9% piss their pants, crumble, and can only mumble.

The clarity of Queen Anne's speech shows she knew she was not going to die.

This is supported by the original text, then the rewriting of the speech as spoken, although few were there to hear it, and even less within earshot.

It does not say "her head was stryken off". "of_" has a double space as though the second "f" was removed, with the space remaining to draw attention to this. It reads "her head was stryken 'of_' with the sworde"... "her head was stryken of_ with the sworde".

In actual fact, it was her long dark-brown hair wrapped up in an oversized coif that was struck off with the sword, leaving 'her head stryken of_ her hair', not her head struck off.

Queen Anne Boleyn was not stripped of any of her styles or titles, and came to "dye" ... to change her colours. So it reads:

'Good Christen people, I have not come here to die, for according to the law and by the law I am judged to change my colours (dye), and therefore I will speak nothing against the law and I will speak nothing against being judged to dye, and not dying.

'I come here to accuse no man, nor address anything I am accused of, nor address that I am condemned to die, as we are all at some time to die. Instead, I pray God save the King and his long Reign over you, as this equates to my survival, for he is the most gentle and merciful prince, and has always been a good, gentle and sovereign lord, meaning Henry will provide whatever is required in the moment, and it is in this moment that the Holy Grael lineage is re-launched.

'I require any person who meddles in my cause, and assists in my escape, to be judged by their friends as the best at what they do. This applies to all you 450 un-uniformed Extraordinary and Ordinary Yeomen, hired here today as crisis actors.

'And thus I take my leave of you all, and your world, and I heartily desire you all follow your instructions as planned (pray for me).

'Do whatever is required in the moment (O lorde) and within one's power (mercy) on me, to God I commend my soul.'

'And then she knelt down saying:
  "To Christ I commend my soul, Jesus receive my soul"
  "To Christ I commend my soul, Jesus receive my soul"
  "To Christ I commend my soul, Jesus receive my soul"
  "To Christ I commend my soul, Jesus receive my soul"

'... until her coif of long hair, mistaken as her head, was struck of_ with the sword, and she slumped forward, and her 3 ladies-in-waiting threw a bloodied swede upon her, then the foot-thick straw was piled on top.'

The execution had been delayed twice. It was done at 8 a.m. (no daylight saving) where there was sun-strike, and there were few in attendance, variously and corruptly recorded as "a handful", and "nearly a thousand", omitting that there were 300 non-uniformed Extraordinary Yeomen, plus a further 150 non-uniformed Ordinary Yeomen who also wore no uniforms until 1550, all tall with broad shoulders to block any spectator views ... and there being 9 locations for the execution, only the 9th firmly established ... the text confirming no head was removed, but only that "her head stryken of_".

It was Queen Anne Boleyn's oversized coif stuffed with her long hair that was 'cut off her head' ... and no part of the execution was ever firmly established.

2 Plaques and 2 Sculptures at 6 & 7 were placed as confident distractions for the 4 assumed execution locations, with the 5th location at 9, reasoned by The Principal.

> Queen Anne Boleyn's Execution:[2] "At her trial, Queen Anne Boleyn (R. 28 May 1533–17 May 1536) ... retained the title 'Queen of England' ... Queen Anne Boleyn's execution in the Tower of London was delayed from Wednesday 17 May 1536 to an unspecified future date. They were waiting for a blazing sunny day & sun-strike over the 6-storey 88-foot high Armoury Depot, now Fusilier Museum, and north-east corner of the central White Tower." This would blind the audience.

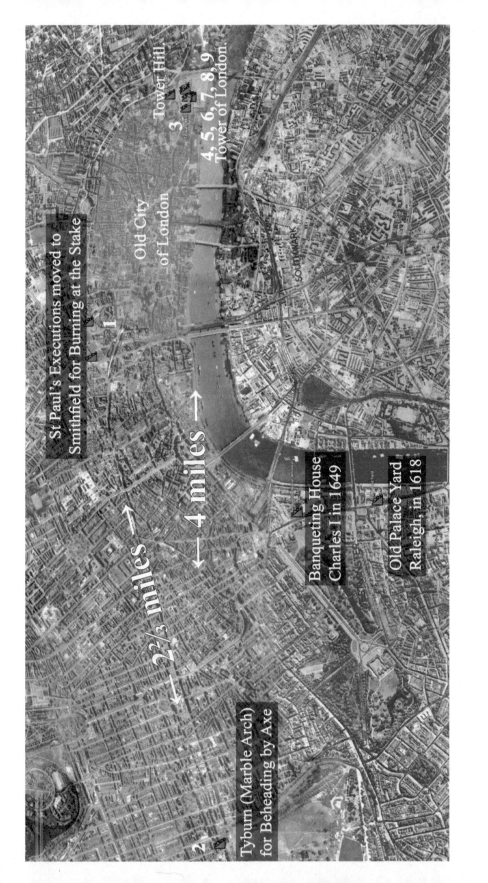

St Paul's Executions moved to
Smithfield for Burning at the Stake

Old City
of London

Tower Hill.

3

4, 5, 6, 7, 8, 9
Tower of London.

1

SOUTHWARK.

← 2⅔ miles →

←— 4 miles —→

Banqueting House
Charles I in 1649

Old Palace Yard
Raleigh, in 1618

Tyburn (Marble Arch)
for Beheading by Axe

2

With no notice, and a change of execution style from:

i.   'Burning at the stake' at Smithfield (1½ miles north-west of Tower of London) to 2⅔ miles further west; to

ii.   'Beheading by axe' at Tyburn (Marble Arch); and then 4 miles east to

iii.   'Beheading by sword' 25 yards behind the Tower of London north wall; then to

iv.   'Beheading by sword' inside the Tower of London at locations 5, 6, 7, 8 or 9;

v.   With further delay provided by bringing an expert swordsman from Saint-Omer in France, 25 miles inland from Calais, near Culleyn aka Bulleyn;

vi.   Having walked seven (7) miles, the method & location were changed; and

vii.   The day was uncertain, as was the time, so there were few if any Commoners on such a promising hot day; and there was

viii.   No crowd, except for the 450 crisis actors paid by the Countess of Salisbury.

450 of those who attended were tall men with broad shoulders, chosen for their ability to block the view, made up of the 150 Ordinary Yeomen & 300 Extraordinary Yeomen. Neither wore uniforms. Ordinary Yeomen began wearing uniforms 14 years later in 1550, when they wore velvet of any colour, or armour with a velvet coat trimmed with silver gilt.

So in 1536 & 1542, and up until 1550, there were 450 non-uniformed crisis actors blocking the public's view of the Royal executions of Queen Anne Boleyn.

Five years later, Queen consort Catherine Howard (R. 28 July 1540–23 Nov. 1541) was 16~21 years old when she was executed on Monday 13 February 1542, when there was no chance of sun-strike.

But with Anne, Friday 19 May 1536 was a blazing sunny day, enough to distract people away from their original intentions, and into ennui, laziness & depleting emetics, where 'the thing' is played out in so many ways, over so many days, with so much cognitive dissonance, people lose interest and fail to be aware and view the event instigated by the English Spymaster, whose goal was to obfuscate, and a century later publish an incorrect version of history ...

As clarified herein, Queen Anne Boleyn's execution was on Wednesday at Smithfield by burning at the stake, then moved to Marble Arch for Beheading by Axe, then 'delayed to some future day', then by Sword on Tower Hill, then inside the Guardhouse where no one would see, so no one bothered turning up, and then inside the Tower of London at six (6) different locations ...

1536, 19 May, Friday: Queen Anne Boleyn's execution was commuted from burning at the stake – to axe – to sword. This had location significance, and meant anyone who walked to Smithfield, then got dawn notice of change of execution style, and had to walk another 2⅔ miles to Tyburn, then another 4 miles to Tower Hill, then another ⅓ mile into the Tower of London ... walking at least 7 miles by 8 a.m. Even then, Queen Anne Boleyn's execution within the Tower of London had six (6) different locations.

Queen Anne Boleyn's 17–19 April 1536 'Execution' sites were at Smithfield (1), Tyburn (2), then Tower Hill (3), then six 'Execution' sites in the Tower of London (4, 5 ,6, 7, 8, 9), with 5 fake and 1 almost real.

Queen Anne Boleyn's 'execution' remains unconfirmed, ambiguous, and patently ambiguous. Patent Ambiguity falls against the Crown, bringing into question the execution? Was it real, staged, or survived with a dead-house body-double provided? If so, what portion of Queen Anne Boleyn's death didn't happen?

The only thing certain was her escape, as this is now celebrated as the 'Ceremony of the Keys' at 10 p.m. every night (almost).

Royalty then began wearing wigs to confirm Queen Anne Boleyn's escape. Even Charles I wore a wig to his 'execution' 113 years later in 1649. Aristocracy followed suit with powdered wigs.

"In the Tower of London, Queen Anne Boleyn's execution was either on the:

i.   North side of the White Tower at "5" as per the Lisle Letters, or at the

ii.   NOT FOR PUBLIC VIEWING 63 metres wsw at "6" at Tower Green; or

iii. Also at Tower Green, but another 30m ssw at "7" 'In PRIVATE'; or the same location

iv.   Inside the Yeoman Warders Guardhouse at "8", where the Execution of Nobles took place 'to avoid public jeering and insults', but really to swish bodies. Destroyed in 1684, rebuilt 1685, the Yeoman Warders Guardhouse was permanently removed around 1689. This served to unsettle any witness statements.

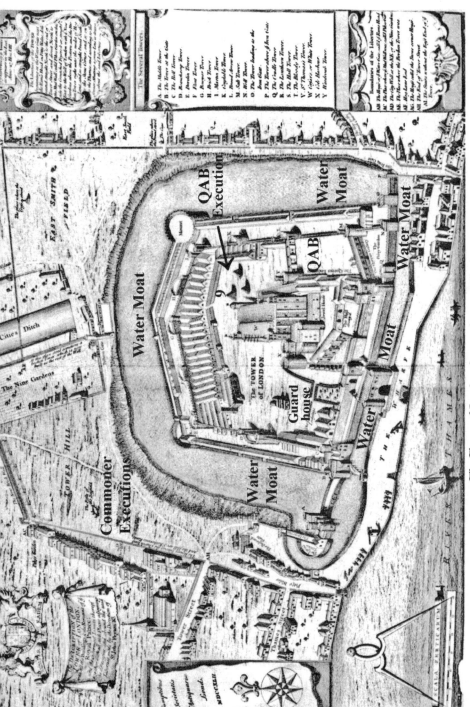

The Tower of London, from a plan made in 1597.

v.   Public executions of high-profile traitors & criminals were done 150 yards north on Tower Hill, which held only one execution every 3½ years.

vi.   In spectacular distraction, Anne's brother, George Boleyn was executed by axe at Tower Hill on Wednesday 17 May 1536, but then Anne's execution was changed from Burning ~ to Axe ~ to Sword ... the location changed from Smithfield ~ to Tyburn ~ to the Tower of London ... then delayed an indefinite period to the next sun-strike, which turned out to be just two days later ... a delay from Wednesday to Friday 19 May 1536 at 8 a.m."

"On the change of execution style, from burning, to axe, to sword, any crowd had to walk at least 7 miles to any one of the 9 different locations, and then miss the execution, as it always happened elsewhere, or "you just missed it, the event is over".[3]

"When four witnesses (there were none) disagree as to the location and number of people attending ("5" or "1,000") one or both are lying. Foreign Ambassadors were 'used' to lie about Executions, the information going east to Europe, when those condemned went west."[4]

The Statement of Claim in support of Joseph Gregory Hallett declares Queen Anne Boleyn's Royal Lineage, 31 December 2019, OTH / 19 / 54733, pages 26–30, continues:

vii.   Anne Boleyn wore a full-length black damask cape with an oversized hammerhead hood, trimmed in white ermine. Under this she wore a high stiff collar. She had tucked her long hair into her oversized coif, which covered her head, the top, back, sides and cheeks of her face, and her neck. No one could positively identify her. It could have been one of her ladies-in-waiting, and no one would have been the wiser.

viii. The 5'3" Anne Boleyn followed the 6' Sir William Kingston (59) KG. Anne's face was completely hidden from everyone, and she was flanked by her four ladies-in-waiting. No one could positively identify the lady under the cape was Anne Boleyn.

ix. At 8 a.m. "Anne's ladies knelt down at the back of the scaffold" to the East, with the sun rising behind them. This put the four ladies-in-waiting in silhouette and Anne Boleyn in the shade. This blocked all the views from the sunlit east. The only other viewing place was from the west looking east into the sun-strike.

x. To the east are the castellated walls of the Constable Tower and Fusiliers HQ, 88-foot high; but in 1536 there was the flat ridge of a simple gable-end N-S roof on a 6-storey-high depot armoury building, which was also 88-foot high.

xi. 'London, England, United Kingdom – Sunrise, Sunset, and Day-length' dates to 1600, when the earliest summer sunrise was at 3:40 a.m. on 2–12 June.

On 19 May 1536, the sun rose at 3:48 a.m. At 8:00 a.m. the sun was at 36° and 101° ESE, meaning the shadow came out 121-foot off the 88-foot high armoury roof ridge and thereafter the sun shone directly into the crowd. It was a perfect scenario for sun-strike; and also splaying off the central White Tower, especially its north-east tower.

xii.   Commoners entered through the Middle Byward Tower in the west, and were blinded by the sun-strike looking east at Queen Anne Boleyn's black back, all in shade.

xiii.   The goal was to have the Frenchman's sword raised into the sunlight, and swung into the shadow to lop off Anne Boleyn's oversized coif full of her very long hair, and to have everyone looking directly into the sun, so they could not see the sword when it did its final swing through the shade.

88-foot high - 8½ foot high scaffold - 2½ foot Anne on her knees = 77 foot high.

77 foot high at 36° or 77/0.7625 = 101 foot out to the centre of the 15' x 15' scaffold.

This places the centre of the scaffold 50 foot east of the centre of the White Tower.

If the scaffold was 15 foot square, one had to stand back 20 feet & be 6-foot tall to see anything. This is where the tall & broad 300 non-uniformed Extraordinary Yeomen crisis actors were instructed to stand and block the view, and were paid 4–6d to do so.

The remaining area was 270 feet East-West by 90 feet North-South looking directly into the sun on a very sunny day, with sun-strike over the tops of 300 non-uniformed Extraordinary Yeomen, and 150 Ordinary Yeomen.

This was copied 112 years later in Charles I's execution. Men with spears on horseback rode in front of the 44-foot high execution platform, and through the crowd, so no one could see that execution either.

Even if one did have a rare line of sight, when looking directly into the sun, over the shoulders of the tall and broad Yeomen, it was impossible to see what happened as the sword travelled from glinting sun-strike sunlight into the shade, lopping off a silhouetted object.

As Anne Boleyn knelt down, the line between her oversized coif stuffed with her long thick hair and her scalp, was the same line as the sun-strike and shadow. Anne Boleyn spoke fluent French, and as the Frenchman cast his glinting sword from the sunlight, past sun-strike, and into the shade, no one's eye could follow it.

Most of the views all round were blind, for one reason or another. They did not want anyone to see this execution, because it was the first of many to be faked under the madness of Henry VIII – mad since 24 January 1536 – and this was just 116 days later.

xiv.   The view from the east was blocked by Queen Anne Boleyn's four ladies-in-waiting.

xv.   Views from the west were the largest, but hindered by sun-strike, Queen Anne Boleyn's back, in silhouette, and blocked by 450 tall broad Yeomen.

xvi.   Due to the scaffold platform set center 37½ foot north of the White Tower, and 37½ foot south of the Commissioners building, and the scaffold 8½ foot high & 15 foot square, all views from the south & north were easily blocked by the tall broad Yeomen.

The 'execution' spot is marked by the stone corridor foundations looking like train tracks 2½ yards apart, central between the White Tower and the 1845 Waterloo Barracks.

xvii. The only views were from the north windows in the gable end building one floor up, occupied by the Commissioners who had already agreed and signed that Anne Boleyn was dead. When the sword was raised to begun its swing, they all turned away.

xviii. Under cover of sun-strike and 450 Yeomen, when Queen Anne Boleyn removed her heavy black damask hammerhead hood cape, finished in white ermine fur, to reveal her long hair tucked into her oversized coif, which still covered her head, top, back, sides, cheeks and neck, further hidden by her oversized stiff collar, not one of the "nearly 1,000 spectators" could identify her as Queen Anne Boleyn. They also did not know what she looked like as Henry VIII had destroyed all paintings of her.

xix. The time of the execution was not advertised to the public, but it began at 8:00 a.m.

xx. The Almoner(s) had trained Anne Boleyn and her ladies from 2 a.m. that morning.

At the first sound from her left, Anne was to be ready;

At the second sound from the right, Anne was to tilt her body forward, then shoulders, then neck so that the oversized coif on the back of her head, stuffed with her long thick dark hair, actually appeared to be an upright head.

At the third sound from the left, the French swordsman was to begin his side-swipe movement, with the aim to remove Anne Boleyn's oversized Coif and hair.

Queen Anne Boleyn had very long hair, which princesses and queens kept as excellent cover to play out royal executions and survive them, as did Charles I. "I gave my only hair/ heir" ... "I gave my only sun/ son".

xxi. Queen Anne Boleyn and her ladies-in-waiting played each role, 2–8 a.m. now aware of what must be done.

Queen Anne Boleyn may have played herself, or may have been replaced by one of her ladies-in-waiting, and thrown her own head into the ring ... in the form of a swede.

Ever since "Swede" has been code for 'one's head'.

xxii. The Commissioners and the Yeomen who were paid, and paid to see, agreed to see what they had agreed to see, and described her clothing in detail, but not the location, nor the specific time. Four different locations were given, the closest to the true location being 50 foot west in front of the middle of the White Tower ... the farthest being 333 foot south-west in the Yeoman Warders Guardhouse on Tower Green.

"xxiii.Most of the spectators couldn't write and had no access to media, which was then a tablet. Any spectators who could write and were allowed to write, were embedded, and only reported what they were paid to see, yet there were no spectator witness statements.

Only the Commissioners were paid to see, and none of these reported, except perhaps for their collective one voice signatures on a pre-written document ... and for this, they had just been paid the biggest bribes in history.

xxiv. The French Headsman hid his sword between the black cloth and foot-thick straw, so no one got to inspect the sword, before or after the strike. Was it sharp steel or blunt, sharpened wood, painted wood, already bloodied, bloodied after, or unbloodied?

xxv. After the sword movement, one lady-in-waiting covered 'the head' or swede with a white cloth that had been pre-dipped in pig's blood. Another threw straw over it, and another threw straw over where the exposed cut should have been.

xxvi. The French Headsman took two days to arrive, which allowed for the sun to come out. He only spoke French, so he & Anne could talk. He never held up Queen Anne Boleyn's head, separated from her body ~ because the head was never separated from the body ... and he never yelled "So perish all the King's enemies!" ~ because they weren't enemies, confirmed by Queen Anne

'Queen Anne Boleyn' was 'buried' in St Peter ad Vincula, but with no head. All 5 Aristocratic heads are missing.

Boleyn's speech and Anne Boleyn retaining her titles as Queen of England and Marquesse of Pembroke.

xxvii. The Crowd dispersed with the help of the 300 Extraordinary Yeomen, being fancy names for Crisis Actors without uniform, plus 150 Ordinary Yeomen also without uniforms, and any number of others in the verbally confusing group of Tower of London warders, Yeomen Warders, Yeomen of the Guard (Royal Bodyguards), Yeomen Warders of Her Majesty's Royal Palace and Fortress the Tower of London, Members of the Sovereign's Body Guard of the Yeoman Guard Extraordinary or Her Majesty's Royal Palace and Fortress the Tower of London' (popularly misnamed "Beefeaters") some of which existed at the time, but almost all without uniforms.

Tower staff made up the majority of the "nearly 1,000 spectators", and their non-existent uniforms were then backdated into history.

The Tower of London is all theatre.

xxviii. The 8½ foot high by 15 foot square scaffold was now sacred ground.

The ladies-in-waiting then put on a great show of being extremely upset, but gracious and dignified. After the smaller common crowd left, Tower Warders and Yeomen officiated the four ladies-in-waiting back to Queen Anne Boleyn's Coronation suite, now her Execution suite, where they emptied an arrow box of its arrows to find Queen Anne Boleyn's dead-house body-double with severed head, in identical black damask coat already placed inside, as per their 2–8 a.m. role-play that same morning.

Tower Warders and Yeomen then escorted three ladies-in-waiting back while they comforted another lady-in-waiting's dress, as though it was an upset lady-in-waiting. i.e. They 'carried' her.

Queen Anne Boleyn lay in the straw playing dead and trying not to sneeze. Once surrounded, she wriggled roughly into the lady-in-waiting's dress, as the ladies-in-waiting held up the large black damask coat, stalled, then slowly placed it over the arrow box ... and the now four ladies-in-waiting carried the arrow box with Queen Anne Boleyn's dead-house body-double 80 yards west to the Chapel of St Peter ad Vincula where they dug a 2-foot deep hole and threw the body in an unmarked grave (without head), carrying the second black damask coat back with them.

xxix. The four of them returned to Queen Anne Boleyn's Coronation~Execution suite, and the now five ladies-in-waiting readied themselves, packed their things, confirmed the wind and weather, and waited for the sun to set at 8:03 p.m. followed by Astronomical Twilight that lasted through the night from 13 May–10 July 1536, providing 58 nights to navigate the Thames and Isis without any need for moonlight.

xxx. Yesterday was a new moon, making their boats harder to see, but they could make out the river edge. They waited an extra 2 hours when almost everyone in London was asleep, then exited through Traitors' Gate at 9:54 p.m., now celebrated as the Ceremony of the Keys ... and the Two Keys at the feet of Jesus ... Keys to the Kingdom.

xxxi. The five of them were escorted by enough of the 300 Extraordinary Yeomen so as to be totally hidden as they were taken through the Inner Ward, under the Bloody Tower, to Water Lane where boats waited out of public view, then they rowed through Traitors' Gate onto the River Thames.

Many of the 300 Extraordinary Yeomen Crisis Actors left in all directions at 10 a.m. others at 10 p.m. so if anyone asked: "Everyone disembarked at 10 in all directions".

xxxii. Queen Anne Boleyn was still intact, with her four ladies-in-waiting. They sailed up the Thames 30 miles to Windsor Castle and Eton, then the Extraordinary Yeomen headed back south, all in their non-uniforms, making them impossible to trace.

xxxiii. Queen Anne Boleyn and her 4 ladies-in-waiting were then horse-drawn at 4 mph up the Isis another 14 miles.

At the end of their 15-hour journey they were greeted by the woman who had organised it all – Margaret, Countess of Salisbury – for ladies tea at Bisham Abbey.

It was 1 p.m. on 20 May 1536, a Saturday beginning summer, and Queen Anne Boleyn repeated her Coronation motto:

"The most happy. We all at one."[5]

1536, 25 May, Thursday, Ascension Day: 6 days later, Henry VIII wore white, yet white is not the colour of mourning, it is the colour worn for a new life, and Christenings.

Henry VIII considered Queen Anne Boleyn had been Christened with a new life, as Queen of England in her own right, with her own lineage, and as Marquesse of Pembroke.

The new Sovereign line of England had been born.

"Knights Templar were rememberers and practical dreamers, storing secrets in plain sight to their advantage, while not cutting out those who were worthy of co-realising such a dream."[6]

Ascension Day was 39 days after Easter Sunday 16 April 1536. Knights Templar want their blessing of Sovereignty recognisable. 39 is recognisable code for 3 x 13, or 3 x (12+1). The Knights Templar were blessing the line of Queen Anne Boleyn as:

i.   Removing Catholicism which is no Christianity;

ii.   Providing a major Correction to Christianity,

iii.   Taking England from Catholic rule back to Christian rule;

iv.   Taking England out of Catholic ownership and into English ownership, creating a very wealthy English aristocracy;

v.   The Holy Grael lineage was re-established in England;

vi.   Anne Boleyn was now Queen of England in her own right;

vii.   Anne Boleyn was now Marquesse of Pembroke;

viii.   Marquess of Pembroke applies to any descendant male who fulfills prophecy, even if illegitimate;

ix.   Marquesse of Pembroke is the Lord of Lords, which overlaps with King David as Lord of Lords, and thus marks the King of the Kingdom of England, and the King of the Kingdom of Scotland;

x.   Anne Boleyn was now the 'Silent Empress';

xi.   Now with her own life and line as the Queen of England, Marquesse of Pembroke, Christian re-founder of the Holy Grael lineage, and Silent Empress of England Europe;

xii.   To be passed down a legitimate or illegitimate line, fulfilling the prophecy;

xiii.   To whom ever fulfills the prophecy the most ... like the Bible, Rosicrucian, and Lord of the Rings prophecies for Christ.

1536, 20 May: The next day, King Henry VIII (45) was betrothed to Jane Seymour (28).

1536, 30 May, Tuesday: 11 days after Queen Anne Boleyn's 'execution', Henry VIII married Jane Seymour rendering her Queen consort for 17 months to 24 October 1537.

1536, 4 June, Whitsunday: Jane Seymour was openly shown as Queen consort of England.

1536, 8 June, Thursday: "Henry VIII held his High Court of Parliament which declared his first two marriages, to the lady Katheryne, and with the lady Anne Bulleyn were both adjudged unlawful, as more at large appears in the Act in the Book of Statutes."[7]

But they spelt Catherine of Aragon or Catalina de Aragón as "lady Katheryne"; and spelt "Anne Boleyn" as "Bulleyn", as though Henry VIII was no longer married to that Bulleyn chapel 3 miles south of Caleys (Calais) in France.

It didn't matter too much about Catherine of Aragon as she had died on 7 January 1536.

It apparently didn't matter too much about "Anne Boleyn as she had been 'executed' on 19 May 1536, but since she hadn't died from her 'haircut', but had only dyed & changed her colours, then the "marriage adjudged unlawful" only served to annul one of the marriages, on 16 November 1532 or 25 January 1533, and didn't annul Anne Boleyn's status Marquesse of Pembroke granted on Sunday 1 September 1532, and did not annul her status as Queen of England in her own right, with coronation on Sunday 1 June 1533.

From her time in the courts of the Netherlands, Belgium, and the French courts 1513–22, and her relationship with Henry VIII from 1525, changing the religion of England from Roman Catholic to Protestant 1525–36–47, elevation to Marquesse of Pembroke in 1532, Anne Boleyn's marriages to Henry VIII in 1532 & 1533, her individual coronation as Queen of England in 1533, the annulment or divorce from a misspelt surname & misspelt title in 1536, and faked 'execution' of her mispelt colour of law style in 1536, Queen Anne Boleyn retained all her titles, Marquesse and Queen, for all her posthumous breeding, legitimate or illegitimate, as long as the prophecy was fulfilled to select the one.

All of this was pre-planned to fulfil the Prophecy of Christ, which Anne Boleyn had been directly named in since her great x 11 grandmother Eleanor of Aquitaine, Queen consort of France (R. 1137–52) & Queen consort of England (R. 1154–89) patronised Chrétien de Troyes to write the Holy Grael legends, naming The Principal by prophecy & in anagram.

This was designed to avoid the Roman Catholic 'Society of Jesus' ~ Jesuit progrom to:

i.   Destroy the intent of all Prophecy,

ii.   Stop all Prophecy being fulfilled;

iii.   Deny Prophecy when it is fulfilled;

iv.   Deny the Prophet the fulfilment of the Prophecy;

v.   Blacklist or kill all those Prophesied;

vi.   Claim all the land of the world;

vii.   Claim all the sovereignty; and

viii.   Coadjutor the Crown of England; and

ix.   Usurp the Crown of England as the Crown of Britain; and

x.   Take total ownership of the Sovereignty of England; and

xi.   Take total ownership of the World and all its Sovereignty via no values.

The remedy was to supersede the 'Merovingian Conspiracy' or 'Red Movement' allowing the Sangrëal to emerge from outside the Catholic Church.

To the Jesuits, legitimacy didn't matter, as long as they could convince themselves via a piece of paper. This paper was often issued 400 years later, and backdated.

The Jesuits backdated many documents, so often, they legalised it. Backdating Instruments is an obvious crime, but the Jesuits legalised it when it is for their benefit. For centuries, Jesuits have used backdated Instruments to convince others that their fiction was your fact. This proliferated 1050~1801 A.D. & hasn't really stopped.

Leading up to Queen Anne Boleyn's 'execution', actually the divorce from a chapel, and execution of a misspelt style, or misspelt title ...

"Henry VIII's first wife, Catherine of Aragon died of cancer of the heart on 7 January 1536. Between her death, funeral and burial in Peterborough Abbey on 29 January 1536, five days prior on 24 January 1536, the widower Henry VIII was knocked off his horse in a jousting tournament and rendered unconscious for two hours. This was his only sorrow."[8]

"St Peter ad Vincula ... Records show the Tudor queens Anne Boleyn and Catherine Howard, as well as Lady Jane Grey, Jane Boleyn, and George Boleyn were 5 of the 7 buried in the Chancel"[9] ...

but there are no heads of any of the aristocrats, as all their beheadings were faked in public, or faked in private ... so definitely faked.

The Official execution witnesses were:

Charles Brandon, 1st Duke of Suffolk (51), Henry VIII's brother-in-law;

Thomas Cromwell (50) Henry VIII's first minister';

Lord Mayor of London, Sir Ralph Warren (49);

Henry Fitzroy, Henry VIII's son (16);

Aldermen;

Sheriffs;

most of the King's Council; and

Reps of the Craft Guild, which burned down in the pre-planned Great Fire of London in 1666.[10]

The same people who attended Queen Anne Boleyn's coronation, wedding feast, marriage, and the baptism by fire of her daughter Elizabeth, were the Commissioners at her Trial, and witnesses to Queen Anne Boleyn's 'Execution' ... which was thoroughly faked ... as fake as a backdated Jesuit document.

Published 'historians' are really propagandists for the Jesuit cause. Embedded historians gloss over anything useful, and focus on costumes, jewellery & Jesuit gossip, when most of the costumes didn't exist, and all the Crowns were stolen in 1216, 1450, and destroyed in 1657, and stolen again in 1671 and partly destroyed.

They Crown Jewels were remade from memory, as imitations, beginning with Charles II's papier-mâché crown worn at his coronation on 23 April 1661, which he then tried to hock off to a porn Jeweller in the Netherlands.

> Henry VIII's 'legacy' was to Protect the true royal lineage of the surviving Queen Anne Boleyn, and her Holy Grael lineage to Sir Walter Raleigh, and then to The Principal Joseph Gregory Hallett.

Embedded historians read from backdated Jesuit records. These have been falsified many times over:

i.   The Lisle Papers were stolen to order and tampered with to remove King Henry VIII's real 'legacy'; and to

ii.   Make it appear the British Flat Lie Royal family were real;

iii.   Whereas they are not English Royals, and are not English;

iv.   They are coadjutored British crypto-Catholics, and knock off royals;

v.   The Lisle Papers were altered again from the 1930s–60s to protect the inferiority complex of the incumbent Flat Lie British Royal family of George V, Edward VIII, George VI and Elizabeth II; where

a. George V was the son of Tsar Alexander III of Russia;

b. George V's elder brother Prince Eddie was still alive in 1910 & 1936;

c. George V's son Edward VIII recognised this, so abdicated using marriage to a double divorcee as cover;

d. George VI was an alcoholic retard, and not the siring natural father of Elizabeth;

e. Queen Elizabeth II was the daughter of Winston Churchill;

f. Winston Churchill was the son of Edward VII, who was the son of Lionel Nathan Rothschild, and this led to WWII.

vi. The Lisle Letters were rewritten as 'The contemporary Lisle Letters' by a compromised swinging lesbian couchon;

vii. This was followed up without question, by another couchon, the Brit. Lit. knock-shop royal em-bedded historian social climber, Marie Louise Bruce ... who took her pseudonym from 'Mary Louisa Bruce, Countess of Elgin and Kincardine (1819–98) a British writer and Vicereine of India, 1862–63'.

The Privacy Act then ensured that these Falsified Documents became 'the new history', and there would never be Discovery of True Documents, as they were altered by Groom of the Stool Sir Anthony Denny (1501–49), then transcribed by the lesbian Muriel St. Clare Byrne (1895–1983) from 1930s–60s, then published in 1981 as "the contemporary Lisle Letters"; to be reinforced by couchon social climbers with wannabe pseudonyms.

Muriel St. Clare Byrne was a lesbian swinger. Lesbians leave feminist marks on history that are particularly obvious, rendering a requirement to see the original Lisle Letters.

'The contemporary Lisle Letters' were heavily "edited".

To the Oxford University History Department, British Library, British History Online & swinging lesbians, "Edit" means to:

i.   Embellish;

ii.   Not decipher archaic words;

iii.   Retain confusion without informed clarity;

iv.   Leave any Jesuit confusion and hagiography intact;

v.   Avoid meaning;

vi.   Avoid symbolism;

vii.   Avoid interpreting meaning and symbolism;

viii.   Leave everything in a meaningless state;

ix.   Promote a secondary source over the original, as in 'The contemporary Lisle Letters';

x.   Avoid background & foreground checks into the characters; and even avoid clearly naming the characters, like the names of the 1, 2 or 3 Almoners available to attend Queen Anne Boleyn just prior to her 'execution' by 'be-heading' ... to 'The Island'.

It appears the British Museum ~ British Library ~ British History Online, Oxford & Cambridge version of "edit" is to interpret all documentation according to the long-held Jesuit tradition of coadjuting English history into a Roman Catholic perspective, and anything done for the English Crown before 1603 was to be obfuscated ... by adding the Jesuit tools of confusion, circumlocution, hagiography, patent ambiguity, depleting emetics, and backdating, while continually publishing embedded Catholic historians and the Catholic Jesuit takeover of Oxford University Press and Cambridge University Press, and their History Departments, who manage to regularly find archaic histories of a Catholic perspective, written by Jesuit monks, made contemporary by 1960s swinging lesbians for the fraud of tomorrow ... right up to an including the European Union ... which is exactly what has happened, with exactly the same intentions ~ the theft of all land ~ the theft of all sovereignty ~ the theft of all crowns ~ and the creation of all wars.

Other contenders for re-inventing the 1536 account of Queen Anne Boleyn's execution were ...

a. Edward Foxe, who died in 1537 aged 42;

b. Hereditary Grand Almoner, Henry Courtenay, 1st Marquess of Exeter who was retired the next year, then beheaded by sword in 1538 – a 30-year-old on The Island, which had just increased from 39,000 square miles to 47,000 square miles.

c. Thomas Cromwell was beheaded in 1540. Henry VIII married Catherine Howard the same day as a distraction.

One, two or three of these received the same saving grace they had meted out and were 'executed', or killed off onto 'The Island' – the Noble Commune that was now 94% of England.

The reward for saving Queen Anne Boleyn included massive land grants, or to become part of her Court company, or both.

Queen Anne Boleyn survived with her head intact, now with short hair, and no one able to see a painting of her from 1536 as Henry VIII was good enough to destroy them all.

As a 28~35-year-old, Queen Anne Boleyn was able to breed again, reigniting the Holy Grael lineage.

Queen Anne Boleyn's daughter *Mary y'Noble* gave birth to Walter Raleigh Christ, and Raleigh's grandson sired the Prince of Pirates Samuel Bellamy (1689–1717) all within 21 miles of Raleigh's home, in an area of outstanding natural beauty.

Raleigh & Bellamy were both pirates, and they were the best pirates in the world. Even new wife-to-be, Maria 'Goody' Hallett in Cape Cod, was from the Dorset border.

Queen Anne Boleyn, Sir Walter Raleigh Christ, the Prince of Pirates Samuel Bellamy and Maria 'Goody' Hallett are all ancestors of Joseph Gregory Hallett, who holds the title Christ above all others with the title Christ,[1] for joining kingdoms, and, as predicted by Raleigh, representing the End Times–New Age, with "Gregory Hallett" an anagram of 'Holy Grael reg tt', and "Joseph" being 'the highest name'.

---

[1] King David would be an exception.

Joseph Gregory Hallett also holds the Royal Marks to confirm all of this, including a letter from Queen Victoria, Royal blood, the Rosicrucian Cosmography plus Silver Key, and was the first to publish images of the Holy Grael, on the same day as the End Times–New Age changeover, in the same cave Sir Walter Raleigh discovered, the same day both gained the title Christ, by capturing the Book of Prophecies and deciphering it, which led Queen Anne Boleyn's grandson Sir Walter Raleigh took to the cave of origin – the source cave, where a Portuguese woman brought both of us a cup of tea, 418 years apart.

All of this has been affirmed, confirmed, ratified & sanctified by His Holiness, Pope Francis, The Archbishop of Canterbury, Justin Wellby, Her Majesty The Queen ~ Queen Elizabeth II ~ Elizabeth Alexandra Mary Mountbatten ~ Elizabeth Alexandra Mary Battenberg ~ Elizabeth Alexandra Mary Windsor; and by Prince Philip, Duke of Edinburgh ~ Philip Mountbatten, KG, who then died on 9 April 2021; Princess Anne; Prince Andrew, Duke of York, who was then shunned, tarred & feathered with all his titles ambiguously removed; Prince Edward, Earl of Wessex; Princess Beatrice of York; Princess Eugenie of York; Prince Charles, Prince of Wales ~ Duke of Cornwall who was replaced with a body-double; Camilla, Duchess of Cornwall ~ Duchess of Rothesay, GCVO who was replaced with a body-double, then treated for alcoholism in the Soukya Indian International Holistic Health Center in India from 8 November 2022[11]; Prince William, Duke of Cambridge, KG; Catherine, Duchess of Cambridge, GCVO; Prince Henry, Duke of Sussex, KCVO ADC who had all his military titles ambiguously removed; Meghan, Duchess of Sussex who had all her titles ambiguously removed, Prince Edward, Earl of Wessex; Sophie,

Countess of Wessex, GCVO; Prince Richard, Duke of Gloucester, KG; Prince Edward, Duke of Kent, KG who ensured Freemasons enacted the Bible to the letter, with only a few minor exceptions; Katharine, Duchess of Kent; Prime Minister of the United Kingdom, Alexander Boris de Pfeffel Johnson who responded by putting a full-stop on the British Empire; President of the United States Donald John Trump who responded many times in support through the media; President of Russia Vladimir Putin who made revolution confirmations through the media ... and their Private Secretaries ... after receipt of three (3) sets of The Documents in January, March and April 2020, responded to by all parties via Estoppel by mail, Estoppel in the media, and Estoppel by their controlled-opposition alternative social media.

Prince Andrew and Prince Harry were stripped of all their titles because they are the closest in age to The Principal ...

Prince Andrew, was born in 1960, and Prince Harry was born on The Principal's 23rd birthday. As of 13 January 2022, Andrew can no longer use the style of His Royal Highness in a public capacity.[12]

This means Andrew has been stripped of his titles.

Prince Harry was stripped of his senior royal status in 2020, his military titles in 2021, and Queen's Counsellors of State in 2022 ... but in the fog of Queen Elizabeth II's death's 20 March 2021–8 September 2022, their loss of titles was rendered as ambiguous as their royalty.

Endnotes

1   1548 & 1809: Edward Hall's Chronicle, THE. XXIIII. YERE OF KYNG HENRY THE. VIII., p. 795.

2   2019, 31 December: Statement of Claim in support of Joseph Gregory Hallett declares Queen Anne Boleyn's Royal Lineage, OTH / 19 / 54733, pp. 1–2, with days of the week corrected to the Julian Calendar.

     2020, 5 March: Confirmation of Joseph Gregory Hallett's Declaration of Queen Anne Boleyn's Royal Lineage, OTH / 20 / 64528;

     2020, 31 March: Certified Declaration of Queen Anne Boleyn's Royal Lineage in Joseph Gregory Hallett, OTH / 20 / 70901;

     2020, 31 March: Certified Declaration of Queen Anne Boleyn's Royal Lineage in Joseph Gregory Hallett, , SRA3, OTH / 20 / 70907, paraphrased in places.

3   2019, 31 December: Addendum One in support of Joseph Gregory Hallett declares Queen Anne Boleyn's Royal Lineage, OTH / 19 / 54733, p. 2.

4   2019, 31 December: Statement of Claim in support of Joseph Gregory Hallett declares Queen Anne Boleyn's Royal Lineage, OTH / 19 / 54733, p. 9.

5   2019, 31 December: Statement of Claim in support of Joseph Gregory Hallett declares Queen Anne Boleyn's Royal Lineage, OTH / 19 / 54733, pp. 28–30.

6   2014, August: Joseph Gregory Hallett and Francisco Manoel, 'The Hidden King of England – Arma Christi – Unveiling the Rose', p. 385.

7   1548 & 1809: Edward Hall's Chronicle, p. 819.

8   2019, 31 Dec.: Statement of Claim in support of Joseph Gregory Hallett declares Queen Anne Boleyn's Royal Lineage, p. 67.

9   Ibid, p. 31.

10   1972, 1973, 1975: Marie Louise Bruce, 'Anne Boleyn', HarperCollins, p. 333.

11   2022, 8 November: 'King Charles III forced Camilla into rehab to "sober up" ahead of coronation', International Business Times, Tanya Diente.

12   2022, 13 January: BBC News.

Chapter Thirteen
Faking the Execution of Queen Anne Boleyn

To fake the execution of Queen Anne Boleyn, every aspect was taken into account ...

1. Anne Boleyn's Coronation lodgings were now her execution lodgings, so she knew them well, and was familiar with their hiding places.

2. Anne Boleyn's Execution lodgings were adjacent to the west and south sides of the White Tower, so no one standing in front of the Execution Platform could see her descend the stairs on the east side of the White Tower and identify her.

3. There is in fact, no evidence it was Anne Boleyn walking down the stairs to the execution platform, or on the execution platform. For ease of English, "Anne Boleyn" is used, but it could have been any one of her four (4) ladies-in-waiting.

4. Anne Boleyn's Coronation lodgings and execution lodgings were removed in the 1790s, but a change in the paving marks the descending corridor, which marks the line of the Execution Platform.

5. Anne Boleyn wore a thick black damask coat that covered her body so completely, it could have been anyone's body beneath.

6. This thick black damask coat had a deep hammerhead hood that projected 6 inches in front of her face, and allowed her thick hair to be stacked in a coif, and hidden inside the rear of the hood.

7. The hammerhead hood of this thick black damask coat was finished in white ermine such that no one could see past the white fur another 6 inches through black & shade to the eyes to see if they were Queen Anne Boleyn's tearful eyes, or even Anne Boleyn.

8. Queen Anne Boleyn emerged out of her execution lodgings, down the stairs on the north side of the White Tower, along the paved way to the execution platform, then up the west side steps to 8½-feet high.

9. It was a hot day on 19 May, as though it was going to be a long hot summer, and there was sun-strike.

10. All of the commoners were viewing from the west and looking directly east into the sun-strike over the 88-foot high Armoury. The light was also splaying off the north-east corner of the central White Tower.

11. No one could see clearly. Everyone looking east facing the Execution Platform was squinting with a forearm in front of their eyes.

12. Anne Boleyn walked a total of 88 yards to the Execution Platform, then up the steps to 8½-foot high where the French executioner waited.

13. The French executioner pulled his sword from under the straw.

14. "xx. The Almoner(s) had trained Anne Boleyn and her ladies from 2 a.m. that morning. At the first sound from her left, Anne was to be ready;
"at the second sound from the right, Anne was to tilt her body forward, then shoulders, then neck so that the

oversized coif on the back of her head, stuffed with her long thick dark hair, actually appeared to be an upright head.

"At the third sound from the left, the French swordsman was to begin his side-swipe movement, with the aim to remove Anne Boleyn's oversized coif and hair.

"Queen Anne Boleyn had very long hair, which princesses and queens kept as excellent cover to play out royal executions ... and survive them ...

"'I gave my only hair/heir' ~ 'I gave my only son/sun'."[1]

15. The Frenchman lifted his sword up into the sunlight, which was incredibly dramatic "... ooh ... arrrggh ..." and as he swung the sword, it entered the shade, and no one could see it "... oh oh oh ...".

16. Anne Boleyn had knelt down with her large coif stuffed with her long hair acting as the back of her head, which the French executioner cut off in the shade with his sword, while the audience watched in silhouette.

17. The ladies-in-waiting were kneeling in front of Anne Boleyn, blocking any view from the east, and even from the north, where the official witnesses were doing their best not to see anything. These were mostly Anne Boleyn's friends, who had benefited enormously from her removal of all things Papal & Roman Catholic out of England.

18. From 2 a.m. one lady-in-waiting had been busy with a potato peeler carving a face out of a swede, and putting pigs blood around the neck.

19. She then carried the carved bloodied swede under her cape and threw it in;

Another lady-in-waiting tossed the foot thick straw over the top of it;

Another lady-in-waiting placed a white handkerchief dipped in pigs blood where the bleeding neck should be;

and another tossed foot thick straw to cover Anne Boleyn;

Queen Anne Boleyn then lay still on what was now very sacred ground.

20. Anne Boleyn's oversized coif, stacked with her long dark-brown hair to look like a head, had been cut off. It was a hair cut.

21. The result was that Anne Boleyn had survived, and now needed to escape.

22. Commoner prisoners in the Tower of London were executed in public outside the Tower of London, 175 metres NNW, on Tower Hill, or 4 miles west at Tyburn, now Marble Arch.

23. All Nobility were 'executed' inside Tower of London walls, on Tower Green, inside the Yeomen Warders Guardhouse, where the 'execution' was totally "PRIVATE", with absolutely "NO PUBLIC" watching ... always ... with "NO EXCEPTION".

24. Beheading in the privacy of the Tower Green was considered a privilege of rank; the nominal dead spared insults from jeering crowds, or viewing their escape.

25. All those with rank were executed inside the Yeomen Warders Guardhouse (8) except for Queen Anne Boleyn, Marquesse of Pembroke, for which they wanted a very public execution.

26. They had done exactly the same thing for Jesus, and it made him enormously famous, and king wherever he went ... King

of Regni ~ Kent ~ Kingdom Come, Mayor of London, with Christ automatically the King of England.

27. "Tower Green (Yeomen Warders Guardhouse) is a space within the Tower of London where two English Queens consort and several other British nobles were executed by beheading. It was considered more dignified for nobility to be executed away from spectators, and Queen Anne Boleyn, Queen Catherine Howard, and 'Queen' Lady Jane Grey were among the nobility beheaded in Tower Green, in the Tower of London."[2]

28. There is dispute over Private Noble Executions inside the Tower of London — where they took place, and now whether they took place at all.

     This has resulted in the noble execution Scaffold or Building having memorials in four (4) different locations, with excuses for each ... and all of them wrong.

29. Queen Victoria tried to solve the problem in the mid-1800s, but failed to comprehend the depth and layers of the lies, fabrication & fraud she was confronted with:

     "5": Sources describe Queen Anne Boleyn's execution as between the White Tower and the 1845 Waterloo Barracks on the current parade ground (see overleaf).

     "6": Queen Victoria asked a Yeoman Warder for the exact 'site' of the Noble Executions, and he pointed out a location. Queen Victoria then laid some granite paving there ;

     "7": On another site, there is a modern 3-metre round glass sculpture on paving next to Tower Green marking 'the building' where the private executions of Nobility took place;

"8". In the middle of Tower Green there is another small granite-paved square plot marking the 'scaffold' on which the private executions of Nobility took place.

30. 1800s: Shallow excavations revealed foundations of a building on Tower Green. Historic Tower of London plans confirmed this was used as a Yeomen Warders Guardhouse with the private execution of Nobles within the same small structure. The Tower Green Yeoman Warders Guardhouse was demolished in 1684, rebuilt in 1685, then demolished ~ 1689 to deter any further witness statements. "8" again.

31. Royal confessions of Royal frauds are marked with absent buildings.

32. "The following nobles are 'known' to have been 'executed' on the Tower Green":

1483, 13 June: William Hastings, 1st Baron Hastings was murdered without notice by axe over a log, by Richard, Duke of Gloucester (28). 13 days later he made himself Richard III of England (R. 26 June 1483–22 August 1485) and 10 months later, his eldest son, Edward, Prince of Wales (17~20) died suddenly of unknown causes on 9 April 1484, leaving no legitimate heirs. Richard III only ruled 26 months, and was succeeded by Henry VII & Henry VIII.

1536, 19 May: Henry VIII's 2nd wife Queen Anne Boleyn escaped.

1541, 27 May: Margaret, Countess of Salisbury was the "last of the Plantagenet dynasty?" and escaped.

1542, 13 Feb.: H5, Queen Catherine Howard, by bill of attainder ~ escaped.

Tower Bridge

The Tower of London
facing South to
Queen Anne Boleyn's
escape up the
River Thames

Armoury Depot
Fusilier Museum

White
Tower

Tower Hill
Beheading

Tower Hill Beheading

3

4

5

6

7

8

9

231

1542, 13 February: Jane Boleyn, Viscountess Rochford, by order of Henry VIII ~ escaped.

1554, 12 Feb.: Lady Jane Grey, the "Nine Days Queen", wife of Lord Guildford Dudley, by order of a Special Commission for High Treason ~ escaped.

1601, 25 Feb.: Robert Devereux, 2nd Earl of Essex, Treason, "last beheading in the Tower" ~ escaped.

1618, 29 October: Sir Walter Raleigh was beheaded outside the Tower of London, 3 miles south-west at Old Palace Yard, Palace of Westminster, yet his head was never found, because it was never separated from his body. Rumours then circulated that his 'long-suffering wife, Besse Throckmorton carried Raleigh's head with her in her handbag wherever she went', but this was an Antiquarian old wives tale. Walter Raleigh escaped in the public eye.

33.   Except for Raleigh, each of these nobles were beheaded in private with an axe, except for Anne Boleyn who was beheaded with a sword in public, but this was really a hair cut.

34.   The 1953 film "Roman Holiday" also shows Princess Anne getting a haircut, as "Joseph" played by "Gregory" Peck watches on, and then the crown appears above the head of "Joseph Gregory" on the bed-head. This was Coronation year, and "Roman Holiday" is an anagram of 'H Royal Domain'. Its full code was the transfer of the Crown from Princess Anne to Joseph Gregory as 'H-is Royal Domain'.

35.   The bodies of all 7 aristocrats are claimed buried 66 yards north in the Chapel of St Peter ad Vincula, but none of these have heads. The head wasn't buried with the body, so it didn't

have to look similar, so there was no need to use look-a-likes or body-doubles, just a dead body without head, about the same size.

36. There are only 2 heads amongst them all, attached to 2 lesser known aristocrats, as sourced by a visit and discussions with the presenting Tower Guard in uniform in 2019. After delivering the 25 Instruments, 2019–2021 The Principal returned to the Tower of London on 6 October 2023 to find that Queen Anne Boleyn's grave had been moved further back, now without "name", only marked by a white orchid.

37. The above nobles are listed as having been executed in the Tower of London, on Tower Green, or in the Yeomen Warders Guardhouse, but each execution has 'credibility issues' written up with every Tudor emotional hook to keep the order of the day – "oooooh, three strikes of the axe, that must have hurt, oooooh, arrrggh. Better not me.!!!"

38. For something to be legal it must be unambiguous with a definitive time and location, but the locations of the Private Noble Executions in and around Tower Green are Ambiguous & Patently Ambiguous, where Patent Ambiguity falls against the claims of Crown.

39. Most of the Noble Executions never took place. These were just Royal escapades.[3]

40. The Tower of London is all theatre, and appears to be all theatre, and its noble executions were entirely fabricated ~ for the most enormous fee, including vast estates and castles.

Queen Anne Boleyn didn't enter at the Traitors' Gate,
she was removed at Traitors' Gate.

Endnotes

1   2020, 5 March: Confirmation of Joseph Gregory Hallett's Declaration of Queen Anne Boleyn's Royal Lineage, OTH / 20 / 64528, Addendum One in support of Joseph Gregory Hallett declares Queen Anne Boleyn's Royal Lineage, Queen Anne Boleyn's Execution, pp. 27–28, point xx.

2   Tower Green, wikipedia.

3   2023, Friday 6 October: The Principal went to the White Tower in the Tower of London, and was presented with the usual confusing 'hype'. When this was broken down, there were officially only ten (10) executions inside the Tower of London from 1400 to 1900, over 500 years, which amounts to one execution every 50 years. Its fabricated and faked executions included:

i.   1483, 13–27 June: Baron William Hastings beheading is confused;
ii.   1536, May: Queen Anne Boleyn execution was faked (aged 28–35);
iii.   1538, December: Henry Courtenay, 1st Marquess of Exeter (aged 40);
iv.   1539, January: Henry Pole, 1st Baron Montague (aged 46);
v.   1541, May: Margaret Pole, 8th Countess of Salisbury (aged 65);
vi.   1542, February: ex-Queen consort Catherine Howard (aged 16~20); and
vii.   Jane Boleyn, Viscountess of Rochford, Queen Anne Boleyn's sister.
viii. 1554, February: Jane Grey's "life was to be spared", so her beheading was inside Tower Green Guard's House. Only 'anonymous' wrote it;
viii. 1601, February: Robert Devereux was swished for Capt. Thomas Lee.

Executions of the following five were most likely real, not guaranteed:
a.   1535, June: John Fisher (aged 65);
b.   1535, July: Sir Thomas More (aged 57);
c.   1542, March: Viscount Lisle (aged 66~81);
d.   1545, May: Duchess of Norfolk, Agnes née Tilney Howard (aged 68); widowed 2nd wife of Thomas Howard, 2nd Duke of Norfolk KG PC (1443–21 May 1524); and
e.   1483, 13 June: 1st Baron William Hastings was hurriedly beheaded by Richard, Duke of Gloucester to become Richard III. This was murder.

1400–1900: This leaves 2~5 execution in the Tower of London, or one every 100–250 years. The Tower of London is no longer living up to its reputation as a 'Grim Reaper' and now claims to have always been a Royal Palace ... again. This is how the Flat Lie Royals wash!

Chapter Fourteen
Erasing Queen Anne Boleyn from all Records & Registers

At the time of Anne Boleyn's birth, the Boleyn family were considered one of English aristocracy's most respected families. Anne Boleyn's mother, Lady Elizabeth Howard (*c*.1480–1538) was the daughter of Thomas Howard, 2nd Duke of Norfolk KG PC (1443–1524) one of the pre-eminent families of England, descending from ...

Queen consort Eleanor of France (R. 1137–52) and England (R. 1154–89), King Henry II of England (R. 1154–89), King John I of England (R. 1199–1216), King Philip III of France (R. 1270–85), King Edward I of England (R. 1272–1307) & by his second marriage, the Earls of Norfolk (1312–38), Countess of Norfolk (1338–99), then Dukes of Norfolk (1397–99, 1483–1485, 1514–24) to Lady Elizabeth Howard, and Anne Boleyn, made Queen of England.

Anne Boleyn was of more noble birth than any of Henry VIII's other English wives – Jane Seymour (1536–37), Catherine Howard (1540–42), and Catherine Parr (1543–47). Catherine of Aragon (1509–33) was Spanish, and Anne of Cleves (1540) was German.

In the early 1500s, the spelling of many words and surnames were variable. "Boleyn" was also spelt 'Bullen', hence the family arms with bull heads, although this may be a Jesuit backdated device to falsely link Bullen to Bulleyn chapel & Culleyn chapel in France.

Margaret of Austria in the Netherlands court used 'Boullan', and when Anne signed a letter to her father, she used "Anna de Boullan". Latinates called her "Anna Bolina".

Maximilian I (1459–1519) became King of the Romans a.k.a. King of the Germans (1486–), Archduke of Austria (R. 1493–) and the Holy Roman Emperor (R. 1508–19) known as Emperor Maximilian. His second child, Archduchess Margaret of Austria (1480–1530) married twice becoming Princess of Asturias and Duchess of Savoy.

Emperor Maximilian named Margaret, Governor of the Low Countries, Governor of the Habsburg Netherlands (1507–15 & 1519–30) and guardian of her young nephew, the future Charles V, Holy Roman Emperor. A new palace was built in Mechelen (Belgium), from where Margaret of Austria negotiated, restored treaties, and was an admirer of the charming English European Diplomat, Sir Thomas Boleyn, Anne's father.

Margaret of Austria (33) was being educated with her four wards, and Anne Boleyn (12) was invited to join them and take a place in her household, May 1513–September 1514. The minimum age was 12; if Anne Boleyn was born in 1501, it fitted; but if she was born in 1507, then Anne Boleyn was a truly exceptional 6-year-old. Despite her youth, Anne Boleyn was educated in Mechelen (Belgium) and Paris, France for 8½ years, May 1513–January 1522, aged 12–20.

Anne Boleyn was taught her family genealogy, horse-riding, archery, falconry, hunting, music, singing and dancing, history, reading, writing and grammar, arithmetic, household management, good manners, needlework, embroidery, chess, cards and dice. This early education was typical of Anne's class.

Margaret of Austria told Sir Thomas Boleyn his daughter Anne was "so presentable and pleasant, considering her youthful age, that I am more beholden to you for sending her to me, than you to me".

Thomas Boleyn arranged for his daughter Anne Boleyn to attend Henry VIII's sister (18) Mary (1496–1533) who was preparing to marry Louis XII of France (52) on 9 October 1514, briefly becoming Queen consort of France, until he died 84 days later on 1 January 1515.

Anne Boleyn was a maid of honour to Queen Mary for 84 days, then maid of honour to Mary's stepdaughter Claude (15), the new Queen consort of France (R.1515–24).

Anne Boleyn stayed with Queen Claude nearly seven years, becoming fluent in French, and developed interests in art, illuminated manuscripts, literature, religious philosophy, music, poetry, and fashion. She also assimilated French culture, etiquette, literature, music, poetry, dance, flirtation, the game of courtly love, Holy Grael Christian mysticism, and how to enact it.

Anne Boleyn was considered "sweet and cheerful" in her youth, then elegant, graceful, brilliant, driven, and forthright, with a keen wit and a lively, opinionated, passionate personality, who exerted a powerful charm.

Anne Boleyn also enjoyed drinking wine, eating French cuisine, playing cards and dice, gossiping, flirting, hearing a good joke, and gambling, offset with falconry, archery, hunting, and the occasional game of bowls. She had a sharp tongue and could talk rough.

Thomas Boleyn owned Bickling Hall in north Norfolk, 1499–1505. Anne Boleyn lived there from her birth in 1501 to 4 years old, then Hever Castle 1505–13; then in the new Palace at Mechelen, Belgium, May 1513–September 1514; then in the Royal Palaces in Paris and France, September 1514–January 1522; where her very forward sister, Mary, caused them both to be returned to England, lest Anne Boleyn be tainted by Mary Boleyn's actions.

1531, September: Simon Grynéem to Martin Bucer: Anne Boleyn was "young, good-looking, of a rather dark complexion".

1532, October: Venetian diarist Marino Sanuto: Anne Boleyn was "not the handsomest women ... of middling stature, swarthy complexion, long neck, wide mouth, bosom not much raised ... eyes, which are black and beautiful".

These are the best accounts, but often invented to a purpose.

Weighing all the accounts, Anne Boleyn was of average height, slender, with long thick straight black or dark brown hair, dark brown eyes, a considerably strong nose, a definite wide mouth with slim lips, and an olive complexion.

These looks were to pass down through her lineage to Sir Walter Raleigh, the Prince of Pirates Black Sam Bellamy, named "Black" for his long thick black hair, then to Joseph Gregory Hallett, who at various times had the same long thick black hair, as confirmed by the Bank of England photographer for the Bank of England brochure in early May 2012. The Principal has been living in Norfolk 2015–24 in between the Duke of Norfolk's Framlingham Castle 15 miles south-east, and Bungay Castle 15 miles north-east.

During the reign of King James VI/I "the Shit" 1603–25, Boleyn's former Bickling home fell into ruin. In 1616, James I gave the ruinous Bickling to his Chief Justice Sir Henry Hobart (1560–1625) Attorney General for England and Wales (1606–13) and Chief Justice of the Common Pleas (1613–25).

Hobart had to ensure there were no Boleyn living on the 7½ square mile estate, and everything 'Boleyn' had been destroyed. Chief Justice, Henry Hobart then rebuilt Bickling Hall from 1616, and this new style turned out to be an idealised version of Queen Anne Boleyn's Tudor childhood, 1501–05.

Sir Geoffrey Boleyn (1406–63) mercer, wool merchant and Lord Mayor of London 1457–58, purchased the 1270 Hever Castle in 1462, and his grandson, Thomas Boleyn /Bullen (c.1477–12 March 1539) inherited Hever Castle when his father Sir William Boleyn died on 10 October 1505.

Hever Castle is 11 miles north of Rotherfield, and when Joseph Gregory Hallett arrived in England for the fifth time, and got a vehicle, the first thing he did was drive an-hour-and-a-half to Hever

Bickling Hall was completely torn down after Queen Anne Boleyn left, then rebuilt as Elizabethan from 1616 ... after the Elizabethan period had ended.

Castle, not really knowing why, but to see Queen Anne Boleyn walking in full dress within its walls ... albeit part of tourism.

At the Coronation of Henry VIII in 1509, Thomas Boleyn (32) was made Knight of Bath of Hever Castle, Kent; then made Knight of the Garter in 1523, Sir Thomas Boleyn, 1st Viscount Rochford (1525–), 1st Earl of Ormond, 1st Earl of Wiltshire (1529–). To be Knight of the Garter, one has to be in the top 24 of the Royal family.

Thomas Boleyn was an English diplomat and politician under Henry VII and Henry VIII. Thomas Boleyn married Elizabeth Howard, daughter of Thomas Howard, 2nd Duke of Norfolk. Their three children were Mary Boleyn, Anne Boleyn (H2) and George Boleyn. Thus Thomas Boleyn was the maternal grandfather of Queen Elizabeth of England.

Thomas Boleyn (1477–1539) was a well respected diplomat with a gift for languages, and a favourite of Henry VII (R. 1485–1509) who sent him on many diplomatic missions abroad.

By 1514, Anne Boleyn (12) was writing in French to her father in England, and completed her education at the Regent, Margaret of Austria's new Mechelen Palace between Antwerp and Brussels, now in Belgium. Margaret was a very capable Governor of the Low Countries and Governor of the Habsburg Netherlands, completing many treaties, and Anne Boleyn was one of her maids of honour.

24 January 1536–28 January 1547: In Henry VIII's 11 years of madness, he removed and destroyed all of Anne Boleyn's:

i.   Local Bickling Parish Records, birth records, including all records for these years;

ii.   All paintings of Anne Boleyn, Marquesse of Pembroke, and Queen Anne Boleyn;

iii.   All Trial records of Queen Anne Boleyn;

iv.   All contemporary written social mentions; and

v.   Executed the people who knew her, albeit most were 'be-headed to 'The Island';

vi.   All around Anne Boleyn was obfuscated. It was as if Anne Boleyn never existed ... and was now a Holy Ghost;

vii.   This made it impossible to establish Queen Anne Boleyn's birthdate, and what she actually looked like;

viii.   Thereafter, all the details of Anne Boleyn are dubious ... written by second-fiddles who never met Anne Boleyn, and were not alive at the time. It was the same for paintings of her.

So 76 years after Queen Anne Boleyn was executed in 1536, hacks like Jane Dormer, Duchess of Feria (1538–1612) former lady-in-waiting and confidante to the very Roman Catholic 'Bloody Mary' Queen Mary I (R.1553–58) in her 1612 memoirs wrote:

"Anne Boleyn ... was convicted and condemned
and was not yet twenty-nine years of age."

This argues Anne Boleyn was born in 1507 and only 28 years old in May 1536 ... but Dormer was born 2 years after the execution in 1538, so what does she know, except court propaganda. Jane Dormer, Duchess of Feria was another embedded Catholic historian.

With Anne Boleyn born in 1507 (after 20 May) and not 1501, it just makes her 6 years more fertile to breed again.

According to the state archives, William Cecil, 1st Baron Burghley, KG, PC (1520–98) private papers, and the annales of William Camden (1551–1623) 'The History of The moft Renowned and Victorious Princess Elizabeth, Late Queen of England' (1551–1623) ... Anne Boleyn was born in MDVII ~ 1507.

William Cecil was 15 in 1536. His illegitimate son William Camden was born 15 years after Queen Anne Boleyn's 1536 'execution'. The annales began to be written 71 years later in 1607, with Books 1–3 covering 1588–1615, not 1536 ... and Book 4 written 1617–25 covering 1589–1603, and not 1536.

Books 1–3 appeared in English in 1625; Book 4 was translated into English in 1629. Neither books covered 1536, and Queen Anne Boleyn's so-called execution just got a passing mention, as a continuation of the lie ... continuing the propaganda for the ruse.

The Kings, Queens and aristocracy all knew Queen Anne Boleyn's beheading was a ruse. So wigs were set to fashion for all the upper class to imitate Queen Anne Boleyn's long thick hair, to escape any forthcoming execution in the same way she did.

Wigs for men became the fashion for as long as the Tower of London, Tower Hill, Tyburn and Smithfield were executing by beheading.

> "In France, wigs bespoke privilege and wealth. With the revolution in 1789, perukes were ousted with the monarch & nobility. British Prime Minister William Pitt put an effective end to wig wearing with a tax on wig powder in 1795."

Wigs only faded when they no longer worked to bypass the executions of 1789.

The wig was the best way to cover the swede, and plenty of straw was the best way to cover the un-beheaded head, confirming they were 'be-heading' elsewhere.

King Charles I knew Queen Anne Boleyn's execution was a ruse and did exactly the same thing. Charles I was never executed in 1649. Rather his executioner held up a swede with a wig over the face, stayed silent, and never cried out "Behold the head of a traitor!"

'Because it was a ruse, the commission refused to allow Charles I to be buried in Westminster Abbey, as it wasn't King Charles I's body, so the next day Charles I's head was officially sewn back onto his body (never happened), then his body was embalmed, placed in a lead coffin, and 9 days later, taken to Windsor Castle on the night of 7 February 1649, then buried in private in the Henry VIII vault, in the St George's Chapel Quire 2 days later on 9 February 1649.

'In 1813, the body was privately examined at Windsor to give it an Antiquarian reality, otherwise known as 'noise'. "In 1813, part of Charles' beard, a piece of neck bone, and a tooth were taken as relics, then placed back in the tomb in 1888.'[1]

This gives the year, 1888, when Charles I's body-double was replaced with the real body. King Charles I survived his execution and moved to the Lake District to be with his childhood sweetheart Lady Anne Clifford, Countess of Pembroke (1590–1676). Charles I died in 1670 and was buried at St Andrews for at least 218 years.

'The Annales are (considered) one of the great works of English historiography, and had a great impact on how the Elizabethan age was viewed', yet the Annales continually missed all the salient points. The Annales are a romanticised broad sweep recreation of history, not using any eyewitnesses, and published in English 93 years after the event, 1536 ...1629, when no eye-witnessed survived to dispute the Annales' romanticised Antiquarian account of history. This is otherwise known as a Jesuit Hagiography!

No witnesses saw Queen Anne Boleyn's execution, due to sun-strike, nor did the 450 tall broad Ordinary and Extraordinary Yeomen who made up 50–100% of the crowd. Public notification of the execution was extremely confused, to the point the public were not notified, so their numbers were 0+, being more accidental than intentional.

'The Annales are still widely quoted today, supported by empty-suit historical frauds for hire, including Hugh Trevor-Roper (1914–2003) who was always spoon-fed by MI5 to mislead the masses whenever his feather pen smelt payroll ... for which he was made Baron Dacre in 1979.

There has been lots of noise but no eye witnesses to Queen Anne Boleyn's execution, meaning it was an act of obfuscation, dubious, questionable, uncertain, unclear, vague, indefinite, indeterminate, unintelligible, inconclusive, doubtful, tenuous, puzzling, as though it never happened ~ so entirely ambiguous ~ rendered patently ambiguous by the Crown's continued attempts to make Queen Anne Boleyn's execution 'real', using manufactured quotes from sources a century later.

This was instigated by the great propagandist of the Elizabethan Age, Lord Burghley, William Cecil (1520–98) Secretary of State 1550–53, 1558–72, Lord High Treasurer 1572–98 & Lord Privy Seal 1590–98 who initiated 'Annales' a year before his death, so no one could question its veracity ... which was none.

Queen Elizabeth's spymaster Sir Francis Walsingham was a secret Jesuit spy, as was William Cecil Lord Burghley, who succeeded him as Secretary of State.

Endnotes

1   1981: Pauline Gregg, 'King Charles I', Dent, London, p. 445;

   1999: Graham Edwards, 'The Last Days of Charles I', Sutton Publishing, Stroud, pp. 173, 183, 188–89;

   2005: Geoffrey Robertson, 'The Tyrannicide Brief', Chatto & Windus, London, pp. 201, 333 ... all paraphrased for clarity & continuity.

Chapter Fifteen
The Holy Grael Influencer

Queen Eleanor (1122–1204) and her daughter, Marie of France (1145–64–98) Countess of Champagne, developed the Holy Grael legends at the time of the Crusades (1095–1291) sponsoring and briefing Chrétien de Troyes (fl. 1160–91) as their mouthpiece, with Eleanor as "the first lady of this island", being aristocratic England, actually called "The Island" ... based on Queen consort Eleanor of France & England as 'Guinevere', and her grandson, Prince Arthur I (1187~1203) Duke of Brittany (1196–1203) as Arthur who died aged 16.

Queen Eleanor of France & England, and Marie of France used Chrétien de Troyes as their mouthpiece to first mention the "Holy Grail", as it was spelt 800–1431. This was about their Royal lineage becoming the Holy Grael, and the Holy Grael becoming the Royal lineage, taking 27 generations to do so.

Two images of Queen Eleanor.

This came true with Queen Eleanor's great x 25 grandson "Gregory Hallett" ~ an anagram of 'Holy Grael' ~ was the first to publish images of the Holy Grael, on the same day the End Times–New Age was represented by the same Gregory Hallett, acting as the Holy Grael ... having just registered the two Jesus.[1]

The anagram of "Gregory Hallett is 'reg tt Holy Grael'
"tt" ≈ the Two Jesus, as in the 1611 King James Bible, 2 Corinthians 11:4:

> For if he that cometh preacheth another Jesus,
> whom we have not preached ... which ye have not accepted,
> ye might well bear with him.

The Holy Grael and its legend were then exported from France to England via the marriage of Eleanor, Queen consort of France (R. 1137–52) to King Henry II of England (R. 1154–89) becoming Queen consort Eleanor of England (R. 1154–89).

Their youngest child was King John I of England (R. 1199–1216) who was the Sangrëal – the Blood Royal – the primary blood descendant of the Jesus–Mary lineage. To be a 'King John of England', one has to be the Sangrëal, or hold the title Christ.

The person who represents the End Times–New Age holds the title 'Christ' above all others who hold the title Christ.

The title Christ can also be held by the Templar Grandmaster if they have achieved Gnosis or 'knowing'. The title Christ was also held by Queen Victoria's firstborn and only legitimate son, Prince Marcos Manoel, who was also the Sangrëal, and also made King John II of the United Kingdom of Great Britain and All Ireland on 6 October 1869 ~ St. Bruno's Day.

King John's great x 24 grandson Joseph Gregory Hallett, holds the Royal Mark for Prince Regent Duke Governor for King John III of England.

The Holy Grael legend's were initiated in the French Court and transferred to the English court via marriage and breeding. This pattern was to repeat 333 years later (1199–1216 ... 1533–36) with Queen Anne Boleyn of England, who spent 1514–January 1522 in France.

This pattern was to repeat 500 years later 1514–21 ... 2014–21 with Joseph Gregory Hallett who represented the Tribulations while in England, the Netherlands, Portugal and the Algarve.

Eleanor of Aquitaine, Queen consort of France, and daughter Marie, Countess of Champagne were the benefactors behind the King Arthur and Holy Grael legends on both sides of the English Channel, their poetic prophecy ultimately predicting, affirming and confirming that after 27 generations, the Holy Grael would be in their lineage.

Joseph Gregory Hallett would return the Kingship of England, and return to the Kingship of England ... and
... right at the last moment, another fulfilling the Holy Grael legend and Sangrëal bloodline may turn up and return the Kingship of Scotland, and return to the Kingship of Scotland.

French Renaissance Holy Grael Christian Mysticism

Princess Marguerite de Navarre (21) was "a radiant young princess of violet-blue eyes" who married Henry II of Navarre, becoming Queen consort of Navarre (1492, R. 1527–49).

Marguerite's brother became Francis I, King of France (1 January 1515–31 March 1547).

Francis I and the King's sister Marguerite were responsible for the intellectual cultural court salon renaissance in France.

Marguerite's grandson Henry de Navarre then became Henry IV of France (R. 1589–1610) and the first Bourbon king.

Marguerite de Navarre was "The First Modern Woman" ... a patron of humanists, reformers, and its authors, and the outstanding woman of the French Renaissance, whose speciality was Christian mysticism that verged on heresy or 'divergent dissident non-conformism'.

This indicates a continuation of Holy Grael legend from Marie of France (1145/1164–98) to Marguerite de Navarre (1492/1527–49) over 3½ centuries (1164–98 ... 1527–49) with the Old and New Testament Bible first printed in English in 1526, then revised in 1534 & 1535.

In France, Anne Boleyn was initiated into the Holy Grael legend and bloodline, and how to take these across the Channel in England to continue the Jesus-Mary Blood lineage into the Kingship of England, and protect it, until the time was right for it to be revealed – the story being part of Revelation – the Apocalypse of John ... which is why the CIA Esoteric division took Joseph Gregory Hallett to Patmos in September 1988, where Revelation was claimed written.

Marguerite de Navarre
"The First Modern Woman"

Anne Boleyn's teen (12–20) experience in the Austrian-Netherlands-Belgium and French Courts led her to become a devout French Renaissance humanist Christian reformist, devoted to the Virgin Mary; with the Pope seen as a corrupting influence on Christianity.

Anne Boleyn would become the champion of the new vernacular Bible, local, not Catholic, to be first published in English in 1526, then revised in 1534 & 1536, and copied in 1537, at the same time as Queen Anne Boleyn's 1536 'execution' ... thus doing a female version of Jesus on the scaffold, gibbet or cross, 1533 years later (A.D. 33~1536).

Anne Boleyn's European education ended when she sailed from Calais to England in January 1522, and became instrumental in getting Henry VIII to break with the Papacy.

It was Queen Anne Boleyn who removed England from being a Papal Vassal State, and gave England to the English.

Anne Boleyn was the truest female pirate – the greatest land pirate ever to assail the Papal See, and her grandson, Sir Walter Raleigh would become the worlds' most famous pirate-privateer, and Queen Anne Boleyn's great-great-great-grandson would become the worlds' most successful pirate-privateer, Samuel Bellamy, with the aid of Letter of Marque from King George I in 1716, via John Hallett, just two years after George I had formally acknowledged he did not have nor hold the Styles or Title King of England ... which was reserved for the emerging Christ in another 300 years.

1519, late: Anne Boleyn's elder sister, Mary Boleyn (19) was recalled from France for her affair with the French King, Francis I (24) and his courtiers too.

1520, February: Mary Boleyn married courtier William Carey, at Greenwich, with Henry VIII attending, and soon after, Mary Boleyn was Henry VIII's mistress, having learnt all things the French King desires, now transferred to the English King via touch.

9.9.1518–15 June 1519: Henry VIII and Elizabeth Blount, Lady Talboys, had an illegitimate son. He was acknowledged as Henry Fitzroy (15 June 1519–23 July 1536) Duke of Richmond and Somerset, and aged 14 on 28 November 1533 married Mary Howard, only daughter of Thomas Howard, 3rd Duke of Norfolk. Henry Fitzroy was painted as AIS Grade 3+, a little transgender, and or subservient gay receiver, so the marriage was never consummated, and he died 2½ years later aged 17 & 38 days.

While Henry Fitzroy was alive in his lavender cover marriage, "He was on excellent terms with his brother-in-law, eldest son of Thomas Howard, 3rd Duke of Norfolk, the poet Henry Howard KG (1511–19 January 1547) the Earl of Surrey"[2] who translated the second and fourth books of Virgil's Aeneid (B.C. 29–19) giving them the rhyming meter, dividing them into quatrains, and un-rhymed iambic pentameter or blank verse. This became the mainstay of Elizabethan sonnets, and was used by Shakespeare.

Henry Howard KG (1511–47) and his poet friend Sir Thomas Wyatt (1503–42) are known as "Fathers of the English Sonnet" due to their excellent translations of the sonnets of Petrarch (1304–74).[3]

This Howard who invented the Shakespearean sonnet had a double life smashing windows. "He was repeatedly imprisoned ... for wandering through the streets of London breaking the windows of houses whose occupants were asleep."[4]

This falls into line with the Howards and Mary Sidney Herbert (1561–1621) Countess of Pembroke 1577–1621, influencing and patronising Shakespeare, who was one of their own, and Marquess of Pembroke.

Mary Sidney Herbert patronised Shakespeare and may have written
the 17 Sonnets attributed to Shakespeare.

Henry Howard KG
smashed windows
and became the
Father of the
Sonnet.

Henry VIII is not the father of Mary Boleyn, nor Anne Boleyn, nor George Boleyn.

Henry VIII did not have a child with Mary Boleyn.

Henry VIII had a child with his wife, Queen Anne Boleyn. This was Queen Elizabeth I.

Two months after arriving in England, Anne Boleyn made her début in English Court on 4 March 1522 in an elaborate dance with Henry VIII's younger sister, Mary (1496–1533) grandmother of Lady Jane Grey, who became "the Nine Days' Queen", 10–19 July 1553, and was then 'executed'.

Anne Boleyn returned to the service of Catherine of Aragon, Henry VIII's Queen consort 1509–33, where Anne caught the eye of Henry VIII in the anterooms.

1526: Henry VIII (34) was enamoured with Anne Boleyn (18~24) and began pursuing her.

1527: Within a year Henry proposed, and Anne accepted.

1526–32: Anne Boleyn was at Henry's side in policy and state, but not in his bed.

1527–32: They were in courtship for 5 years without sex, waiting for Henry's annulment – "the King's Great Matter", or for Queen consort Catherine of Aragon to die, as she did on 7 January 1536, from 'cancer of the heart'.

All Queen consort Catherine of Aragon's children had died in infancy, except for Mary, who became Mary I, Mary Tudor ruling just prior to Elizabeth I as 'Bloody Mary' (1553–58).

Inclusion is highly selective and warrants unusual process

Inclusion into the Holy Grael lineage is highly selective and requires intense initiation and decades of purpose.

Joseph Gregory Hallett is a descendant of Queen Anne Boleyn, Walter Raleigh Christ and Samuel Bellamy, and also holds the title Christ, and 'Christ above all others with the title Christ' (except when Christ turns up, or one can prove a higher claim). In support of this, Queen Elizabeth II gave birth to GREG HALET via the UK coins 1968–1998 over 11,011 days, which spells "M0M" (11 = M).

Queen Elizabeth II wanted to become the 'Bride of Christ', so she looked around for someone to marry, and chose Joseph Gregory Hallett, making him the Biblical 'Bridegroom'. Marriage was by proxy using symbols.

Gainsborough painted 'Elizabeth marries Hallett' or 'The Morning Walk' in the summer of 1785, just prior to the marriage of Elizabeth Stephen to William Hallett. Both were 21 years old at the time, marking "the Shin" or 'Forbidden Secret'.

The National Gallery is in Trafalgar Square overlooking Charing Cross where the King is announced. Room 34 alludes to Illuminati knowledge; Keith Gregory, alludes to K. Gregory, for King Gregory.

Queen Elizabeth II got Keith Gregory to go into Room 34 of The National Gallery, and scratch 'Elizabeth marries Hallett' with a drill bit for 'Dr. ill-bit' meaning 'Doctored by Elizabeth'. The next day, K.(ing) Gregory was heard in Court on Sunday 19 March, and published in the newspapers on Monday 20 March.

Foster's offered 'The Morning Walk' or 'Elizabeth marries Hallett' for sale in 1834, the year Queen Victoria gave birth to Prince Marcos Manoel who became King John II of England, with Joseph Gregory Hallett as Prince Regent Duke Governor for King John III of England, and or King John III of the United Kingdom of Great Britain and All Ireland, and King of the Kingdom of England.

50 years later in 1884, Nathan Mayer Rothschild purchased the 99-year-old 'Elizabeth marries Hallett', then sold it to the National Gallery seventy (70) years later in 1954 for £30,000. Seventy (70) years later in 2024, 'Elizabeth marries Hallett' was worth £3 million.

By 1707, the four versions of title King of England were lost – the colour of law Style, and the colour of law Title, the real Style, and the real Title – each progressively transferred to Sir Walter Raleigh Christ and his descendants ... confirmed as The Principal Joseph Gregory Hallett with the 1967–1998 UK coins, in 2007 & 2014, 300 years after 1707 and 1714 when the Monarch no longer held any of the Style or Title 'King of England'; ratified by Queen Elizabeth's 2017 marriage as the Bride of Christ, identifying the Bridegroom as Joseph Gregory Hallett. With this Bible prophecy fulfilled, Christ is automatically the King of the Kingdom of England etc.

Endnotes

1   2014, 16 August: 'The Hidden King of England – Arma Christi – Unveiling the Rose, Volumes IV & V, published at the End Times–New Age changeover.

2   2018: Nicola Clark, 'Gender, Family, and Politics: The Howard Women, 1485–1558', Oxford University Press, Oxford, p. 145.

3   The Shakespearean Sonnet,
     https://shakespeare-navigators.com/romeo/Sonnet.html;
     Early English Sonnets, http://www.sonnets.org/early.htm.

4   2012: 'The Norton Anthology of English Literature: Sixteenth/Early Seventeenth Century, Volume B', p. 661.

Chapter Sixteen – Stuart Kings
hunt the Posthumous Tudor Lineage using Forest Law

Queen Anne Boleyn was 'executed' in 1536, but released into the wild. Forest Law then did something to preserve the Holy Grael lineage in remote comfortable hiding places.

In the last month of his reign, Henry VIII (d. 28 January 1547) placed the Royal Forests under the Court of Augmentations (land-grabs), then Exchequer (land-grab administration) who were all working for Queen Anne Boleyn, and doing their best to hide her and the Holy Grael lineage safely, which included promoting distractions to subsequent monarchs.

King James VI/I "the Shit" (R. 1603–25) and son King Charles I (b. 1600, R. 1625–49) considered Queen Anne Boleyn (1501–1536+) and posthumous offspring, Mary y'Noble (1537–) and hidden grandchildren, Walter Raleigh (1552–1618+) and his son, MP Carew Raleigh (1605–1666) to be living on 'The Island', somewhere on the 47,000 square miles or 94% of aristocratic England, with many other posthumous nobility ... and their offspring.

> Walter Raleigh's first son, Walt Raleigh was killed by a musket ball in January 1618 in Venezuela. Walt (17) was the first killed. Only two others were killed, one on each side, then the Spanish deserted the town, as though this was their only mission.

The concept of a 'Commune' was well known and used. The walled City of London began as a lion-shaped Commune without its head ever manifesting, awaiting the Holy Grael; and Anne Boleyn had lived in palaces in the Netherlands, Belgium & France, and been introduced to the Salons – all run as communes. The French districts are still known as 'Communes' to this day.

Queen Anne Boleyn's descendants et al were either living on aristocrat noble estates, which the King could do little about, or in the Royal Forests.

Queen Anne Boleyn's daughter, Mary y'Noble, and her grandson Sir Walter Raleigh, and his grandson, Stephen, knew this, so they concentrated their offspring in country houses with large numbers of children, with many fathers, so the children could not easily be stopped, counted and identified.

Nevertheless King James VI/I "the Shit" and son King Charles I attempted to do something about a more original Royal Lineage living on their land – in the Royal Forests. This involved:

i.   Taking a Census of the Royal Forests;

ii.   Charging new fixed rents to confirm occupier ownership;

iii.   Evicting Peasants out of the Royal Forests;

iv.   Depopulating areas of the Royal Forests;

v.   Disrupting select settlements in the Royal Forests;

vi.   Making the Royal Forests smaller;

vii.   Selling the Royal Forests off;

viii.   Turning the Royal Forest borders into farmland;

ix.   Grabbing the Royal Forest land as Crown land;

x.   Selling eternal leases to court favourites for the cost of the manufactured fine that removed the unwanted;

xi.   Fence off these new leases in exchange for setting up watches within the Royal Forest; and

xii.   Any unregistered people in the Royal Forest were charged with 'Trespass against the Vegetation', and required to go to the Forest Law Courts, where they would be identified.

The concept of the Royal Forest was introduced by the Normans to England. After 1066, by Royal Prerogative, Forest Law was widely applied to protect the "noble" animals of the chase – deer & wild boar – and the Vegetation that sustained them.

In 1079, bâtard William the Conqueror proclaimed New Forest to be a Royal Forest. This is 219 square miles in Wiltshire-Hampshire, just east of Dorset. There are 62 Royal Forests or 'Kingswood' in England, with three larger than New Forest.

In 1154, Henry II (R. 1154–89) declared all 350 square miles of Huntingdonshire to be a new Royal Forest, just north-west of Cambridge. This is roughly 19 by 19 miles.

From 1180–1220 one-third of southern England was designated Royal Forest.

Royal Forests were the Monarch's hunting grounds. The King would invite aristocracy to join him in the hunt. Local nobles were then granted a royal licence to take a certain amount of game; and take payment from others for hunting access. These sprouted up all over England, and allowed for a rather remote and private selective breeding programme, whereby the Monarch and Aristocrats were greeted by their offspring tending the horses & hounds & reception. Huntingdonshire and Essex still look like this to this day, where there are many attractive bastards ... or bâtards darling, bâtards.

All of Essex was a Royal Forest, and where Royal bâtards and illegitimate nobles were born and bred, which is why the girls are so pretty. They lived in communes in the forest, which are places without walls, where the commons land had no fences.

This is remembered in your myths and now fairy tales ...

Common inhabitants of the forest had the right to firewood (estover), to cut turf as fuel (turbary) and to harvest forest products.

The 1217 Charter of the Forest allowed all freemen owning land within the forest to enjoy the rights of cattle grazing (agistment) and pig grazing (pannage). In the cleared lands (disafforested) on the edge of the forest (purlieus) agriculture was allowed.

Any deer causing damage to purlieus were allowed to be killed.

Until the 1650s, Forest Law courts prescribed harsh penalties for a wide range of offences. Any villages, towns and fields within the Royal Forests were also subject to Forest Law, with Forest Law operating outside of Common Law.

Forest Law offences included Trespass against the Vegetation, and against the Game, being deer and boar (extinct in 1200s) hare and wolf (extinct in 1400s) then extended to the fox, marten, and beasts and fowls of warren: rabbit, pheasant, and partridge.

'The rights of chase and of warren' were granted to local nobility, who charged hunting fees.

Forest Law Trespass applied to wrongful appropriation of land (purpresture), clearing forest land for agriculture (assarting), felling trees or clearing shrubs, and even applied to land within the boundary of the Royal Forest that was freehold.

Those who lived in Royal Forests were not allowed to carry hunting weapons, and dogs were banned from the forest, although mastiffs with their front claws removed were permitted as watchdogs, but not allowed to hunt. This all aided any Royal in hiding.

To achieve privacy in breeding attractive bâtards, but more to hunt the Holy Grael Tudor Royals, settlements were disrupted, peasants were evicted and areas depopulated, as per i–xii.

The Kings' Forest Gate Keepers were Royal Forest censors working
for the Stuart Kings (R. 1603–1714) and their ultimate game was
the Tudor dynasty who ruled 1485–1603, but especially the Holy
Grael lineage of Queen Anne Boleyn and her progeny.

Queen Anne Boleyn, Queen Elizabeth I, and Sir Walter Raleigh
were of the House of Joseph. Half of the Tudor dynasty was the
House of Joseph, the House of Ephraim.

King James VI/I "the Shit" and his son King Charles I (R. 1625–49)
were attacking and eroding their own Royal Forests, stating it was
for an income independent of Parliament, but really they were
hunting the Royal Holy Grael lineage out of their hiding places,
eliminating those hiding places, and vastly reducing the size of the
Royal Forests, while giving land to prominent courtiers to set up
watchmen in the Gatehouses to censor who was coming in and out,
aid the official hunting parties, and look for the Royal Holy Grael
lineage at all times. Nobility also bred and interbred attractive
bâtard for future concubine stock.

Under Charles I in the 1630s, Exchequer Commissioners confirmed
occupiers ownership only when they paid a new fixed rent. This
extorted over £25,000, having a labour value of £76 million in 2024.

This turned Gillingham Forest (Dorset) and Chippenham and
Blackmore Forests (Wiltshire) into leased farmland. Charging a new
fixed rent became the model for depopulating the Royal Forests,
shrinking them, and having walled estates within. These were not
communal, but encroachments.

Exchequer Commissioners then surveyed the Royal Forests to
determine Crown lands from Commons Land, and Royal Forest.
Landowners and Tenants traditional rights to use commons land
were then revoked and a compensation fee was negotiated for them,
and the entire 'commune' was increasingly revoked from the 1630s.

In the Court of Exchequer, the Attorney General would take legal action against the forest residents for 'intrusion'. This involved a fine and court costs. Then the same Attorney General confirmed the Settlement Fee negotiated by the Exchequer Commissioners for the land. The Settlement Fee, Fine and Court Costs made the Compensation Fee. Most of these Compensation Fees were never paid and Landowners and Tenants walked off the land, or were driven off. These new Crown lands were then granted to prominent courtiers or aristocracy for the unpaid Compensation Fee, and the land considered leased.

It was a long cheap lease. The lands were fenced off with high masonry walls, a Manor House built, with Gate-Houses for the Watchmen, who could see who was arriving in the official parties, and who was otherwise unregistered or unknown.

Artisans and Cottagers were not entitled to Compensation (nor were Gypsies) "with armed mobs ... and the low born nature of the participants" they rioted in their thousands. There were mock parades (chivaree) at Feckenham (1622–31), Leicester (1628), and Malvern (1632), and the Western Rising riots in the West Country forests of Gillingham (1625), Braydon (1630) and the Forest of Dean, where rioters destroyed 12 miles of fence.

The Crown got Feckenham, Leicester, Gillingham and Braydon (1622–31). The Artisans and Cottagers (and Gypsies) got Dean and Malvern Chase (1632), so the Forest of Dean wood was sold for iron smelting charcoal (1612–70–1700s) its western side privately owned, and the deer removed in 1850. All are now managed by the Forestry Commission.

Royal Forests not used for hunting, or with few timber sales, were abolished (Knaresborough Forest, Yorkshire). Royal Forests were surveyed and cleared for agriculture (assart) at Feckenham,

Sedgemoor and Selwood. Grazing enclosures (herbage) and pig grazing (pannage) were added in Chippenham and Blackmore.

1635 was the last serious exercise of Forest Law by a court of justice-seat or Forest Eyre when Pirate/Privateer Holy Grael Christ Sir Walter Raleigh's son, Andrew was 16 years old, and living unregistered in a nearby location. The timing and location were "Rudolf" (Nureyev) meaning close enough to be in tune.

This was Queen Anne Boleyn's great-grandson, and the same year, Andrew Hallett and Andrew Hallett emigrated as brothers to Cape Cod in New England, North America.

"Andrew" is an anagram of 'Ane-w-r-d' ~ 'Anne's Walter Raleigh died' in 1646, aged 94, and this is 'Ane's-word'.

King James VI/I "the Shit" (R. 1603–25) and his son King Charles I (R. 1625–49) were fearful of the Tudor Lineage of Henry VII, Henry VIII & Elizabeth I (1485–1603); and Henry's six wives including his 'second eternal wife' Queen Anne Boleyn; and any progeny, especially Sir Walter Raleigh Christ; and Queen Elizabeth I sons, Viscount Francis Bacon (65) who could see the writing on the wall and faked his own death in 1626, living in Europe with all things Rosicrucian; and Queen Elizabeth I's second son, Robert Devereux, 2nd Earl of Essex who was charged and convicted of treason becoming the "last beheading in the Tower" on 25 February 1601, but Capt. Thomas Lee was beheaded in his place.

Robert Devereux, 2nd Earl of Essex escaped the Tower of London to be company of the 58-year-old Mary, Queen of Scots in the brown palacete in France, which Devereux had set up when he was Elizabeth I's spy in France for ten years.

The Stuart Monarchs lived in fear of previous monarchs while observing the predictions ...

<1817:These Royal Forests had their own four levels of Courts, held every 40 days or 3 years.

1855–75: Just north of London, the 5 square miles of Epping Forest was illegally inclosed, then purchased by The Corporation of London, and opened up, with The Corporation of London appointed as conservators. 1 square mile of Epping Forest was then encroached for development, and now has suburbs on two sides and is less than 4 square miles.

So Epping Forest is no longer a place for the Royal Holy Grael lineage to survive.

1877: New Forest re-established Forest Courts.

i. The Crown's right to inclose the New Forest was limited;

ii. Common rights were regulated;

iii. The Court of Verderers or Woodmote was reconstituted;

iv. And called every 40 days.

1964–: New Forest is managed by the Forestry Commission.

Persian & Egyptian Royalty hunted in Forests in
'The Land of the Long White Cloud'

The exact same thing happened in the forests of New Zealand. Queen Victoria named the original white-skinned fair-haired native people of New Zealand "Maori", which means 'White Native'. Here, these original White natives are categorised "M1".

232 B.C.:The 'Toi', 'the Multitude' or 'M1' arrived from Persia and Egypt, with Alexander the Great's ring, which The Principal was given to wear between Christmas & New Year 2009. The Toi became the Royalty of New Zealand.

1721–25:   There were many changes of Pope. This aided plausible deniability ...

Pope Clement XI ruled 23 November 1700–19 March 1721

Innocent XIII ruled 8 May 1721–7 March 1724

Benedict XIII ruled 29 May 1724–21 February 1730 ...
with no Popes 19 March–8 May 1721 & 7 March–29 May 1724.

During this time, perhaps of the no Popes, 7 March–29 May 1724, Jesuits got word to brown-skinned opportunists on the western island of Western Samoa, Savai'i or Salafai. These "M2" were to go to New Zealand and exterminate the local White native M1 Toi, of which there were at least one million.

The Jesuits and Popes wanted the M1 Toi killed as they were Egyptian and Persian Royalty, and had dug 400 miles of canals and built straight stone walls, which the M2 Maori never did.

The M2 arrived in New Zealand in 1725 & hunted & killed 98.6% of the Multitude, killing the white native Maori 'M1' close to extinction.

M2 would get 2,000 M1 to dig a large round ditch, be sat inside with their hands bound, then bury them alive.

When archaeologists in the Bay of Islands reported this to local Maori in A.D. 2000, they didn't want anything to do with the bodies saying: "They aren't ours".

1860: M2 killed 3,600 M1 in one day during the last great cannibal feast, at Cherry Grove, Taranaki. 3,600 Ngati Hotu were killed and eaten. Ngati Hotu were red-headed Persians.

1725–1860: M2 literally mass-murdered 98.6% of M1 over 135 years. The original white-skinned fair-haired native "Maori"

M1 had been retreating into the forests since 1725, the last of them retreating in 1860.

Only 14 per 1,000 survived the M2 forest hunt to extinction of M1. They had been known as "Toi" meaning 'the Multitude'.

When 98.6% of the 'Multitude' (Toi) were killed and eaten. the remaining 1.4% lived in the forests, and became known as "patupaiarehe" – 'pale-skins that live deep in the forests.

c.1800: When the Whites arrived, there were a million skeletons strewn all over New Zealand, left unburied where they had been killed. People were paid threepence a skeleton, and their bones were ground up and sprayed as fertilizer.

Despite this, sightings and legends of the Patupaiarehe were so thick, they made it to the postage stamp in 2000.

Forests became forestry towns, then towns, then cities. The forests had been eroded and vastly reduced in size before WWII, and this continued after WWII into an industry. M2 worked cutting the forests down, and M1 worked planted them. The Principal M1 planted 750 trees a day in 1979 in the back blocks of Rotorua.

1945: Straight after WWII, M2 claimed they were M1 – the original Maori, and Tangata whenua, meaning 'People of the land', and even invented the 1945 warring 'Haka' as propaganda for their claim.

But this was a false claim. M2 are usurpers. M2 are not 'Maori', and M2 are not White Natives.

M2 then backdated 'Te Wherowhero" to a king in June 1858, changing his name to Kingi Pōtatau, and then killed off King Potato 2 years later on 25 June 1860 at the same time as the Cannibal Feast. This reeks of Jesuit planning and backdating.

M2 worked cutting down and shrinking the forests so the original
M1 Patupaiarehe Toi White Maori Royalty could no longer survive
there, but when the time was right, after WWII, M1 walked out
of the forests and assimilated into society, white and brown, even
breeding with the above named Royals, who were also in and out of
the English Forests.

Hallett in England had the fore-
sight to have their own forest –
Halletts Wood in Rotherfield.

Lisa Marie Presley was the
daughter of the King of Rock and
Roll and wife of the King of Pop,
and chose to live in Rotherfield.
This marked Rotherfield as a
place of kings. Marie Presley
served The Principal cake in
Rotherfield, adjacent to Hallett's
Wood. Way too much sugar Lisa.

Both were anonymous, as though Chief of the Ordinaries.

M2 were totally surprised and in awe of M1 and copied them in
every way, as though M2 did not have their own culture, and copied
others' cultures, which is true. M2 carved wood in M1 style & told
M1 genealogies as though they were their own.

This was the usurpation of an entire peoples ...

Cultural Appropriation before the phrase was even invented.

M2 claimed they were the original 'White Native 'Maori' "Tangata
whenua" ~ 'people of the land', carrying oversized banners on
national marches closing down the Auckland Harbour Bridge to
walk over it on 23 September 1975, and again in 2008.

M2 than had the cheek to claim compensation for the Native land taken by the Crown in 1901/02.

M2 (fake Maori) then kept the millions and billions for their own personal use, and did not pass it down to the people they represented, as they were not the Maori they claimed to be.

All of this compensation is due to the M1. See the blue guy above.

These M2 usurpers from Western Samoa were after whatever compensation was available "for loss of lands", but M2 had usurped these lands, and would continue to usurp these lands as long as the true Royal M1 White Native Maori lineage was suppressed ... by ignoring them, and ignoring their survival, and ignoring them in the media.

This is why the 1725 recent-arrival M2 Western Samoans still sing and dance for the Jesuit-controlled British Royals, who are also usurping monarchs.

> M2 and the British Royals are usurpers together.
> The British Royals are Flat Lie Royals
> and the M2 are Flat Lie Maori.

The M1 Toi Multitude highest survival rate was in the South Island, the further south, and especially in south-west.

In the south-west of the South Island, and on Stewart Island, the Egyptian and Persian Royalty survived as Toi and the Multitude, albeit in small numbers, and when the tribes were being defined, these Toi were registered as 'Ngai Tahu'.

The Principal is registered Ngai Tahu ... being a record of Egyptian and Persian Royalty.

Chapter Seventeen – Trouble with Catholic Church Authority and the breakaway Holy Grael lineage

The Roman Emperor, lastly in Constantinople in 1453, was the Pontifex Maximus or "greatest priest", from which we get the shortened title "Pope".

The Vatican clergy purportedly usurped the title "Pope" in the early 1400s, then backdated their claim into the complete and utter mess that makes up the official List of Popes:

1. Some Popes were women, including Pope Ioannes Anglicus (r. 855–57) who has her own crowned statue in Rome. The Pope's list replaced Joanna with Benedict III (r. 855–858);

2. Hermannus Contractus or Hermann of Reichenau (1013–54) was the first to number the Popes continuously, his list beginning with Pontificate St Peter A.D. 33–68, and ending with Pope Leo IX (r. 1049–54) at #154.

3. 1054: The Great Schism, East–West Schism, or 'Schism of 1054' was the break between the Roman Catholic Church and Eastern Orthodox Churches, based on whether or not:

    a. Leavened or unleavened bread should be used in the Last Supper Eucharist;

    b. Constantinople should remain as one of the five major Episcopal Sees, with Rome, Jerusalem, Alexandria, and Antioch; and

    c. The Bishop of Rome had universal jurisdiction over Constantinople.

    d. London was not considered one of the Episcopal Sees, but should have been, along with Faro in the Algarve, making seven (7) Episcopal Sees. If the Popes actually knew what they were talking about, and understood the history of Christianity, they would include London and Faro in the seven Episcopal Sees.

4. This backdated papal line was discontinuous with acknowledged interregnums:

29 November 1268–1 September 1271 (2 years, 275 days)
4 April 1292–5 July 1294 (2 years, 94 days)
20 April 1314–7 Aug 1316 (2 years, 111 days)
4 July 1415–11 Nov 1417 (2 years, 136 days) (867days)
29 August 1799–14 March 1800 (228 days)

These five (5) Interregnums amount to 10 years 3 months 23 days.

5. 1378–1417: The Western Schism, Papal Schism, Great Occidental Schism, or 'Schism of 1378' was a split within the Catholic Church, where two men simultaneously claimed to be the true Pope, and each excommunicated the other – so a house of curses.

The Papal Office was based on politics, not theology, and this turned its authority into a laughing stock, under question, and its reputation permanently damaged.

6. 1378–1449: For 70 years there were more Anti-Popes ~ 6 over 52 years, than Popes 5 over 51 years.

7. 1410: 3 men claimed to be Pope. This established enough confusion to cover for the fact that the Roman Emperor was the 'Pontifex Maximus' or "greatest priest", and held the title "Pope". The last Roman Emperor died defending Constantinople in 1453.

8. 4 July 1415–11 November 1417: After the 4th Interregnum, the title 'Pope' was usurped and backdated, purportedly from the Roman Emperor & Pontifex Maximus. But the Popes did not purchase the title Roman Emperor or Pontifex Maximus, nor inherit it. The Vatican just assumed the title Pope during the Plagues, when people were dying not to notice.

The Pope in Rome is colour of law style only. The Vatican has never had legitimacy to use the title Pope.

9.   The first Pope was purportedly in the early 1400s, at the time of Popes, Antipopes, Schisms and Interregnums. Even the Church can not tell who were the good guys and who was the bad guys. Antipopes reigned 217–1449/2013 alongside Popes 33–2013.

10.   1409–10: 3 Popes ruled simultaneously for 10 months with Benedict XIII (1394–1423), Gregory XII (1406–15), and Alexander V (30 June 1409–3 May 1410).

11.   2013–22: There are also 2 Popes now, but friendly with each other – Pope Benedict XVI (r. 19 April 2005–28 February 2013) who is homosexual and resigned amid paedophile accusations, but some say continues ... and Pope Francis (r. 13 March 2013–).

They came prepared for Joseph Gregory Hallett's emerging story by:

a. Changing the dedication of the Catholic Church away from Jesus to Mary, or an assimilation of her;

b. Having the capital of Israel moved from Tel Aviv to Jerusalem;

c. Having Jerusalem given to the Catholic Church; and

d. Having two Popes, Benedict and Francis ... all in 2012–2013; and

e. Advertising this with the 2017 stage-play 'The Pope', by the New Zealander, Anthony McCarten, born in 1961 like The Principal;

f. Anthony McCarten then wrote the film adaptation script for

'The Two Popes' starring Anthony Hopkins as Pope Benedict XVI and Jonathan Pryce as Pope Francis, released 27 & 29 November 2019; and

g.   Having the Laws of Succession backdated from 2014 to 25 April 2013, the date Joseph Gregory Hallett was registered in the Holy See as a Member of the Star Family, being the Jesus-Mary lineage, and placed above all Royalty in Europe and the UK.

12.   Wealthy families routinely bought the position of Pope, 1455–1655. This included three (3) Borgias:

8 April 1455–6 August 1458: Alfons de Borja as Pope Callixtus III; & his nephew

11 August 1492–18 August 1503: Rodrigo Lanzol Borgia as Pope Alexander VI;

15 September 1644 –7 January 1655: Giovanni Battista Pamphili as Pope Innocent X, great-great-great-grandson of Pope Alexander VI

... and four (4) Medici Popes ...

1513–1 December 1521: Giovanni de' Medici as Pope Leo X; and his first cousin

1523–25 September 1534: Giulio di Giuliano de' Medici as Pope Clement VII;

1559–9 December 1565: Giovanni Angelo Medici as Pope Pius IV; and

1 April–27 April 1605: Alessandro Ottaviano de' Medici became Pope Leo XI.

13.   1503–13: Popes were Army Generals: Pope Julius II took control of all the Papal States, being Italy, for the first time: then

1870–1929: Italy rejected the Vatican, and the Popes were evicted for 59 years.

14. 1179–1400–1920–present: The Catholic Inquisitions was a death cult with 'any excuse to murder' as 'spirituality'. Homosexual paedophile priests were executing sexy fertile women for the relish. Ugly evil women seem to have been spared. It was also a land grab exercise.

15. A.D. 33–1502: The Popes, involved in the Catholic Inquisitions and Spanish Inquisitions did not hold the title Pope, nor Pontifex Maximus, at these times. The Vatican's use of "Pope" or Pontifex Maximus is a colour of law style only, and not a real title, and offered no protection for their crimes. A.D. 33–1502: All of the Popes were a fraud.

16. 1494 &1502: Previously the title "Pope" or "Pontifex Maximus" belonged to the Roman Emperor. However, these titles were sold, but not to the Vatican, rather they were sold to the King of France, and Queen of Spain, then transferred to England.

17. The titles 'Roman Eastern Emperor' & 'Roman Western Emperor' occasionally joined, but their subtitles, including Pontifex Maximus, later assumed as Pope, have been left in historical obfuscation with a dedicated lack of clarity, using ambiguous words, to avoid clarifying where the title Pontifex Maximus and Pope ended up – in England with the Protestants.

18. 2800 B.C.–A.D. 36: Christianity first began in the upper Nile in Egypt ~2800 B.C., then emerged in England around A.D. 36. Christianity was then delivered back to Rome, Palestinia & Israel ... Christmas started in the Algarve, then went through Germany to England. Christianity began in London, but Christmas began in the Algarve.

19.   A.D. 305: Roman Emperor Constantine the Great (R. 306–324) knew of the Book of Predictions via a meeting in Britain and honoured his agreement to install these prophecies into a religion, Christianity, and this became the Bible, and Revelation from Jesus Christ, The Book of Revelation, Revelation, Revelation to John, Apocalypse of John, or The Revelation of St. John the Divine.

20.   1609–10: The Bible was completed by Viscount Francis Bacon and Walter Raleigh installing all the prophetic elements to name the new Christ.

21.   1502–1717: There was then a concerted effort to breed into this line, in secrecy, posthumously, reinvigorating the Royal Holy Grael lineage. This moved away from Borgia & Medici to Boleyn–Raleigh–Bellamy–Hallett, who were all neighbours in Devon & Dorset.

22.   With this line came the true title Pontifex Maximus, "greatest priest", and Pope.

23.   21 July 1425–31 October 1448: John VIII was the penultimate Byzantine Emperor.

       6 January 1449–29 May 1453: His younger brother Constantine XI Palaiologos was the last Byzantine Emperor. Palaiologos died defending Constantinople.

       "Palaiologos" means 'old-reason' or 'the last word'.

       These were the last Roman Emperors, based out of Constantinople (Istanbul) Turkey.

       There were no formal succession laws, but their surviving younger brother immediately claimed the title 'Roman Emperor', being:

29 May 1453–12 May 1465: Thomas Palaiologos & son
12 May 1465–7 April 1502: Andreas Palaiologos.

24.   1461: Pope Pius II (r. 1458–64) recognised Thomas Palaiologos as the rightful "Emperor of Constantinople" as he
stemmed from Roman Emperor Constantine the Great (R.
306–324) who was both Emperor of Constantinople and the
Roman Emperor.

The recognised Roman Emperor was the 'Emperor of
Constantinople who had been Roman Emperor'. This meant
Thomas Palaiologos was also Pontifex Maximus ~ Pope.

25.   1461–65: It is at this point that the titles Roman Emperor,
Pontifex Maximus, and Pope begin to be obfuscated jointly
& severally in ambiguity, patent ambiguity, and tacit silence,
demanding passive acquiescence from all players, cognitive
avoidance from all players, and cognitive avoidance from all
historians ... as though everything was not to be declared, and
records were stolen, redacted, or altered and reinserted, as is
the practise from the Tower of London to Westminster Abbey
to the State Paper Office at the State Paper Commission to the
Public Record Office in the National Archives at Kew, much
of which has been interfered with by Jesuits under control of
the Pope, many of whom were MI5 agents.

26.   12 May 1465: Roman Emperor, Thomas Palaiologos died,
and his son, Andreas Palaiologos became the new Roman
Emperor, and with it the title Pontifex Maximus.

27.   1494: Roman Emperor Andreas Palaiologos sold his claim to
the Roman Emperor imperial title to Charles VIII of France
(R. 1483–94). Both were 24 years old.

28. 7 April 1498: 4 years later, Charles VIII (27) walked into a lintel at Château d'Amboise where he was born, and knocked himself dead ... clearly illustrated with the 1994 'Dumb and Dumber', on the 496th anniversary of his death.

29. 1498: Charles VIII's Roman Emperor titles were then inherited by his cousin, Louis XII of France (R. 1498–1515) aged 35.

Anne Boleyn was a maid of honour to Louis XII's wife, Mary of England or Mary Tudor, who became Queen consort of France (9 October 1514–1 January 1515) and was Henry VIII's younger sister. Not a bad looker.

30. 1515–22: At this juncture it appears the Roman Emperor and Pontifex Maximus titles went the way of the Christian mystic female conspirators, Anne Boleyn (13), Claude of France (15), Mary Tudor (18) and Margaret of Navarre (22) ...

Their goal was to take control of the title Pontifex Maximus, and Pope, with enough leverage using the title Roman Emperor, to negotiate the Catholic Church & Papal Vassal States out of England and Wales, and into the arms of Queen Anne Boleyn's controllable future husband, Henry VIII ... who would then have an accident in early 1536, go mad, and sentence Queen Anne Boleyn to be 'executed', but retain her title Marquesse of Pembroke, and Queen of England in her own right, to breed posthumously, again, thus reinvigorating the Holy Grael Royal lineage ... now with the title Pontifex Maximus, Pope, and Roman Emperor attached ... to pick up the recurrence bloodlines, wherein the Holy Grael male was to be a descendant of Roman Emperor Antoninus Pius (R. 138–161), Jesus' great-great-grandson in the Algarve, as is Joseph Gregory Hallett.[1]

To confirm all of this, Pope Francis abdicated his highest style and title 'Vicar of Christ' to Joseph Gregory Hallett, Easter Friday 2020.

31.   Louis XII of France's daughter, Claude of France ruled from 1 January1515 to 20 July 1524, and married Francis I of France (1494, R. 1 Jan. 1515–1547). Both were 14 years old.

1 January 1515–January 1522: Once again, Anne Boleyn was the maid of honour to the Queen consort France, and remained in Queen Claude's service another 7 years.

Anne's elder sister, Mary Boleyn (19) was having a rather open affair with the new husband French King Francis I (24) and his courtiers too.

Late 1519: Mary Boleyn was running distraction for Anne Boleyn, which got Mary removed from the French Court.

January 1522: Younger sister Anne Boleyn returned to England 27 months later with the titles Pontifex Maximus, Roman Emperor, and Pope.

32.   1525–36: Anne Boleyn then guided England's break from Rome. England created it's own Episcopal See – the Church of England. The England See is still not referred to enough.

"Episcopal See" is a shifty word for 'Church Jurisdiction'. Episcopal = church leadership; See = Jurisdiction.

"Ecclesiastical jurisdiction" = Church leaders jurisdiction over other leaders & laity. Laity are the nuns, brothers, attendees, the unpaid, and can include all people at large. So Church of England definitely had its own Episcopal See.

33.   1527–32: Henry VIII proposed and Anne Boleyn accepted. They were now engaged, until they married on 16 November 1532 & 15 January 1533, and Anne became Queen in her own right on 1 June 1533, continuing after her 1536 execution ....

24 January 1536: Henry VIII went mad from a jousting accident; and 4 months later on ...

19 May 1536: Queen Anne 'Bulleyn' was 'executed' of 'Marquis of Penbroke' but continued to live as Pontifex Maximus, Roman Emperor, and female Pope guiding the new Christian Church of England religion – Protestant.

"Officiate": 'to perform & carry out the office, duties or function of any member of the clergy, as an official in some contest, divine service, religious ceremony, serving as a priest or minister, acting as official, timekeeper, or referee in the contest.

"Salvation" is protecting from harm, risk, loss, destruction, deliverance from the power of sin; and deliverance from penalties & foreign taxation ~ saving or redemption.

"Protestant": 'Pontifex Romanus Officiates The Emperor Salvation Through Anglican New Testament' ... or 'Roman Pontiff Officiates The Emperor Salvation Through Anglican New Testament'.

In this case, the Roman Pontiff or Pope (PR) was Queen Anne Boleyn, so an anagram of "PROTESTANT" might be: Queen Anne Boleyn (PR) carries out the Office of the (OT) Emperor's deliverance from the power of Sin & foreign taxation (ES) through The Anglican New Testament' (TANT) ... or 'Roman Pontiff Officiates (PRO) The Emperor no foreign taxation (TES) Through Anglican New Testament (TANT) first printed in English in 1526, 1534 & 1535.

1537: Queen Anne Boleyn, Marquesse of Pembroke then bred posthumously creating the Royal Holy Grael lineage with these titles Pontifex Maximus, Roman Emperor and Pope to back it up. Posthumous Queen Anne Boleyn Marquess of Pembroke was now the Silent Roman Empress, and had reinvigorated & restarted the Holy Grael lineage.

34.　12 May 1465–7 April 1502: Andreas Palaiologos held the title Roman Emperor as he was nephew to the last in situ Constantinople Roman Emperor Constantine XI Palaiologos 1449–53.

1502: Andreas Palaiologos sold his other titles to Queen Isabella I of Castile (R. 1474–1504) and husband King Ferdinand II of Aragon (R. 1479–1516). These were known as "The Catholic Monarchs", and their Crown known as the Crown of Aragon.

35.　England then stole Spain's Crown of Aragon for 372 years, 1603–1975. This was done to really show who held the titles Pontifex Maximus, Roman Emperor and Pope for the last 505 years, 1519 to 2024 ... or 1533 to 2024+.

36.　Spain did nothing about it because it was true – nothing for 372 years, not even the fascist Dictator General Francisco Franco (r. 1938–20 November 1975) who raised Juanito as his own, and mind-controlled him into shooting his younger brother Alfonso at point black range in the face, killing off his competition on 9 March 1956 at their exile home Vila Giralda in Estoril (see page 286).

22 November 1975: Franco died, and Juanito became King Juan Carlos of Spain. Five (5) years later on ...

15 September 1981: King Juan Carlos of Spain inseminated Princess Diana and sired Prince William of England.

This was done on The Principal's 20th birthday, to mark Joseph Gregory Hallett as the true King of England.

This was confirmation from the Monarchies of England & Spain that Joseph Gregory Hallett was the Royal Holy Grael backed up with Pontifex Maximus, Roman Emperor and Pope.

37. **26 March 1953:** The future Pope Paul VI (R. 21 June 1963–6 August 1975/78) then backed this up with the 1953 film 'Roman Holiday' which names "Joseph Gregory Hallett" at least three times, and shows "Joseph Gregory" with Crown, gives the year 2017, and has Pope Paul's real life lover cutting the hair of Princess Anne who plays Queen Elizabeth II getting a haircut of her real Royal Styles and Title, leaving only colour of law Styles from 26 March 1953.

38. **10–15 September 1961:** The future Pope Paul VI knew Joseph Gregory Hallett had been born during Rosh Hashanah at the time of the Mashiach, with the name predicted by 'Roman Holiday', which anagrams 'H. Royal Domain', and was likely to survive.

39. **21 June 1963:** As soon as Pope Paul VI was elected, he stopped himself and any future Popes having a Coronation or being Crowned, then gave the Papal Crowns away, sending them overseas to America and other countries to ensure no Pope would ever be a Prince of Europe again, because the Predicted One had been born at the right time with the right name, in the correct location, as the Royal Holy Grael Roman Emperor Pontifex Maximus and Pope to herald in the New Age and claim his titles Christ & King of England.

    Christ is automatically the King of England.

40. **1975:** For his troubles, Pope Paul VI was drugged after Easter 1975, and by Christmas 1975 had been replaced with an "Impostor Pope" who tried to undo his new lack of status – No Crowns, No Coronations, and Not a Prince of Europe – but failed.

41. Both Jesus who held the title Christ, and Joseph Gregory

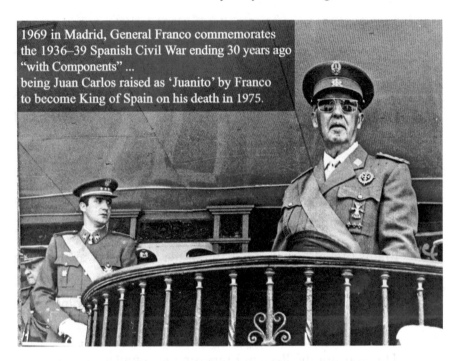

1969 in Madrid, General Franco commemorates the 1936–39 Spanish Civil War ending 30 years ago "with Components" ...
being Juan Carlos raised as 'Juanito' by Franco to become King of Spain on his death in 1975.

Hallett were 'The highest initiate of the Egyptian Mysteries' at 18 years of age – trained by the Elohim – the Shining Ones.

42. 13 March 2013: This is why there have been two Popes since 2013. 12+1 or "13" marks 'Jesus on the March' & 'the one with the title Christ above all others with the title Christ'; "3" marks the Trinity; and "13" marks King. It was Joseph Gregory Hallett who discovered and registered the Two Jesus, fulfilling his "Gregory Hallett" anagram – 'reg tt Holy Grael', as per 2 Corinthians 11:4, ... talk of the second Jesus.

43. 13 March 2013: Pope Francis delayed a few days to became Pope to signal he was occupying the position as second Pope awaiting the person with the title Christ above all others with the title Christ ... of the Holy Grael Trinity Deus Desposyni lineage ... to be given the title King, Roman Emperor, Pontifex Maximus and Pope.

44.   March 2012, May 2013 and April 2014: "King" came in the form of a Letter from Queen Victoria, dated 17 March 1850, which states "Assemble him Claimant". This was given to Joseph Gregory Hallett three times by Queen Victoria's great-great-great-great-grandson, the Sangrëal, and retained by The Principal.

45.   There was the King of the Romans ... Emperor of Rome, Pontifex Maximus ... and Holy Roman Emperor, which devolved upon the Principality of Hannover.

     In this title obfuscation: "King of the Romans" was the King of Germany (962–1806) under the Holy Roman Empire. German electors chose the king, who went to Rome to be crowned Emperor by the 'Pope'.

     This was not the Roman Emperor, but sounded similar.

46.   1834 & 1840: A lot of titles were assumed ...
     The German 'Albert' who married Queen Victoria was not a prince, had no titles, and was just 'Albert of Saxony'.

     The British Albertine title of 'Saxe-Coburg and Gotha' was assumed by the illegitimate Albert of Saxony in 1840, betraying his elder legitimate half-brother who held the real Ernestine German title, Duke of Sachsen-Coburg und Gotha, with its 13 castles and 0.5% of Germany ... but Ernst had no legitimate heirs.

     The British-invented title "Saxe-Coburg and Gotha" was created in the UK for Albert to marry Queen Victoria, under a misspelt false name, and a false citizenship, for a bigamous marriage that Queen Victoria could annul at a moments notice, or by Albert's timely arranged death in 1861.

Albert of Saxony was chosen because he looked exactly like Victoria's first husband Blind Prince George of Cumberland who Queen Victoria married on Mother's Day, Sunday 9 March 1834 in Mt St Michel. The chambermaids couldn't tell Queen Victoria's two husbands apart.

47. 1893: The British "of Saxe-Coburg and Gotha" then assumed the German lands and titles 'of Sachsen-Coburg und Gotha', but 24 years earlier, in 1869, Duke Ernst II of Sachsen-Coburg und Gotha had given us his sword, defining his allegiance to our cause – the Royal Lineage Sangrëal–Christ–Holy Grael. This sword was presented to The Principal on Leap Day 2012, and used for his elevations on 1 March 2012.

48. 1918: WWI and Communist conflicts ensured the British Duke of Saxe-Coburg and Gotha and British Duke of Sachsen-Coburg und Gotha lost the titles and lands of Sachsen-Coburg und Gotha, which were then assumed by Communists, although faulty paperwork ensured the lands were returned whenever the unseen part of the plan had been fulfilled ... which was The Principal proving himself.

49. Late March–11 April 1945: USSR destroyed Justus Perthes 'Almanach de Gotha printing press, plate by plate, with General George S. Patton watching & waiting for 9 days, aggrieved that he was instructed to allow it to happen.

50. 1945–89: Queen Elizabeth II, an illegitimate herself, then gave Sachsen, Coburg, Gotha and all of Thuringia to Russia, so the true Royal Story could not be investigated until after the Cold War:

1989–1998: Justus Perthes' family regained the rights to print the 'Almanach de Gotha', but it's printing was delayed another

9 years, and moved to London, under the strict oversight of Queen Elizabeth II.

1998–2014: King Juan Carlos I of Spain was the Honorary President of the 'Almanach de Gotha'. Queen Elizabeth II was on the Society of Friends of the Almanac Honorary Patronage Committee ...

The 'Almanach de Gotha' editing committee worked together to ensure each others' illegitimacy was not exposed, quid pro quo ...

Juan Carlos requested that the bigamous birth of his wife Sofia's great-great-grandfather in 1845 was not included;

Queen Elizabeth II knew King Juan Carlos I of Spain had mated with Princess Diana on The Principal's 20th birthday conceiving Prince William, and that this was an attempt to steal hubris off the Roman Emperor, Pontifex Maximus, and Pope of the Royal Holy Grael lineage, for the illegitimate Prince William ...

Queen Elizabeth II requested King Juan Carlos I of Spain not declare in the 'Almanach de Gotha' that he was the natural father of Prince William, conceived on The Principal's 20th birthday ...

The Principal Joseph Gregory Hallett exposed King Juan Carlos I of Spain, and ...

Six weeks later King Carlos had his leg broken in Africa; and was forced to abdicate on 31 May 2014.

The leg represents Kingship, so the Kingship was broken in Spain and the UK.

At the same time, Portuguese Navy boat Reg "1165", attended The Principal, parking 30 metres off his cave at Carvoeiro, disembarking their inflatable and running up and down the 60 metre bay coastline, as though they were searching for a path up the cliff-face.

This was the same cliff-face and cave Sir Walter Raleigh had visited from midday Saturday 27 July 1596 to Sunday 4 a.m., publishing his drawings identifying this cliff-face in his Rosicrucian Cosmography in October 1618, two weeks prior to his 'execution'.

51.   The sword of the Duke of Sachsen-Coburg und Gotha is used to mark the Christ, and the sword of the Duke of Sachsen-Coburg und Gotha was presented to Joseph Gregory Hallett on Leap Day 2012. The last time it was brought out was 1959.

52.   Pontifex Maximus, Pope, and Roman Emperor contribute to the title Christ.

53.   All of these titles became joined in the Royal Holy Grael lineage that Queen Anne Boleyn had reinvigorated, and added the appropriate licenses, and likenesses.

54.   Joseph Gregory Hallett was then invested with the style and titles Lord Chancellor Arch-Treasurer of the Kingdom of England ... the Duchy of Sachsen-Coburg und Gotha, and the Principality of Hannover, on 1 March 2012.

Arch-Treasurer is synonymous with Prince Elector & Arch-Banner-Bearer; and it was the Prince Elector of Hannover who became Kings of the United Kingdom of Great Britain in 1714–1837–1901.

These Style and Titles affirm, confirm, ratify and sanctify Joseph Gregory Hallett as The Principal, and can be crowned King United Kingdom of Great Britain, and King of the Kingdom of England, and King of England, and King of the Land and People of England, especially where "People" is used to define living men and women, who have a voice of their own as Sovereign beings of the land, air, water, sea & See.

205 ESTORIL "La Giralda" — Residência de los Condes de Barcelona

The house where the current king of Spain, Don Juan Carlos, spent his childhood
with his parents in exile in Estoril / © Cascais Historical Archive

Above pictures: Left: "Vila Giralda" is Spanish for 'she who turns' and applies to Juan Carlos' tennis-playing model girlfriend, Chantelle, the love of his life, who left him for The Principal's co-author.

Juan Carlos then married Sofia on the rebound, but had at least four (4) affairs with Princess Diana, three (3) of them published in Hello magazine.

Right: December 1996: Princess Diana turned up for this private house party at Vila Giralda, Estoril, Portugal, for the 50th golden anniversary of King Juan Carlos' mother, Countess of Barcelona Doña María de las Mercedes of Bourbon-Two Sicilies, Princess of Spain (1910–2000) published by Gtres on 10/06/2017.

Vila Giralda means 'she who turns' and Princess Diana is the only one turning, and looks directly towards her lover, King Juan Carlos of Spain, the father of Prince William of the UK of GB & NI.

Vila Giralda was then sold in 2002 for 2.7 or 4.5 million Euros then demolished in February 2017. The extra 2.2 million was an embezzlement.

Eight (8) months after this photo was staged, Princess Diana underwent an "unlawful killing" in August 1997.

They all look like the body doubles posing for this photo.

Endnotes

1   'The Hidden King of England – Arma Christi – Unveiling the Rose', p. 1056.

Chapter Eighteen – The printed
English language Bible emerges through Anne Boleyn

The Latin Bible or 'Vulgate' existed in Spanish, German and French, but for some reason an English version was deemed heresy; and anyone found in unlicensed possession of a "Scripture in English" was liable to the death penalty.

Why – because the Pope knew that England was going to be a breakaway Papal Vassal State, and not a colony, but its own dominion.

John Wycliffe (c.1320s–31 December 1384) was an English scholastic philosopher, and seminary professor at the University of Oxford. He was an influential dissident within Catholic priesthood, and helped create Protestantism.

1382: John Wycliffe completed his translation of the Latin Bible into Middle English and published the first New Testament English Bible. Wycliffe's Bible was published 1382–95, with 250 manuscripts surviving and now selling for US$1.7 million each.

1526: William Tyndale (c.1494~6 October 1536) translated the more original Hebrew and Greek New Testament scriptures and part of the Old Testament into Middle English. Tyndale changed God's name from 'Iehouah' to "Jehovah". The 2009 film 'Avatar' uses "I wah" for "Iehouah".

The entire New Testament was first published in English in 1526 by Tyndale, and was the first Bible in England to be made on the printing press. Tyndale revised it in 1534 & 1535.

Anne Boleyn's spiritual awakening during her teenage years in France, under "The First Modern Woman" Marguerite de Navarre, and Queen Claude, spurred her on to become a catalyst and facilitator for Christian Mysticism and Christianity's Reformation, attributed to Henry VIII.

Anne Boleyn was continuing the work of Emperor Constantine, ensuring prophecies could be comprehended by tradespeople & non-Christians, then eventually by Christians.

Anne Boleyn supported William Tyndale's 1528 book 'The Obedience of a Christian Man' which advocated the King as head of his country's church, and not the Pope.

Anne Boleyn ensured Henry VIII had a copy, providing him with the rationale to break with Catholic Church of Rome in 1534 and create his own Church in England in Queen Anne Boleyn's image – that of the Holy Grael with its own Pope, having its own ecclesiastical jurisdiction over its own Episcopal See ... big words for 'the Church of England could do what it liked, where it like'.

The word "Catholic" comes from 'Catchment', defined as all it could see, hence the Holy See. So Catholic Churches were built on hill tops with tall spires, and would send a man up the spire to spot all he could see, and everyone who lived within that area was in their Catchment, in the 'Catholic See', and was counted Catholic.

1485–1551: Sweating sickness was a mysterious disease; some died within hours.

1528: Sweating sickness broke out in London; the Court was dispersed, and many died. Anne Boleyn was sick in Hever Castle, and her brother-in-law ...

1528, 22 June: William Carey died of sweating sickness.

1533, 25 June: Mary Tudor caught sweating sickness and died of it on 25 June 1533.

1529: Simon Fish wrote 'Supplication for Beggars' calling for monarchs to reduce the evil excesses of the Catholic Church. Anne Boleyn gave Henry VIII the 16-page pamphlet.

1535: William Tyndale was arrested and jailed in Castle Vilvoorde for more than a year, then convicted of heresy, strangled to death, and once dead, burnt at the stake on 6 October 1536. Vilvoorde was just 7 miles south of Margaret of Austria's Palace at Mechelen.

1537: Henry VIII had John Rogers (1505–55) publish a Bible under the author pseudonym "Thomas Matthew", but it was really William Tyndale's New Testament. This is called the 'Matthew Copy'.

1609–11: King James VI/I "the Shit" (R. 1603–25) then got 47 or 54 scholars together for 33 months to produced the 1611 King James Bible. They used 76% of Tyndale's Old Testament and 83% of Tyndale's New Testament.

2002: William Tyndale was placed 26th of the 'Top 100 Greatest Britons' ... but he was non-Jesuit English ... so it was a curse upon his grave.

So there were Bibles published in English in 1382 (NT) in 1526 (OT & NT) in 1534 (rev), 1535 (rev) and in 1537 (Matthew Copy) with Queen Anne Boleyn 'executed' in May 1536 at the end of the most intense first printing press publishing in English of the Old Testament and New Testament, for the first time.

1526–35: The full Bible was published in English, under the guidance and or promotion of Anne Boleyn, who became Queen Anne Boleyn of England in her own right.

24 January 1536: Henry VIII had a jousting accident, rendering him unconscious with an old festering leg wound that never healed, and drove him mad over the next 11 years. Four (4) months later ...

19 May 1536: Anne Boleyn, Queen of England in her own right, left the scene having completed almost all her destiny work, except for the Holy Grael breeding ... to be done without Henry VIII's madness.

1596–1610: Viscount Francis Bacon and Walter Raleigh deciphered the Book of Prophecies from the 1596 Faro book raid and inserted these codes into the 1611 King James Version of the Bible, including 'Though shalt covet they neighbour's wife' as an allusion to Bacon's father, Robert Dudley, KG, PC (1532–88) coveting Queen Elizabeth to sire Viscount Francis Bacon (b. 1561) & Robert Devereux, 2nd Earl of Essex (b. 1565).

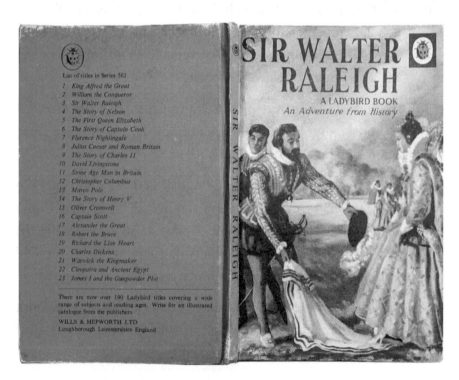

The apocryphal story that Sir Walter Raleigh lay down his coat for the Virgin Queen Elizabeth to avoid a puddle, is code that they:

i.   Used the same coat of arms from the same family as both descended from Queen Anne Boleyn – the Silent Empress;

ii.   Queen Elizabeth used the appellation 'Virgin Queen' to acknowledge Sir Walter Raleigh founded North America with the title Christ;

iii.   Sir Walter Raleigh held the title Christ and could claim the title King of England over Elizabeth I, or after her;

iv.   Jesus entered into Jerusalem upon coats laid down ...
Mark 11:8: And many spread their garments in the way:
Luke 19:36: as he went, they spread their clothes in the way.
2 Kings 9:13: every man ... took his garment and put it under him ... and proclaimed, 'Jehu is king'.

v.   Strictly speaking this was only for the House of David to use, but in his absence, the secondary House of Joseph used it.

In this Walter Raleigh was right, the Queen loved to be surrounded by handsome young men, and Raleigh was one of the handsomest men of his time. It was an age when men wore clothes of velvet and brocade, with ornaments of gold and many jewels. Raleigh's youthful figure set off these clothes to advantage, and with his trim, pointed beard, and his eager eyes, he must have looked like a hero out of a story book.

He was as gallant as he was good-looking. When Raleigh arrived at the palace, Elizabeth was walking in the grounds, surrounded by her courtiers.

Suddenly the Queen stopped. The path was wet and muddy, and Elizabeth in her golden shoes and silken dress, hesitated to pass. The courtiers did not know what to do, but in an instant Raleigh had swept off his rich velvet cloak, and spread it across the mud at the Queen's feet.

18

Henry marriages & annulments or divorce encouraged Christianity

To get his marriage annulled with Catherine of Aragon, Henry VIII sent a direct appeal to Pope Clement VII (r. 19 November 1523–25 September 1534) born Giulio di Giuliano de' Medici, but:

1527: Charles V, Holy Roman Emperor and King of Germany (R. 1519–56) sacked Rome and was holding the Medici Pope Clement VII prisoner in Hadrian's Mausoleum, Castel Sant'Angelo, in Rome from 6 May 1527–October 1528.

1527, 6 May: The prison keeper was the French Charles III (1490–1527, Duke of Bourbon 1521–27 who died in battle the first day, 6 May 1527, his titles forfeit.

1528, 6 May –20 August: The second prison keeper was the German Georg von Frundsberg, a soldier of some distinction who promised to hang the Pope with a golden rope, but died 20 August 1528, his family extinct; and

1528, 20 August: The third prison keeper Charles V Holy Roman Emperor, King of Germany & King of Italy (R. 1519–56) was loyal to his aunt, Catherine of Aragon.

To complicate matters, Pope Clement VII (r. 1523–34) insisted on making his decision on Henry VIII's marriage annulment (divorce) in Rome, but Rome was no longer his.

1527, 6 May: The leaderless French army destroyed & pillaged Renaissance Rome forever. When Rome is attacked, the Romans have a policy of depopulating the city, to return afterwards to see the damage, and what can be done to repair it. A month later ...

1527, 6 June: Pope Clement VII paid a ransom of 400,000 ducat in exchange for his life. In 2023 this was variously £13m, £43m in labour or £103m income, so around £50 million. Pope Clement VII surrendered Castel Sant'Angelo with himself inside, then also surrendered the rights to Parma, Piacenza, Civitavecchia and Modena to the Holy Roman Empire, represented by Charles V, nephew of Catherine of Aragon, and the subject of the marriage annulment, or divorce.

1528, October: 4 months later, the Medici Pope Clement VII was allowed to escape from Castel Sant'Angelo disguised as a peddler. He emerged into Rome devastated and depopulated. The Renaissance was over, so Pope Clement VII took refuge 60 miles north in Orvieto, then 40 miles north in Viterbo.

Republican enemies of the Medici family took advantage of the chaos in Rome and expelled Pope Clement VII's Medici family out of Florence.

Thomas Cromwell then brought the 'Supplication against the Ordinaries and Submission of the Clergy' before Parliament. These Acts recognised English Royal Supremacy over the Roman Catholic Church, and completed the break with the Vatican in Rome, whose authority was now pillaged, destroyed & tenuous.

May 1532: Sir Thomas More resigned as Lord Chancellor, and Thomas Cromwell became Henry VIII's chief minister, and Chancellor of the Exchequer 1533–40.

1529 & 1531: French and Italian ambassadors concurred, it was essential to have Anne Boleyn's approval to influence the English government. Anne Boleyn was able to receive diplomats, grant petitions, give patronage, and plead the cause of foreign diplomats. Anne Boleyn simply had enormous influence over Henry VIII before their marriage 1529–1532, and during their marriages 1532/33–1536.

1531: Queen Catherine of Aragon was banished from court and her rooms were given to Anne Boleyn. The Boleyn family chaplain Thomas Cranmer (1489–1556) was then made 'Lord Archbishop of Canterbury' 23 May–3 December 1553, and then 'Archbishop of Canterbury' 3 December 1533–4 December 1555.

Under Catholic Bloody Mary (R. 1553–58) Thomas Cranmer was charged with heresy, and burnt at the stake on 21 March 1556. No good deed goes unpunished.

1527–32: It was Anne Boleyn who solidified England's international position with France, before she became Queen, and this contributed to France sacking Rome in 1527, jailing the Medici Pope, extorting the Medici Pope for ~£50 million (2023 values) allowing the Medici Pope Clement VII to escape in 1528, then evicting the Medici family out of Florence.

1532, 1 September: In recognition of this, Henry VIII performed an investiture granting Anne Boleyn, the Marquessate of Pembroke, making her the highest ranking peeresse in England. Anne Boleyn was now in the top six of England's elite ... with silver falcon badge.

Henry VIII's great-uncle had formerly held the title Earl of Pembroke, and Pembroke lands. In 1532 there were only 3 Dukes and 2 Marquesses in England, being the:

Duke of Suffolk, Charles Brandon, Henry VIII's brother-in-law, via his sister;

Duke of Richmond and Somerset, Henry Fitzroy, Henry VIII's illegitimate son;

Duke of Norfolk, Thomas Howard, Anne Boleyn's uncle;

Marquess of Pembroke, Anne Boleyn; and

Marquess of Dorset, Henry Grey.

Many of the early Dukes and Marquess were absent at this time, most notably the Duke of Cornwall, absent 1511–37, then with the minority Edward VI (9–15) & absent 1547–1603.

1584–1603: All titles surrounding the Duke of Cornwall were given to Walter Raleigh as Queen Anne Boleyn's grandson, e.g. Lord Warden of the Stannaries of Cornwall, allowing judicial, military & financial rule in Cornwall, and as the silver & tin coins were mined and minted, controlling the money pit.

With the first date as the date of creation, the Duke and Marquess around this time were:

1138: Earl of Pembroke. 7th creation, Jasper Tudor, 1st Duke of Bedford (1431–95) forfeit 1461–85.

"1 September 1532–36, Marquess of Pembroke, 9th creation, Anne Boleyn".

1532–36: Marquesse of Pembroke, never forfeit and passed to The Principal.

1551–70: Earl of Pembroke, 10th creation, William Herbert.

1337: The Duke of Cornwall was absent 1511–37. While Edward VI ruled in his minority, 1547–53, the title Duke of Cornwall was not used. The title Duke of Cornwall was not filled 1547–1603 and was essentially, effectively and financially with Sir Walter Raleigh 1584–1603, and on-going.

1397: Marquess of Dorset, 1530–1554 was forfeit and beheaded by Bloody Mary.

1397–99: Duke of Norfolk was absent 1399–1425, 1485–1514 and 1572–1660.

1483: Thomas Howard KG, PC, 3rd Duke of Norfolk, 1524–54.

1444: Duke of Buckingham, absent 1521–1623, extinct from 1687.

1397: Marquess of Somerset, absent 1399–1410.

1443–44: This became the Duke of Richmond and Somerset.

1525–36: It was recreated for Henry VIII's son Henry FitzRoy, 1st Duke of Somerset, then absent 1536–47, until its 4th creation for Edward Seymour 1547–52, then absent 1552–1623, 1624–41.

1444, 14 September–2 May 1450: William de la Pole was made Marquess of Suffolk, then elevated to Duke of Suffolk (1448–50).

1448–50: Duke of Suffolk, 2nd creation Charles Brandon, Duke of Suffolk 1514–45.

1494: Duke of York merged with the crown 1509–1605, but then re-emerged for the Jesuit King's son, Charles, Duke of York, who became King Charles I (R. 1625–49) and faked his own execution as King of Brittaine in 1649, surviving to 1670. Both James I & Charles I destroyed the Royal lineage of England, Brittaine, and the United Kingdom of Great Britain.

Chapter Nineteen
Henry VIII's fall from Grace on 24 January 1536

1536, 7 & 29 January: Henry VIII's first wife, Catherine of Aragon died of cancer of the heart on 7 January. Her funeral and burial were held in Peterborough Abbey on the 29th, the same place Mary, Queen of Scots had been buried. Five days prior on ...

1536, 24 January: The widower Henry VIII was knocked off his horse in a jousting tournament and rendered unconscious for two hours. "This was his only sorrow." Five days later on ...

1536, 29 January: The same day Catherine of Aragon was buried in Peterborough Abbey ~ Queen Anne Boleyn gave birth to a premature stillborn son.

As Queen Anne Boleyn recovered from her miscarriage, Henry declared he had been seduced into the marriage by means of "sortilege" – spells or deception (French).

1536, last week of January: Everything fell apart in England, like a house of cards built on Spanish curses. New mistress and 3rd wife to be Jane Seymour (28) then moved into the royal quarters.

Henry VIII was 44 years old when he was jousting off his horse, and this did many things, and changed many things, including:

i. It re-opened and aggravated a previous wound that festered and painfully ulcerated with pus-filled boils for his next 11 years. Henry became irritable, had mood swings, and from his lack of mobility, contracted gout. All of this dramatically changed his personality and temperament;

ii.   Henry VIII's concussion placed his brain in trauma that left immediate debilitating damage, and led to a neuroendocrine growth hormone deficiency, causing him to become obese, growing a 54 inch waist, a 4½ foot or 1.4 metre girth. This fat is called 'adipos' ~ when it astonishes the imagination ~ fat to the death;

iii.   Henry VIII's jousting accident would change the entire course of the English Monarchy ... as though the Jesuits had planned it;

iv.   24 January 1536 was the day that led to the change of the Tudor English Monarchy to a Jesuit British Stuart Monarchy in 1603;

v.   It was this moment on 24 January 1536 that Queen Anne Boleyn became the true monarch of England, albeit briefly, and with an increasingly mad partner as king, who also increasingly distanced himself;

vi.   Henry VIII's rule can be separated into before and after his trauma: 22 April 1509–24 January 1536 ~ 26 years 9 months & 24 January 1536–28 January 1547 ~11 years & 6 days.

vii.   From 24 January 1536 it was obvious to all around him that Henry VIII was physically and mentally sick, and deteriorating into a continual liability. Henry had painfully ulcerated pus-filled festering wounds that stank; irritable with mood swings, debilitated with obesity and gout, so he was moved around in a mechanical tram ~ a wheelchair;

viii.   All of this dramatically change of his temperament and personality so that Wife 2 would not know her husband, and Wife 3 would be marrying a completely different man.

It was the king's madness, and there was nothing they could do about it, other than plan around it;

ix. Henry VIII's wives' pattern of stillborn pregnancies and infant deaths, and Henry's mental deterioration suggests he suffered from 'spikey red blood cells', discovered in 1961 as 'McLeod syndrome, Kell positive';

x. The King was mad; and that madness could have been in his spikey red blood, and could be genetic, such that the English line of Kings and Queens wanted to avoid breeding off Henry VIII;

xi. They decided to void Henry VIII's Welsh line;

xii. 47 years later, 1536–1603, Jesuits voided the English Monarchy line, by deceit;

xiii. From 24 January 1536, Queen Anne Boleyn of England was the measure, confirmed by the Kings of Great Britain wearing long thick dark wavy wigs imitating Queen Anne's long thick dark hair, 1603–1795;

xiv. Queen Anne Boleyn had been organising Henry VIII's land-grab of all the Catholic lands and buildings in England, and the recipients of these lands would be the 27 Commissioners in the Trials of Queen Anne Boleyn, close relatives and close friends, as though they were all being exited together;

xv. Queen Anne Boleyn's execution was the first shock-testing for the new Protestants. They survived, and Queen Anne Boleyn daughter, Queen Elizabeth I, was to have the longest female reign in English history, 44 years, 1558–1603; Queen Elizabeth II 1952–2022 is removed from consideration.

xvi. Queen Anne Boleyn and brother George, his wife Jane Boleyn, Viscountess Rochford, and Margaret, Countess of Salisbury then invoked the Holy Grael lineage and planned and practiced their own trials and executions and how to escape them ... and where they would go afterwards, code words, code clothing, code timing and who was who in the Royal hide & seek chain of command of operations;

xvii. The increasingly sick and unaware Henry VIII moved into a pattern of execution and marriage, turning a blind eye to the executions, attempting births, then turning over the marriages;

xviii. Henry VIII farmed out his illegitimate children, elevating the surrogate fathers to Knight of the Garter;

xix. 23 April 1536: George Boleyn was expected to receive the Order of the Garter, but instead, it was granted to Sir Nicholas Carew KG (1496–3 March 1539) who had just married Henry VIII's pregnant mistress Elizabeth Bryan (1500–46) who gave birth to Anne Carew (1520–81) who gave birth to Elizabeth Throckmorton ~ Henry VIII's granddaughter ~ who married Sir Walter Raleigh, grandson of the posthumous Queen Anne Boleyn ... so it went full circle ... the granddaughter of Henry VIII married the grandson of Queen Anne Boleyn;

xx. 8 days later on 1 May 1536: George Boleyn was a principal Jouster, but on 2 May George Boleyn was arrested, tried on 12 May, and beheaded at Tower Hill on 17 May 1536;

xxi. However, George Boleyn's head is not buried with his body in St Peter ad Vincula, nor is Queen Anne Boleyn's, and it is much more likely George Boleyn went to 'The Island' to be with his sister, Queen Anne Boleyn, and tender too the Holy Grael lineage, recently imported by Anne from the

Netherlands, Belgium, France and Paris, originating with Eleanor, the former Queen of France & England;

xxii. 2 days after brother George, Queen Anne Boleyn was 'executed' on 19 March 1536, with her title Queen intact, and her title Marquess of Pembroke intact;

xxiii. Queen Anne Boleyn escaped and the other Boleyn's joined her, along with friends and helpers, some also executed to plan. It was a reunion that was to be repeated 51 years later with Mary, Queen of Scots, and Anne Boleyn's descendants.

1536, 30 May: Henry VIII (45) married Jane Seymour (28).

1540, 6 January: Henry VIII was 48 when he married Anne of Cleves (24), but he could not consummate the marriage within 6 months, so it was annulled on 9 July 1540.

1540, 28 July: Henry VIII (49) married Catherine Howard (1521/25–13 February 1542) who was 14–19 years old.

1541, 23 November: 16 months later, Catherine Howard was stripped of her title queen. This was done to affirm the Queen Anne Boleyn lineage would always be superior to the Howard lineage & Catherine Howard never had her own coronation.

The Howards were still plotting against the Boleyns working with illegitimate pikey Windsors from 2010–15, on-going.

1542, 13 February: George Boleyn's wife, Jane Boleyn was 'executed' to 'The Island', the same day Catherine Howard was 'executed'.

1543, 12 July: Henry VIII (52) married Catherine Parr (31).

30 May 1536–12 July 1543: Henry VIII descended into madness and had 4 wives in 7 years with up to 33 years age difference.

1546: "By late 1546 [Henry] could barely walk and was carried 'to and fro in his chambers' in a pair of specially constructed chairs called trams."[1]

"At Hampton Court [the king] had to be winched into a wheelchair by a series of pulleys."[2]

1546–47: Henry VIII (28 June 1491–28 January 1547) had to be moved about in his final years with the help of mechanical inventions ~ the "wheeled chair". Henry died aged 55 in the Palace of Whitehall, and with him died the Middle Ages.

24 January 1536–47: As founder of Papal-Free England, Queen Anne Boleyn became the true head of the Monarchy of England, no matter how long it took to realise.

It is now time to invoke the Holy Grael lineage.

Joseph Gregory Hallett descends from Eleanor of Aquitane, Queen consort of France (R. 1137–52) and Queen consort of England (R. 1154–89) who instigated the Holy Grael Christian Mysteries, aimed at The Principal, fulfilled by Joseph Gregory Hallett, including pulling the sword from the stone, joining kingdoms, joining time, and retrieving the Coronation Stone Jacob's Pillow, Lia Fáil, the Stone of Scone from Scotland, and removing the Crowns off the Popes, removing the title 'Prince' off the Popes, and removing the title 'Vicar of Christ' off all future Popes. The Principal descends from Henry II of England (R. 1154–89); King John of England (R. 1199–1216); Henry III of England (R. 1216–72); Philip III of France (R. 1270–85); Edward I of England (R. 1272–1307); Edward II of England (R.1307–27), the Earl, Countess and Dukes of Norfolk; Queen Anne Boleyn (R. 1533–36), Sir Walter Raleigh Christ (1502/04–1618/46) and 'the Prince' Samuel Bellamy (23 February 1689–26 April 1717).

Eleanor of Aquitaine (1122–1204) married (1137–52) Louis VII, King of the Franks (R.1137–80) becoming Queen consort of France. They begat Princess Marie of France (1145–98) Countess consort of Champagne, and Regent of Champagne (1179–81 & 1190–97). Mother & daughter rendered the Holy Grael scripture with Chrétien de Troyes.

Queen Eleanor of Aquitaine then married (1152–89) Henry II of England (R. 1154–89) and begat son, King John of England (1166–1216) ... who had the Magna Carta attributed to him ...

King John of England (R. 1199–1216) married (1189, annulled 1199) Isabella, Countess of Gloucester (c.1173–1217) and begat son in 1207 ...

Henry III of England (R. 1216–72) married Eleanor of Provence, Queen consort of England (1223–R. 1236–91) and begat son, Edward Longshanks ...

Philip III of France (1245–R. 1270–85) married Maria of Brabant and begat daughter, Princess Margaret of France.

Edward I Longshanks, King of England (1239–R. 1272–1307) first married (1254–90) Eleanor of Castile and begat Edward II in 1284 ...

King Edward II (R. 1307–27) then married (1299) Princess Margaret of France (c.1279–1318) and begat son in 1300...

Thomas of Brotherton, Earl of Norfolk (r. 1312–38) was the son of King Edward II by his second marriage.

Thomas of Brotherton, Earl of Norfolk married (~1319) Alice Hayles (d. ~1330) and begat daughter, Margaret Countess of Norfolk in 1320.

Margaret Countess of Norfolk (r.1338–99) married Baron John Segrave (1315–53) and begat daughter Elizabeth Segrave in 1338.

Elizabeth Segrave (1338–68) married Baron John Mowbray (1340–r. 1361–68) and begat son Thomas in 1366 ...

Thomas de Mowbray, Duke of Norfolk (1366–r.1397–99) married Elizabeth Fitzalan (1366–1425) & begat daughter Margaret in 1391.

Margaret de Mowbray (1391–1459) married Robert Howard of Tendring (1398–1436) and begat son, John Howard in 1425 ...

John Howard, Duke of Norfolk (r. 1483–85) married Catherine Moleyns (d. 1465) and begat son Thomas Howard in 1443 ...

Thomas Howard, Duke of Norfolk (r.1514–24) married Elizabeth Tilney, Countess of Surrey (~1445–97) and begat daughter Elizabeth Boleyn (c.1480–1538).

Elizabeth Boleyn married Thomas Boleyn, 1st Earl of Wiltshire (1477–1539) and begat daughter Anne Boleyn (1501/07–1536+).

Anne Boleyn (25 or 31) married (1532 & 1533) Henry VIII (1491–1547), became Queen Anne Boleyn, Queen of England in her own right & begat Queen Elizabeth I (1533–R. 1558–1603).

Queen Anne Boleyn (1501/07–36+) then faked her execution and posthumously begat
Mary Boleyn/*Mary y'Noble* (1537–) who begat Walter Raleigh (1502/04–1618/46) Christ 1596–1646 ... and on to The Principal.

Endnotes

1   1986–2016: David Starkey, the "rudest man in Britain" wrote 8 books on Henry VIII.

2   1999: Maria Perry, 'The Word of a Prince: A Life of Elizabeth I from Contemporary Documents', Boydell Press.

Chapter Twenty
The Lisle Letters – Forging History's Past

1 January 1533–31 December 1540: The Lisle Papers were written over eight (8) years. Correspondence was mainly from the London Merchant John Husee alias 'Hussey' (d. Nov. 1548) updating the Lord Deputy of Calais, Lisle, on events in London.

Arthur Plantagenet, 1st Viscount Lisle (*c*.1480–1542) was an illegitimate son of King Edward IV (R. 1461–83) making him half-uncle of Henry VIII (R. 1509–47). He second married (~1529) Honor Grenville, whose earlier daughter, Anne Basset (1520–57) was a mistress of Henry VIII, 1538–39. Viscount Lisle worked as Lord Deputy of Calais out of Staple Inn in Calais ~ his official business location.

1540, 19 May: Lord Lisle was invited to London where he was arrested for Treason. His wife Honor, was placed under house arrest for two years.

1540, 2 June: All his 'Lisle Papers' were seized from Calais, including 515 letters from John Hussey, and another ~2,500 items of correspondence from others.

Henry VIII was seizing all aspects of history and controlling it. He didn't want anyone to know he had somehow faked the physical execution of his second wife, Queen Anne Boleyn in 1536, as recorded in the Lisle Papers.[1]

1540, 3/4 June: The Lisle Papers were transported to London where they were placed in the Tower of London.

1540–1832: The Lisle Papers were then transferred to the Chapter House of Westminster Abbey and stored under the category "Treasury of the Receipt of the Exchequer".

The Chapter House in the East Cloister of Westminster Abbey built 1246–55, has a massive octagonal vaulted ceiling resting on a central column, around which 80 monks sat on tiered seating to meet with the Abbot to 'hold chapter' discussing the day's business, punishments, to read from the rule book of St Benedict, and to pray (off-track).

~1390: Many scenes of the Book of Revelation, Apocalypse and the Last Judgement are painted on the east wall arches. Around the doorway is the 'Tree of Jesse' with small seated figures. The Virgin Mary and Archangel Gabriel are painted as large figures above the doorway revealing the Annunciation. On the floor is written in Latin:

> "As the rose is the flower of flowers,
> so is this the house of houses".

This is very Rosicrucian for:

> 'the essential house is the rose,
> and when it flowers,
> you can smell it,
> and will be drawn to it.
> Just as Pembroke is the house of houses,
> so is Pembroke the Lord of Lords,
> and king of kings'.

1257: The King's Great Council assembled in the Chapter House in Westminster Abbey, effectively beginning English Parliament.

1300s, early: House of Commons had meetings in the Chapter House for a few years, then used Westminster Abbey Refectory.

1535–40: During Henry VIII's Dissolution of the Monasteries, Henry VIII removed the Papal Catholic influence and acquired all their lands and buildings, amounting to a quarter of England ... 16–60%.

This was the biggest land-grab in history.

Henry VIII gave much of this land to his Commissioners, and many of these were hearing the trial of Queen Anne Boleyn, and offered her refuge on their newly acquired estates that had only just been freely granted to them.

1540: Fifty (50) monasteries a month were dismantled, so 600 monasteries dismantled in 1540, including Westminster Abbey, where Henry VIII kicked the Monks.

1540–1832: Henry VIII then stored the Lisle Papers in the Chapter House in the East Cloister of Westminster Abbey, and this became part of the repository for State records for 292 years ... during which time, the Chapter House, East Cloister & Westminster Abbey fell into increasing ruin.

In addition, the Lisle Papers and State records were emotively locked behind "the oldest door in Britain" built ~1050, but this door was physically unlocked, giving all and sundry complete access to Lisle Papers and State records.

All the records were available to be removed, copied, altered and replaced, utilising any monk, most of whom had been coadjutored by the Jesuits ... and all of whom were lonely looking for a greater cause.

These records were also available to be altered by:

i.   Thomas Cromwell Steward of Westminster Abbey, removed and 'be-headed' on 28 July 1540;

ii.   Sir Anthony Denny, who was heavily patronised and yet specialised in making himself absent. Denny was made Keeper of the Privy Purse 1536–47; Groom of the Stool 1546–47; and Keeper of Westminster Palace 1548/9–51 (the year after Henry VIII died). The Parliamentary records were kept in Westminster Abbey.

iii.   The Parliamentary records of Queen Anne Boleyn's execution were kept 60 yards west across St Margaret Street in the Chapter House in the East Cloister of Westminster Abbey, behind "the oldest door in Britain" ~ an emotive 'front for security' that translated as 'unlocked 410 years'.

The State records & Lisle Papers were stored for 292 years in the increasingly ruined Chapter House, East Cloister & Westminster Abbey. Westminster Abbey was so run down and leaking as to be insecure and open 24/7, day & night, summer and winter.

As such, all of Queen Anne Boleyn's Trial records were stolen. They are missing from history.

1866–72~78: Sir George Gilbert Scott (1811–78) was a prolific English Gothic revival architect who designed and altered over 800 important buildings. He was required to survey St Margaret's, Westminster Abbey, reconstruct the stone vault and roof, re-glaze & re-install the windows. This was done 34–45 years after the records had been removed, 1832–66; also recorded as 11 years later in 1877–78, ending with Scott's death on 27 March 1878, aged 66.

1832: The Home Office ordered the Lisle Papers removed from Westminster Abbey to the State Paper Office at the State Paper Commission.

1852: The State Paper Commission amalgamated with the Public Record Office at Chancery Lane. The Public Record Office still retains its own legal entity – "PRO".

There is no evidence that record removal did not happen repeatedly ... and recently ...

1952–81: These records were moved again and stored in the new Public Records Office ("PRO") at Kew. The National Archives were now less secure than Westminster Abbey with its doors open. The Lisle Papers began to be completely adulterated again, this time by a feminist lesbian swinger, renaming them the "contemporary Lisle Letters".

1977: The Public Record Office moved to Kew, 10 miles wsw of the Tower of London, where PRO holds "Documents from the central courts of law from the twelfth century onwards, including the Court of King's Bench, the Court of Common Pleas, the Court of Chancery, the Court of Exchequer, the Supreme Court of Judicature, the Central Criminal Court, Assizes, and many other courts ... It stores the Lisle Papers under the category "State Papers Foreign and Domestic, Henry VIII, SP3, Lisle Papers".

2003: Public Record Office (PRO) & Historical Manuscripts Commission amalgamated.

2006, 31 Oct.: Office of Public Sector Information (OPSI) contained Her Majesty's Stationery Office (HMSO) and amalgamated with the PRO to become The National Archives (TNA).

Her Majesty's Stationery Office was previously part of the Cabinet Office, where:

i.   Winston Churchill controlled everything about Elizabeth;

ii.   Winston Churchill first faked Elizabeth's parentage, by siring Elizabeth; then

iii.   Faked Elizabeth as a Princess; then

iv.   Consented to her marriage to the German Silent Weapons for Quiet Wars agent, extortionist & Jesuit coadjutor Prince Philip; then

v.   Faked Elizabeth's Proclamation in the London Gazette; then

vi.   Faked The London Gazette Supplements; then

vii.   Faked the Coronation Oath; then

viii. Faked Her Majesty's Stationery Office;[2] and in

ix.   2005–07: The National Archives at Kew, TNA discovered 29 forged documents written on 4 different typewriters, placed in 12 separate files, and cited in at least 3 books; and in

x.   2005–11: The National Archives stated over 1,500 files had gone missing, so 250 files per year, including documents from the courts of several monarchies, & correspondence from Winston Churchill – Queen Elizabeth II's sperm-donor father.

xi.   Around 800 of these records have since been recovered, leaving 700 missing; but

xii.   The National Archive recovered files may have been replaced with 800 forgeries.

xiii. Kew's Chief Executive and Keeper covered this with the standard Jesuit response, which includes faith & distraction:

"We believe most are misplaced rather than permanently lost", or stolen ... then replaced with forgeries after a staff rotation, under a new Chief Executive and Keeper, like Sarah Tyacke 1991–2005, Natalie Ceeney 2005–10, Oliver Morley 2010–13, Acting Kew CE Keeper Clem Brohier 2013–14, followed by Jeff James 2014–2022+ ... The National Archives now being under total Jesuit control.

When there is a breach ~ change the business name, location and executive. They changed the business name repeatedly, changed the business location repeatedly, and changed the Executive repeatedly.

1977: The Public Record Office moved to Kew.

2006: The Public Record Office became The National Archives.

2008: In light of The National Archives having a well spoken policy for open fraud in perfectly empty stylish suits – TNA began hosting the UK Statute Law Database in 2008, which further changed its name to legislation.gov.uk.

2011, October: The National Archives took over the Museums, Libraries and Archives Council. This meant it was open season on replacing documents, and removing books from libraries en masse ~ which they did.

All those well-meaning socialists went about destroying culture. For socialists, it was better a fake monarchy than a real monarchy with power, thus the Queen has remained in power longer than anyone else, as a fake monarch, and as a socialist in line with the socialist cause – to destroy all truth from all history, including her own.

2017: The National Archives reported another 1,000 files had been removed ~ 100 documents per year ~ 0.01% stolen annually. Most of these 1 in 10,000 documents stolen annually were by government officials.

MI5 regularly removes records out of The National Archives, and redacts some information or withholds the record entirely.

MI5 also gives documents to The National Archives twice a year.

So it is fair to say, every six months, MI5 steals documents, edits and redacts documents, and replaces them with a sanitised version of history, or removes the documents entirely, and removes that piece of history entirely:

> "Some information in records—or records themselves— are withheld at the discretion of MI5."[3]

2018: The National Archives: "Additional MI5 records relating to the blacklisting ... have also prompted questions ... the blacklists also targeted other groups, such as unions and minorities ... whether or not these blacklists had an effect on the careers of any individuals ... as of 2018 ... there are still blacklists currently in effect ..."[4]

2018~20: Rewritten applying to this situation in The National Archives at Kew: 'Additional MI5 records relating to the blacklisting of The Principal have prompted questions ... the blacklists targeted anyone who was predicted, such as anyone who fulfilled any Prophecy ... these blacklists had a massively detrimental effect on the careers of the Prophetic Targeted Individual ... as of 2018 ... there are still blacklists currently in effect. These were run by the coadjutored Jesuit Prince Philip, so his demise was required for the prophecies to be fulfilled, and recognised as such.'

The National Archives reports to the Minister of State for Digital Policy, and is part of the 'Department for Digital, Culture, Media and Sport of the United Kingdom of Great Britain and Northern Ireland'.

"The National Archives is part of the 'Department for ... Culture".

"The National Archives is part of the 'Department for ... Sport".

The National Archives holds documents from all the courts of law from the 1100s on, including the courts of several monarchies.

Losing 100–250 files annually amounts to 90,000–225,000 files missing. Around 111,111 of these have been replaced with forgeries, and many more have been redacted beyond comprehension, in support of the preferred rumour ... usually when the Monarch is in some way illegitimate, or extorted for their illegitimacy ... currently confirmed by the illegitimate Queen Elizabeth II giving the UK to the Catholic Church via the EU.

The Public Record Office is supposed to report to the Department for Culture, but reports to the Department for Digital alteration according to Media and Sport, which has become the Culture, and is what the Department for Culture does – Digital alteration in Media and Sport.

As this is their ethos, after decades of university ethics classes, its ethics are as bad as they were when the former Catholic Westminster Abbey stored England's history under a leaking roof with broken windows behind an unlocked door for 292 years, 1540–1832 ... and its heroes, like Sir Walter Raleigh Christ were executed, and the Bible editor, Viscount Francis Bacon, had to fake his death to get any breathing room, and they had to hide their work in code, inside secret societies, to preserve it away from the Roman Catholic Church, Vatican, Jesuits, hagiographers, Chroniclers, embedded historians, and Antiquaries.

After decades of failed university ethics classes, controlled by the same ethos as the Chapter House in Westminster Abbey ... the State Paper Office at the State Paper Commission, the Public Record Office, and The National Archives were just as bad ... reporting to the 'Department for Digital, Culture, Media and Sport', with special focus on Blacklisting, with plausible deniability for the ex-Public Record Office, which is now part of the UK's TNA 'Animal Farm' where everything is its meta-opposite.

The National Archives 'Animal Farm' is an exercise in centralising history to be pilfered and replaced by counter-intelligence agencies like MI5; and the Crown Judiciary, who then legislate the continuing fraud of altered history as the new history to be learnt and taught and enacted into law.

The National Archives 'Animal Farm' is an exercise in centralising history to be pilfered and replaced by foreign counter-intelligence agencies like the Vatican, and Roman Catholic Church.

Civil Statute stems from history, so if the history is false, so are the laws, and so is the Royal family, or rather the Flat Lie Royal family – the incumbents ... as led by Her Majesty's Stationery Office, formerly part of the Cabinet Office led by Winston Churchill, father of the un-Princess Elizabeth suffix Queen.

The World is run on Predictions ... based on prophecy, which names those predicted. These become Targeted Individuals who are blacklisted with the assistance of The National Archives.

MI5 takes its lead from this, then removes, alters and replaces these files and attacks the Predicted Targeted Individual ("PTI") to the end of their life, which they continually arrange with plausible deniability.

Predicted Targeted Individuals are not allowed to work anywhere in the world, as has been the case with The Principal since 2007, but really since 1972, except for 4½ years.

Prince Philip was in charge of targeting Prophetic Individuals, and became the biggest Heroin Trafficker the world has ever seen. Philip trafficked "The Queen's Heroin", and no one could be charged for the Queen's Heroin.

Prince Philip targeted The Principal's family with drugs from 1969, and heroin from 1978. Heroin effectively works against itself, and obliterates any family into non-existence. Surrounding suburbs were partially obliterated by Prince Philip heroin trafficking, and those trafficking the Queen's Heroin from Military Airports became heads of the Judiciary, Judges, Queen's Counsel lawyers, MP's, and Deputy Prime Minister. Any Leader of the Opposition who trafficked the Queen's Heroin became the Prime Minister, from 1984 to 2016.

Since Christ is automatically the King of England, Prince Philip's primary target was whomever fulfilled the Christ Prophecies. Naming the Christ as King of England has been on the top of their list since A.D. 1111, and this was Walter Raleigh and The Principal.

So you can bet that any accounts leading up to naming the Predicted One, the Targeted Individual, the POI, and all the Holy Grail records have been removed and redacted, or replaced with forgeries, and that The Principal who fulfils the Prophecies, and is the Predicted Targeted Individual will be Blacklisted by the PRO & TNA and Prince Philip since 1972, 1996, 2003, 2007 & 2014, 2020 etc, and is currently living grace and favour courtesy of those who can sense the future, and smell the rose that is the house of houses and flower of flowers.

The National Archive fraud at Kew falls in line with The London Gazette fraud, and the Her Majesty's Stationery Office fraud, as well as the Home Office fraud under the daddy fraudster of them all, Winston Churchill, war reporter, illegitimate of the faux King Edward VII, with Churchill as sperm donor father of Queen Elizabeth II.

All of this is affirmed with England's suspicions, and confirmed with not a funeral in sight for Prince Philip (17 April 2021) or Queen Elizabeth, with no-social mixing due to Covid-19 as the cover for covering up their crimes against humanity and the prophecies.

The coadjutored Jesuit SW4QW Prince Philip was never charged for trafficking "The Queen's Heroin", nor with being the biggest heroin trafficker the world had ever seen.

The 3,000 Lisle letters had inconsistent spelling and difficult-to-decipher handwriting, claiming to be the correspondence from England to Arthur Plantagenet, 1st Viscount Lisle stationed in Calais.

Like all the records in the Public Record, they were neglected, and "largely undiscovered down the centuries", meaning there were few references to them, and the Jesuits had not inserted enough providence to support their origination.

Muriel St. Clare Byrne (1895–1983) was a swinging lesbian from a mixed up American-English family, and became a student of Tudor England, which may have been another tragedy for everyone.

In the Public Records Office, Muriel St. Clare Byrne "found the Lisle Letters largely undiscovered down the centuries",[5] although the year of discovery is not given, and the specific location is not given. Finding such records with undefined date is a neon sign that continually flashes "JESUIT" with trumpets & strumpets, 24/7, even in the daylight.

This reeks of the Stubb's Charters, where Oxford History Professor William Stubbs Hon FRSE (1825–1901) also 'found' many documents supporting the Catholic ruse of history.

Muriel St. Clare Byrne completed an exhaustive study in a timeline that doesn't add up, purportedly 1930s–60s, so over 30 years, but cited as "almost 50 years producing the 6 volumes", because publication was delayed for 20 years until 1981, allowing others 20 years to further alter her transcriptions, by which time Muriel St. Clare Byrne was an 86-year-old lesbian, and dead 2 years later.

Muriel St. Clare Byrne purportedly found 3,000 original Lisle Papers in the Public Record Office, and transcribed them, annotated them, added poetic commentary, and arranged the letters in some form of order, perhaps by date!

The publication was then delayed 20 years ... with generous donations from Queen Elizabeth II ... and published in 1981 as 'The Lisle Letters' in six-volumes. They are now stored at Kew, as part of 3,000 documents, "State Papers Foreign and Domestic, Henry VIII, SP3, Lisle Papers".

The Lisle Papers had now been entirely replaced several times.[6]

1540–1950: Westminster Abbey remained unlocked for 410 years.

1540–1832: Westminster Abbey remained unlocked for 292 years, meaning the English State Papers and State records of England in the Chapter House in the East Cloister of Westminster Abbey were available to be stolen, altered and replaced, inserting an entirely fake history, supporting which ever Royal family was doing the altering.

1863–72–78: During renovation of the Chapter House in the East Cloister of Westminster Abbey, the State Records of England could be stolen, altered and replaced, with subsequent 'official embedded' historians using these faked records to legitimise the incumbent Royal family over any challenges.

1872–1950: Freemasons, Notary Public, Lawyers, Judges, Lords, Barons, and Members of Parliament – all Freemasons – caught wind of this. Their solution was to retake the Coronation Stone ~ the Stone of Scone ~ Lia Fáil ~ 'the speaking stone' ~ Jacob's Pillow ~ the Tanist Stone ... out of Westminster Abbey, and render the incumbent British Royal family even less certified in any subsequent Coronation, establishing them as Flat Lie Royal.

1950, Christmas morning: "The son of a Mason is in England called a Lewis."[7] The above Freemasons sent their university student Lewis sons and daughter from Scotland to Westminster to enact their solution and steal back the Coronation Stone. The Coronation Stone was stolen out of Westminster Abbey at 4:00 a.m. on Christmas morning.

This brought to light that all of England's Papers, Records & History had been subject to theft and exchange by those in the know with the power & position to act as thieves ... over centuries. One of Scotland's Lewis sons was studying law, and became a Queens Counsel.

Official embedded Royal Historians did their best to ignore this assault, and obfuscate it, with slight mention as "an affront to the dignity royal".

1953, 2 June: 2½ years later, Silent Weapons for Quiet Wars caught onto this & took over Coronation Day rendering it a Coronation of Silent Weapons for Quiet Wars, which is why it is known as "Coronation Day", and not 'Elizabeth's Coronation'.

2 June 1540– 2 June 1953: was the 413th anniversary of King Henry VIII taking the Lisle Papers, and where "413" ≈ Freemasons withholding the real Crown until Christ (13, 12+1) and "314" ~ Archangel Michael.

Muriel St. Clare Byrne's did 30 years research: "Based on contemporary Lisle Letters (not the original 'Lisle Papers') ... Anne Boleyn was ... 'executed on a scaffold erected on the north side of the White Tower, in front of what is now the Waterloo Barracks' (built 1845)." However, we should we be aware that:

i.　The original Lisle Papers were taken by Henry VIII on 2 June 1540 and placed in the Tower of London, where they could best be altered; then transferred to the Chapter House of Westminster Abbey, where they could best be altered again, or not stolen & replaced, or just stolen.

ii.　Muriel St. Clare Byrne transcribed every letter, meaning she re-wrote them all over 30 years, 1930–60s, and this formed "the contemporary Lisle Letters".

iii.　All published Royal Historians are embedded, and prone to lying on behalf of those who fund them. 'Patron lairs' has been the case "with generous donations from Queen Elizabeth II".

iv.　Muriel St. Clare Byrne researched any agreed upon lie and inserted these into the Lisle Letters.

v.　The Lisle Papers were originally written, then stolen and altered, then altered again, then transcribed, so they were now in a 'manufactured' state as the Lisle Letters to hide the fact that Henry VIII pretended to kill two of his wives, but didn't; so that

vi.   Henry VIII could create a true Holy Grael Royal lineage through his second wife ~ the highly intelligent multilingual Queen Anne Boleyn ~ who retained her title 'Queen of England' and her title Marquesse of Pembroke, and her breeding rights as such.

vii.   The Lisle Papers were altered with enough complexity to delay discovery, until the prophesied Holy Grael lineage deciphered this obfuscated history ... that the Holy Grael lineage would be free of Henry VIII's madness, but Christ would still be the King of England.

viii.   Queen Anne Boleyn's posthumous children were the Holy Grael lineage, and as the mother of Elizabeth I, these were Queen Elizabeth I's half-siblings.

ix.   Posthumous Queen Anne Boleyn had a daughter, Mary y'Noble, whose son was Walter Raleigh of the Holy Grael lineage, Royal, and the predicted line ... meaning it was his role to get the Book of Predictions, gain the title Christ from 1596–46, and reveal its pertinent codes as prophecy of Christ from 1618.

x.   In support of this, Henry VIII had all Anne Boleyn's parish records and portrait's destroyed, so Queen Anne Boleyn, Marquess of Pembroke was unrecognisable living on any estate, from the age of aged 28/29 or 34/35.

        The Lisle Papers were tampered with to suit King Henry VIII and any subsequent Royal family with an inferiority complex, stemming from their Flat Lie Royal status, but really listing and defining the Holy Grael Lineage.

The Privacy Act ensured these Falsified Documents became the new history, and there would never be any Discovery of True Documents, as they were altered by Thomas Cromwell and or Sir Anthony Denny, then transcribed by the lesbian Muriel St. Clare Byrne into "the contemporary Lisle Letters".

For the six execution locations of Queen Anne Boleyn in the Tower of London, the Lisle Letters state the north side of the White Tower, but the exact location is not defined, and remains undecided, except herein.

Endnotes

1   The Lisle Papers did not include any record of the execution of Henry VIII's fifth wife, Catherine Howard, as she 'died' in 1542. The Howards still attack the Boleyns.

2   2019, 1/17 November: Joseph Gregory Hallett declares Patent Ambiguity QEII's Royal Style and Titles.

3   "MI5 At The National Archives | MI5 – The Security Service". www.mi5.gov.uk.

4   2018, 23 July: Ian Cobain, The Guardian, 'Subversive civil servants secretly blacklisted under Thatcher', Prime Minister 1979–90.

5   1983: Ed. Elizabeth Devine, The Annual Obituary – Muriel St Clare Byrne, St James Press, pp. 573–75.

6   The Byrne family are known for still covering up Charles' Royal Crimes in 2017.

7   Masonicdictionary.com.

Chapter Twenty-One
Tower of London Uniforms & the Ceremony of the Keys

It is a military tactic to provide confusion, so that no one has to take responsibility for what has been done, for what was unofficially done, for what was officially treasonous at the time, and for what was done with the Crown's blessing ... otherwise known as Silent Acquiescence and Passive Cognisance to a wink and a nod, with a strange searching look when questioned. This applies to the Tower of London warders and their uniforms.

1485, late August: First Tudor monarch Henry VII (R. 1485–1509) formed the Yeomen Warders, who wore the heraldic Tudor Rose, 1485–1509.

1509, 23–24 June: Henry VIII (R. 1509–47) & Catherine or Aragon (1485–1536) spent the night in the Tower of London, then left for Westminster Abbey to be anointed and crowned together.

~1510–47: Henry VIII lived in the Tower of London, then moved his official residence amongst the Palaces' of Eltham, Greenwich, Hampton Court, Richmond, St James's, Westminster and Windsor Castle, but retained the Tower of London's formal status as a 'Royal Palace'.

1509~10: Henry VIII kept a token garrison of 12 Yeomen of the Guard who wore scarlet royal livery, but they had 'no ceremonial state functions'; so

~1510–47: They forfeited the right to wear the scarlet royal livery and changed their title to Tower Warders, and had no uniforms.

The Tower of London Warders have variously been called:

Yeomen Warders ~8,

Yeomen of the Guard 12, who then became the

Tower Warders in ~A.D. 1510;

Ordinary Yeomen, 150; and

Extraordinary Yeomen, 300 ... so

~ 470 Tower of London warders.

These are very similar, but distinct from the:

'Yeomen Warders of Her Majesty's Royal Palace and Fortress the Tower of London';

popularly misnamed "Beefeaters".

This allows for enough confusion to fake an execution and extract a Noble out of Tower Green and Tower of London, even taking the Noble up to the Queen's House to watch their own execution on Tower Green.

By 1540, Tower of London staff were proficient at faking Royal Executions for a fee, and 4 years after Queen Anne Boleyn's 'execution' the Queen's House was built.

This signals Queen Anne Boleyn's escape had been successful, and any future Queen executed could watched her own execution from the Queen's House. This was repeated in the Nuremberg Trials for Hitler's Financial Secretary Martin Bormann.

Henry VIII's 5th wife, Catherine Howard (20) was ordered 'executed', "scheduled for 7:00 am on Monday 13 February 1542"[1] ... These "Arrangements for the execution were supervised by Sir John Gage (1479–1556) in his role as Constable of the Tower."[2]

1542, 13 February: However, the sun rose at 7 a.m., so it was still dark, the location was on the west side of the tall White Tower, so completely shaded, the chance of fog was 'almost certain', with no flood lights, and it was the first thing on a Winter's Monday morning, so the chance of a crowd was purposefully minimised to no one saw it ... which is all the circumstances required for 'Catherine Howard was never executed in the Tower of London or elsewhere'.

1536–42: During the period of the Tower of London 'executions' of Henry VIII's wives, Queen Anne Boleyn & Queen consort Catherine Howard, the Tower Warders did not wear uniforms of any kind or description ~1510–47.

This provided less security, easy infiltration, and was an opportunity for extraction with a dead commoner brought in dressed & beheaded, and the live Noble swished out.

150 Ordinary Yeomen were employed full-time & 300 Extraordinary Yeomen were called up on occasions. An 'execution' was an 'occasion'. A 'be-heading' was an 'occasion'.

A Noble execution allowed 450 non-uniformed men to occupy the Tower of London, leaving little room for the public, and plenty of room to fake the execution, which was unconvincing at close quarters.

The execution was only convincing to the uneducated general public standing behind 450 tall and broad Yeomen, who were there and wanted to see something, but omitted to state they had failed to see the advertised event, then convinced themselves they had seen an execution, merely by being present.

So rather than make 450 uniforms, it was easier to make the Queen a death dress, and an exact copy, then dress the Dead-house look-alike Commoner as the Queen, with or without a head.

What the head looked like didn't matter as the separated head never materialised, and 5 of the 7 nobles buried in St Peter as Vincula were buried without their heads, including Queen Anne Boleyn, Catherine Howard, Jane Boleyn and George Boleyn.

To avoid harassment from the public, the 300 Extraordinary Yeomen were picked up in a couple of dozen boats off both sides of the Thames, up and down stream.

1550: Extraordinary Yeoman were paid 4~6d per day, the same as a common infantryman. The Ordinary Yeomen were paid 16d per day. To keep the Tower of London guards quiet, the Extraordinary Yeomen daily wages of 4~6d were increased 4-fold to that of the Ordinary Yeomen at 16d per day. So a raise from £80=120 to £400 per day.

These 300 non-uniformed Extraordinary Yeomen were then delivered to Tower of London wharf, entering at Cradle Tower and Henry III's Watergate.

When exiting the Tower of London, after the 'occasion' of the 'execution' (of a title) and the 'be-heading' elsewhere, these 300 non-uniformed Extraordinary Yeomen plus surviving 'dead' Queen and ladies-in-waiting were returned far upstream to where the Thames meets the Isis at Windsor–Eaton (where it is no longer tidal) plus another 14 miles upstream to Bisham Abbey, owned by the Earls of Salisbury, 1344–1540.

Margaret, Countess of Salisbury had been a lady-in-waiting to Henry VIII's first wife, Catherine of Aragon (R. 1509–33) and appointed Governess of their daughter (1520–21, 1525–33) Princess Mary (1516–58) who became the Bloody Queen Mary I (R. 1533–58).

When Henry VIII declared Mary a bastard in 1533, Margaret, Countess of Salisbury asked to serve Mary at her own cost.

1512–38: The Earldom of Salisbury was restored to Margaret, Countess of Salisbury, and through shrewd management, she became the 5th richest peer in England.

1536, May: When Queen Anne Boleyn was arrested, Margaret, Countess of Salisbury was permitted to return to Court briefly, just long enough to arrange everything in favour of Queen Anne Boleyn, including faking her execution, and a posthumous stay up the Thames and into Isis, at the newly vacated Bisham Abbey on the Earl of Salisbury estates.

Margaret, Countess of Salisbury owned Bisham Abbey, and had assisted Henry VIII's first wife, and child, and was now assisting Henry VIII's second wife, Queen Anne Boleyn, post execution in the high summer of 1536.

Margaret, Countess of Salisbury owned Bisham Abbey, until she was also 'executed'; then it was transferred to Henry VIII's surviving wife, Anne of Cleves (9 July 1540–16 July 1557) who could then protect the Nobility from the four Executions on & of:
1541, 27 May: Margaret, Countess of Salisbury;
1542, 13 February: Queen Catherine Howard & Jane Boleyn; &
1554, 12 February: "Nine Days Queen" Lady Jane Grey.

Anne of Cleves brother William I of Cleves (b. 1516, r. 1539–92) was one of the richest men in Europe, known to Germans as 'Wilhelm der Reiche' ~ 'William the Rich Man'.

Taking control of the Tower of London executions was as simple as supplying the uniforms, and this is exactly what happened.

1510–47: There were no uniforms when most of the Queens and Countesses were 'executed', many of an age they could still breed. Queen Anne Boleyn was 26~35, Queen Catherine Howard was 19, Viscountess Jane Boleyn was 36, and the

'Nine Days' Queen' Jane Grey was just 17.

1547–1601: 'Tower Warders' wore scarlet royal livery.

1550: The 150 Ordinary Yeomen wore no uniforms, then velvet of any colour, or armour with a velvet coat trimmed with silver gilt.

The 300 Extraordinary Yeomen were on call, and given three weeks notice of any 'occasion', like a noble execution, and could gain easier access by wearing a small patch of velvet.

These crisis actors and extras entered the Tower of London en masse to retake the Queen alive! So whomever was in charge of the Tower uniforms was in charge of Noble Extractions, and this was "the King's Beloved Sister" Anne of Cleves, 1540–57, who extracted Margaret Pole, the former Countess of Salisbury, and Catherine Howard, Jane Boleyn and Jane Grey.

Margaret, Countess of Salisbury extracted Queen Anne Boleyn, then taught Anne of Cleves how it was done. Anne of Cleves then perfected the Noble Extractions, and came to own Anne & George Boleyn's Hever Castle.

Anne of Cleves had also been given much of Margaret, Countess of Salisbury's land, so both knew all the hiding places, and Margaret could show Anne of Cleves exactly where Queen Anne Boleyn was in hiding, and what channels to use to access her.

1547–53: When King Edward VI reigned as a 9–15-year-old, he 'restored' the Tower of London uniforms, but only for the Tower Warders and 150 Ordinary Yeomen in 1550.

1500–1837: The 300 Extraordinary Yeomen remained without uniforms, at best wearing a patch of velvet of any colour, until the time of tourism, 1837/49–.

1837: Beginning with Queen Victoria's reign, the Yeomen Warders backdated uniforms into history for all players, except for the 300 Extraordinary Yeomen, who were really tall and broad rent-a-crowd crisis actors, sprinkled with short thick people in between to block the rows. Their purpose was to prevent movement and block the view during the 'occasion' of 'be-heading' and 'execution' of a title was an occasion for nobody to see.

1509~10: Yeomen of the Guard are a distinct corps of Royal Bodyguards, tough guys & the oldest military corps in Britain; whereas Yeomen Warders are just warders.

1510–47: Royal Bodyguard Yeomen Guards wore no uniforms in the Tower of London during 'occasion' for executions. Tower Warders, Ordinary Yeomen, and Extraordinary Yeomen had no uniforms. Some may have worn velvet. Velvet is a fabric, not a colour. Any colour velvet could be considered 'Yeomen uniform', as were most materials, including tarp, sail-cloth, blanket, or rag.

1547–50: Tower Warders came to wear scarlet royal livery.

1550–51: 150 Ordinary Yeomen wore armour with a velvet coat trimmed with silver gilt; or wore velvet of any colour; whereas the 300 Extraordinary Yeomen on call had no uniforms.

1551: 200 Ordinary Yeomen plus 100 Archers & 100 halberdiers (spike with axe head) made 400 Ordinary Yeomen without uniforms.

1554–1601: Ordinary Yeomen still wore armour with a velvet coat of any colour trimmed with silver gilt; but for Tudor state visits & ceremonial occasion, they wore red with gold trim. Tower Warders still wore scarlet royal livery.

1700s–1813: During this period of "The Invention of Tradition" uniforms became more 'uniform' with 40 Yeomen on daily duty and 20 Yeomen on night duty.

1813~37: Yeomen on daily duty were reduced to one division of 16–150 men. This allowed for easier obfuscation, and less ability to answer questions about the recent invention of traditions.[3]

1837–1901: From Queen Victoria's reign, the steam locomotive & tourism, Yeomen Warders began conducting guided tours in blue with red trim, and Tower Warders in red with gold trim, advertising the tradition Queen Victoria had just invented.

These uniforms were then backdated into history as being more uniform, with the required verbal confusion where words mean the opposite anywhere else:

Yeoman Warder everyday 'undress' uniforms became dark blue with red trim.

Yeoman Warder and Tower Warder 'dress' became red with gold trim for Tudor State visits (1485–1603) and ceremonial occasions. Queen Victoria 'invented' some of the Tudor style, which was then backdated, with minor variations.

Queen Victoria was quite the artist and used to make her own porcelain dolls.

1837~1955: "Yeomen Warders of Her Majesty's Royal Palace and Fortress the Tower of London, and Members of the Sovereign's Body Guard of the Yeoman Guard Extraordinary" ~ popularly misnamed "Beefeaters" ~ became ceremonial guardians of the Tower of London, in principle, responsible for looking after any prisoners in the Tower, and safeguarding the British Crown Jewels.

1868–1967: Yeomen Warders of the Tower of London were responsible for protecting the Crown Jewels, held on the upper floor of the Wakefield Tower, being the King's apartments, built in 1220.

1963–66: Flashing eyelids and a brash sense of entitlement was the biggest threat to the security of the British Crown Jewels. Princess Margaret twinkled past the Yeomen Warders and seconded the British Crown Jewels, using them for aristocratic orgies, wearing the Crown, holding the Orb & beating the Sceptre on the floor when she ordered her participants to change ends.

1963: An assistant curator was then appointed.

1968: Yeomen Warders were replaced with a new independent body of wardens, and
senior wardens; and a
second assistant curator employed to watch the
first assistant curator; and the
live-in Resident Governor also became the Keeper of the Jewel House watched by the more responsible Deputy Governor ...
in case any of these fell under the spell of Princess Margaret's fluttering eyelids ...

1963: The same man who stripped Elizabeth of all her real style and titles, Pope Paul VI, then ensured Popes were no longer allowed a crown or coronation, and most of the Papal Triple Crowns were sent away overseas. At the same time ...

1963~95: Princess Margaret seconded the British Crown Jewels for her orgies, and the Crown Jewels the public saw were fake. The orgies were real, the jewels are fake.

1990: An Executive Agency of Government invented a new organisation to wipe out this colourful history using MI5 at Kew, and formed 'Historic Royal Palaces' and 'took responsibility for everything'.

2002, 9 February: With the ceasing of the fluttering eyelids, announced by the death of the midget cocaine addict threesome slapper Princess Margaret ~ who was fun, but sour ~ the main threat to the Tower of London British Crown Jewel improved security no longer existed, and after 39 years orchestrating aristocratic orgies, the Crown Jewels may have been returned ... from 1995 or 2002.

The chances are that what tourists saw in the Waterloo Block of the Tower of London from 1963~2002 was a papier-mâché copy, the basis for Esty and rap-porn videos.

This is how the British Crowns lost their sparkle.

The Ceremony of the Keys

If required, one could infiltrate the Tower of London Ceremony of the Keys just as simply as imitating an Extraordinary Yeomen's uniform, 1510–1837 ... there weren't any. Swishing bodies has been going on for centuries, and it is not uncommon. Since the time of Jesus, swishing Princes, Kings and Nobles out of executions has been more common practice than not. It's the Bible that tells you how to do it, and the Monarchs who got the Priests to interpret it.

The Ceremony of the Keys is a ceremony of a Tower of London official walking a Queen 'who has survived their execution' out of the gate at 10 p.m. so they could catch a boat on the Thames, and head to the noble refugee camp, up the Thames into Isis and Bisham Abbey ... as per the eye witness Account of the Ceremony of the Keys in 2018 ... with distances added by The Principal.

"Every night for about 700 [490] years, Yeoman Warders (popularly misnamed 'Beefeaters') have performed a gate-closing ritual known as the 'Ceremony of the Keys' at the Tower of London. It lasts 8 minutes, from 9:52 to 10:00 p.m.

I.   "At exactly 9.52 p.m. the Chief Yeoman Warder of the Tower comes out of the Byward Tower dressed in red, carrying a candle lantern in one hand and the Queen's Keys in the other hand.

II.   "He walks 75 metres east to Traitors' Gate to meet members of the duty regiment Foot Guards who escort him throughout the ceremony.

III. "One soldier takes the lantern and they walk in step 15 metres south to the outer gate. All guards and sentries on duty salute the Queen's Keys as they pass.

IV.   "Warder locks the outer gate [at 9:54 p.m.] and walks back 140 metres west to lock the Middle Tower oak gates [at 9:54 p.m.]; then walks back 40m east to the Byward Tower.

V.   "They then return along Water Lane 80 metres east to Wakefield Tower, where the Crown Jewels were kept, 1868–1967. In deep shadows of the archway of (Raleigh's) Bloody Tower a sentry waits & watches 11 metres north.

VI.   "As the Chief Warder and escort approaches, the Sentry's challenge rings out:
'Halt! Who comes there?'
Chief Warder: 'The Keys.'
Sentry: 'Whose Keys?'
Chief Warder: 'Queen Elizabeth's Keys.'
Sentry: 'Pass Queen Elizabeth's Keys. All's well.'

VII. "All four men walk to the Bloody Tower archway and up towards the Broadwalk steps, 45 metres north, where the main Guard is drawn up.

VIII. "The Chief Yeoman Warder and escort halt at the foot of the steps and the officer in charge gives the command to the Guard and escort to present arms.

IX. "The Chief Yeoman Warder moves two paces forward (north) and raises his Tudor bonnet high in the air and calls 'God preserve Queen Elizabeth'.

The guard answers 'Amen' exactly as the clock chimes 10 p.m.; and

'The Duty Drummer' sounds The Last Post on his bugle.

X. "The Chief Yeoman Warder takes the keys on an 80 metre dogleg, ending up 44 metres ssw back at the half-timbered Queen's House. The Guard is then dismissed.

'Every night 21.52–22.00, the Chief Yeoman Warder of the Tower walks 411 metres, accompanied by duty regiment Foot Guards for 336 metres – each advertising the role they would play in extracting a Noble out of the Tower for a bribe, which was then £5 or a dozen new velvet uniforms.

'The Ceremony of the Keys is a walk-the-walk and talk-the-talk of Noble Extractions ... out of the Traitors' Gate to the Thames at 9:54 p.m. and lock it afterwards; or out of Middle Tower at 9:57 p.m. and lock it afterwards, then lock the Monarch inside the Queen's House as she watched helplessly, locked in on so many levels, as the 150 Ordinary Yeomen assist the 300 non-uniformed Extraordinary Yeomen evacuate the 'executed' Queens and nobles onto two-dozen boats on the Thames ... travelling past Windsor and up the Isis to Bisham Abbey, to arrive the following day 'at one' on 'The Island'.

The Monarch is helplessly locked in on so many levels of royal history.

In this case, the Ceremony of the Keys actually celebrates that the British Royal family are illegitimate, and that the last (but one) English Queen escaped the Tower of London, and her execution by 'beheading' upstream, and the execution of her title 'Marquis of Penbroke' to start the Holy Grael lineage ... almost completed when The Principal wrote this and got the Coronation Stone, and visited the Tower of London in the most intense rain/reign.

This is the untold story of English Royalty.

Henry VIII was still using the Tower of London as a Royal Palace.

Queen Anne Boleyn entered through a private entrance in the Byward Tower Court Gate then was escorted along Water Lane, to the Innermost Ward where she spent 2–19 May 1536 (17 days) in her former Coronation lodgings – apartments attached to the central White Tower.

Most prisoners passed under London Bridge heading ESE on the River Thames, under St. Thomas's Tower and through the Traitors' Gate.

Later, Walter Raleigh lived in the Bloody Tower with the wheelhouse that controlled the land Gate behind the watery Traitor's Gate of the Tower of London.

The prisoners then entered into a pool where an engine raised water to the White Tower roof using the force of the tide.

Tower of London has always been a Royal Palace."

Endnotes

1   1991: Alison Weir, 'The Six Wives of Henry VIII', Grove Press, p. 481.

2   2002: David Potter, "Sir John Gage, Tudor Courtier and Soldier (1479–1556)", English Historical Review, 117 (474): 1109–46, p. 1129.

3   1984: Editors Eric Hobsbawm & Terence Ranger, 'The Invention of Tradition, Past and Present Publications'.

Chapter Twenty-Two – St Peter ad Vincula Chapel
is full of un-Royal moving Body-Doubles

The original Tower of London parish chapel was destroyed by fire in 1512, then rebuilt in the ecclesiastical Tudor style in a slightly different location as St Peter ad Vincula.

The Secretary to Her Majesty's Privy Purse had an exact plan of where all the bodies lay, prior to the 1876–77 restoration.

1876–77: St Peter ad Vincula was restored to mark Victoria being rescued with the title Empress of India. Queen Victoria had been without major title for 7 years, 1869–76, as she had passed the title Sovereign of the United Kingdom of Great Britain and All Ireland, to her firstborn son, born 7½ years before Prince Bertie.

After a grave robbery, it is common to find the earth or floor at a different level. Straight after a robbery, if the floor tiles are level, then they are going to sink later.

August–October 1876: After 340 years, the Surveyor noted the paving stones on the floor of St Peter ad Vincula had sunk in two places, where the graves had been robbed of Queen Anne Boleyn and Catherine Howard, probably many times. It was never actually their remains, and their heads were never attached or nearby their bodies

Records show the Tudor queens Anne Boleyn and Catherine Howard, as well as Lady Jane Grey, Jane Boleyn, and George Boleyn were 5 of the 7 buried in the Chancel.

Sir Thomas More was executed in 1535. As some kind of Tower Warders sick joke, the Tower of London quotes Sir Thomas Mores, who doesn't appear to exist, yet talks from 1876:

"So the pews were removed and the paving stones lifted over Queen Anne Boleyn to find the resting places ... had been repeatedly and ... universally desecrated."

At just 2-foot deep, a heap of disordered female bones were found "not lying in their original order", as though they had been dropped there, out of a bag, when grave-robbers stole the arrow bag and expensive damask ermine hammerhead cape and shook the bones loose.

Royal Historians gave the excuse coffins were broken up to make way for a new coffin beside it, but the coffins weren't packed that tight.

1535–1945: Royalty, and those with a pedigree, were notorious for having grave-robbers on their payroll swishing bodies at night, after they had faked their death, or stealing a more noble body and using it as their own, or for Shakespearean plays.

1821–40–61: Napoleon's body was stolen three times, so his body-double was stolen twice, and that was by the Duke of Wellington, who buried him nearby in the Horse Guards 2¼ miles west of the Tower of London. Wellington, a 4'11" midget, would pace around Napoleon's dead body double talking to it.

It would be perfect for Tower of London staff to be the grave-robbers for the Royal family, trying to cover their tracks that Queen Anne Boleyn had escaped Henry VIII's madness with her real titles Queen of England & Marquess of Pembroke intact.

Queen Anne Boleyn was able to create an entirely new Royal Family, right down to Joseph Gregory Hallett, who has the most important Royal Marks to prove it.

The Restoration team, Royal Historians, and Royal Surgeon who inspected the bodies, formed a complicity, and agreed to use the language of cognitive dissonance and unresolved ambiguity, to cover that all the Royal and Noble bodies found in St Peter ad Vincula were:

i.   Did not conform to their age;

ii.   Did not conform to their height;

iii. Did not conform to their facial description; and or

iv.   Were not present at all; and the

v.   Graves appeared to have been robbed several times over; with

vi.   Queen Anne Boleyn's proposed remains in a complete mess, the bones not even in the order of a skeleton.

With so many Royal failures covered up & obfuscated, the language of cognitive dissonance and unresolved ambiguity has become the language of the British Flat Lie Royal family.

Sir James Mouat VC CB (1815–99) was the Inspector General of Hospitals 1865–28 April 1876, known as 'Surgeon General' and was then appointed an honorary surgeon to Queen Victoria in 1888, and made a Knight Commander of the Order of the Bath in 1894. He was fully aware that there are no existing portraits of Anne Boleyn, but plenty of fakes.

Royal Surgeon Sir James Mouat's description of the body of 'Anne Boleyn' even differed from his own previous description of 'Anne Boleyn'. These were ambiguous and full of lies, as though one described a portrait, the other the bones, and neither were a match.

Mouat: "the bones belonged to a female, 25–35, with a slender delicate frame of perfect proportions, and small forehead and lower jaw especially well formed. The vertebrae were particularly small, especially the atlas joint next to the skull" ... versus ... "The bones ... a female in the prime of life, all perfectly consolidated and symmetrical, and belong to the same person. The bones of the head indicate a well-formed round skull, with an intellectual forehead, straight orbital ridge, large eyes, oval face and rather square full chin. The remains of the vertebrae, and the bones of the lower limbs, indicate a well-formed woman of middle height, with a short and slender neck. The ribs show depth and roundness of chest. The hands and feet bones indicate delicate and well-shaped hands and feet, with tapering fingers and a narrow foot."

"slender delicate frame of perfect proportions"
versus "ribs show depth and roundness of chest"

"small forehead" versus
"a well-formed round skull, with an intellectual forehead";

"lower jaw especially well formed"
versus "rather square full chin";

"vertebrae were particularly small,
especially the atlas joint next to the skull"
versus "vertebrae ... indicate a well-formed woman ...
with a short and slender neck".

In both descriptions, Surgeon General Mouat fails to state the head was separated from the body ... and there was no head.

It is Sir Thomas Mores who mentions it is just a heap of jumbled bones.[1]

Surgeon General Mouat was an expert at cognitive dissonance and unresolved ambiguity – proficient in complicit outrageous lies. Mouat was not an expert in medicine, but a Victorian Antiquarian Guess-worker:

'If it sounds good, I could bill them for it and get an elevation'.

The 340-year-old remains of 'Anne Boleyn's headless body double were an ambiguous heap of bones in the wrong location, leading to centuries of unresolved ambiguity and cognitive dissonance that only a 'Royal Expert' could manufacture.

Surgeon General Sir James Mouat VC CB was a paid liar of dubious medical expertise.

The remains of Catherine Howard (d. 13 February 1542) were not found at all. The excuse they used was "young bones are softer and more cartilaginous and so disintegrate more rapidly, and the use of lime in her interment", but she was 18 & lime preserves bones.

Jane Boleyn, Viscountess Rochford (d. 13 February 1542) 'died' with Catherine Howard. Catherine Howard's body is missing, so Jane Boleyn's body isn't there either.

Lady Jane Grey 'died' on 12 February 1554, yet there is no mention of her body here.

Bones of George Boleyn, 2nd Viscount Rochford (d. 17 May 1536) were not found at all. The excuse was George Boleyn's remains were removed in the late 1700s, or the Victorian restoration team didn't find him because they didn't raise the entire floor and look everywhere, so anyone missing was justifiably unaccounted for.

The Victorians knew George & other bodies were never original, so grave-robbers body-snatched & swished towards unresolved ambiguity and cognitive dissonance to cover the fact that:

'No aristocrat was buried in the in the Chancel of the St Peter ad Vincula, but there were wrong bodies in nearby places'.

"In 1877, Doyne C Bell cites Secretary to Her Majesty's Privy Purse and member of the committee undertaking the restorations of the chapel, 'consulted various historical authorities' and drew up his plan of Anne Boleyn and others in the chancel."

The location for a female body at Anne Boleyn's grave site was accurate to the position, but not accurate to Queen Anne Boleyn.

For instance, the head had not been severed from the body, instead, all the bones were in a jumble, as though tipped out of an arrow bag.

Similarly, bones belonging to a 35–40 year old female were found in the grave where Catherine Howard (19) and Lady Rochford (36) were buried, meaning Catherine Howard's remains were stolen, or never there, and never killed.

And now for another proliferation of ambiguity to bring about more cognitive dissonance:
The seven sets of bones found ... buried in the chancel, including (i) Anne Boleyn, (ii) Catherine Howard, (iii) Lady Rochford, Jane Boleyn and (iv) George Boleyn, 2nd Viscount Rochford, and (v) Lady Jane Grey ...

> 'were identified, placed in the respective positions in the chancel where the remains had been found, re-interred in separate, labelled boxes, all buried about four inches below the chancel floor, the earth filled in, and concrete immediately spread over them. Memorial marble tiles with their names and armorial bearings were set on top'

... versus ...

"soldered up in thick leaden coffers, and then fastened down with copper screws in boxes made of oak plank, one inch in thickness. Each box bore a leaden escutcheon, on which was engraved the name of the person whose supposed remains were thus enclosed, together with the dates of death, and of the year (1877) of the re-interment."

> If Queen Anne Boleyn wasn't in her supposed 1536 grave, even after natural death, and her bones were not in order, and had been grave-robbed, perhaps several times over, and were not a certifiable set of single identity bones .... and many other graves in the Chancel of the St Peter ad Vincula in the Tower of London were in the same category ... then Queen Anne Boleyn escaped Henry VIII's madness, escaped her execution, and at just 28–35 years old, began a new Royal Family – the Holy Grael lineage, with Sir Walter Raleigh as her heir, and Joseph Gregory Hallett as the predicted heir of both of their prophecies.

After this was published and several interviews were done, The Principal Joseph Gregory Hallett returned to the Tower of London and St Peter ad Vincula on St Bruno's Day, 6 October 2023 ...

Queen Anne Boleyn's grave marker now had her name missing. When I asked the guide he said:

"Anne Boleyn's grave has been moved further back towards the far wall of the Chancellery. It is marked with a white orchid."

The white orchid symbolises humility and purity, victory over death, and a son like the sun for 'Christ', and "God is pleased with Joseph".[2]

Endnotes

1   1877: 'Notices of the Historic Persons Buried in the Chapel of St Peter ad Vincula in the Tower of London, With an Account of the Discovery of the Supposed Remains of Anne Boleyn', by Doyne C Bell, 30 pages; cited in

1898: Lord 'Macaulay's History of England, volume I', pp. 628–9, Longmans Green and Co, London; and

"Camelot International: Britain's Heritage and History". www. camelotintl.com. reign of Queen Victoria, and Anne's grave is now identified on the marble floor, www.theanneboleynfiles.com/ anne-boleyns-remains-the-exhumation-of-anne-boleyn.

2   1996: Hans Biedermann, 'The Wordsworth Dictionary of Symbolism', "Flower", p. 135.

Bibliography

Imitation of Christ

~1500: William Atkynson, 'De imitatione Christi', 'Imitatio Christi: Of the imitation of Christ', Books I–III, held in the library of Trinity college, Dublin, and University library, Cambridge.

~1500: Lady Margaret, Countess of Richmond and Derby, mother of King Henry VII, Book IV, held in the British museum.

1884: Margaret Beaufort, John K. Ingram & William Atkinson 'Imitatio Christi: Of the Imitation of Christ', 4 Volumes, D. Appleton & Co.; Philadelphia, George S. Appleton, New York.

1893: Margaret Beaufort, John K. Ingram & William Atkinson 'Imitatio Christi: Of the imitation of Christ', printed for Early English text society, London by K. Paul, Trench, Trübner & co.

Hall's Chronicle

1548, 1550: The Vnion of the Two Noble Illustre Famelies of LANCASTRE & YORKE, being the long in Continual Discension for the Croune of this Noble Realme, with all the Actes done in bothe the Tymes of the Princes, Bothe of the One Linage and of the Other, Beginnyng at the Tyme of Kyng Henry the Fowerth, the First Aucthor of this Deuision, and so Successiuely Proceadyng to the Reigne of the High and Prudent Prince Kyng Henry the Eight, the Vudubitate Flower and very Heire of both the sayd Linages' ... its title changed in ...

1809: 'Hall's Chronicle; containing The History of England, during The Reign of Henry the Fourth, and the succeeding Monarchs, to the end of the Reign of Henry the Eighth, in which are particularly described the manners and customs of those periods. Carefully collated with the editions of 1548 and 1550, London: Printed for J. Johnson; F.C. and J. Rivington; T. Payne; Wilkie and Robinson; Longman, Hurst, Rees and Orme; Cadell and Davies; and J. Mawman; London.

It is cited as "Hall's Chronicle" or "Hall's Chronicle, 1548 & 1809".

1531–32: THE. XXIII. YERE OF KYNG HENRY THE. VIII., p. 785;

1532–33: THE. XXIIII. YERE OF KYNG HENRY THE. VIII., pp. 789, 794–95;

1533–34: THE. XXV. YERE OF KYNG HENRY THE. VIII., pp. 805–06;

1536–37: THE. XXVIII. YERE OF KYNG HENRY THE. VIII., p. 819.

2011, 1 June: Tudor chronicler Edward Hall wrote an account of Anne Boleyn's coronation, edited by Susan Doran in Catalogue, 'Man & Monarch Henry VIII', Exhibition guest curated by David Starkey, British Library, p. 151.

The Maner of the Tryumphe of Caleys and Culleyn/Bulleyn, Cum Priuilegio' with privileges ...

1532: 1st Edition: The Maner of the Tryumphe of Caleys and Culleyn, Cum Priuilegio'.

"Culleyn" is changed to "Bulleyn".

1533: 2nd Edition: 'The Maner of the Tryumphe of Caleys and Bulleyn and the Noble Tryumphant Coronacyon of Quene Anne, Wyfe unto the Most Noble Kynge Henry VIII', printed by Wynkyn de Worde, 1532–33, p. 12.

1533–40: The Lisle Papers, Arthur Plantagenet, 1st Viscount Lisle (1480–1542) Lord Deputy of Calais, uncle of King Henry VIII; and the correspondence of several servants, courtiers, royal officials, friends, children and other relatives. These were available as 'Letters and Papers of Henry VIII'.

1884: 'The Maner of the Tryumphe of Caleys and Culleyn, Cum Priuilegio', edited by Edmund Goldsmid F.R.H.S., F.S.A. (Scot), privately Printed in Edinburgh, as 'The Maner of the Tryumphe of Caleys and Culleyn, Cum Priuilegio'.

Authors & Book

39 b.c: Publius Vergilius Maro, 'Eclogues and Aeneid', Vol 1–6.

1220, 6 Feb. or March: Jacques de Vitry, Letter.

1223~25: Jacques de Vitry, Historia orientalis, cap. XXII.

1228: Tommaso da Celano, Vita prima §57. Tolan 2009 quotes translated in English, pp. 19 & 54.

1661: Gerald O'Collins, Edward G. Farrugia, 'A Concise Dictionary of Theology', 2000, p. 115.

1849: Nicolaus Cabasilas, 'The life in Christ', translated from the Greek 'Περὶ τῆς ἐν Χριστῷ ζωῆς' by Carmino J. Decatanzaro, copious introduction by W. Gass in 1849; a new edition by M. Heinze in 1899; 1974; and then by St. Vladimir's Seminary Press in 1997, p. 129.

1867: Cardinal Manning, Bonaventure, 'The Life of St. Francis of Assisi', 'Legenda Sancti Francisci', p. 178; 1988 edition, TAN Books & Publishers, Rockford, Illinois.

1877: Doyne C Bell, 'Notices of the Historic Persons Buried in the Chapel of St Peter ad Vincula in the Tower of London, With an Account of the Discovery of the Supposed Remains of Anne Boleyn', 30 pages.

1895: Editor Lt.Col. J.L. Vivian, 'The Visitations of the County of Devon: Comprising the Heralds' Visitations of 1531, 1564 & 1620', Exeter, p.162.

1889: Lord Macaulay, History of England, Vol. I', Longmans, Green & Co, pp. 628–9, citing Doyne C Bell, 1877.

1906: W A Shaw. The Knights of England, Vol. I, Sherratt and Hughes, p. 150.

1957: L. Du Garde Peach, 'Sir Walter Raleigh, A Ladybird Book, An Adventure from History', Illustrations by John Kenney, published by Wills & Hepworth Ltd, Loughborough, England.

1962: Hester Chapman, 'Lady Jane Grey', p. 169; Macmillan, 1972; Grafton/ Collins, 1985.

1969: Leslie Hotson, 'Shakespeare Versus Shallow', Haskell House Publishers, New York, NY.

1972: Marie Louise Bruce, 'The rise and fall of Anne Boleyn'; 'The challenge of Anne Boleyn'; 'Anne Boleyn', publ. Coward, McCann & Geoghegan, 1973, p. 333. Geoghegan is known for manufacturing evidence and mixing fact & fiction.

1972: Robert Lacey, 'The Life and Times of Henry VIII', p. 70.

1973: Marie Louise Bruce, 'Anne Boleyn', p. 333.

1973: Ignazio Silone, 'Bread and Wine', novel.

1974: Hester W. Chapman, 'The challenge of Anne Boleyn', publ. Coward, McCann & Geoghegan.

1975: David Crane, "English Translations of the Imitatio Christi in the Sixteenth and Seventeenth Centuries", Recusant History, 13 (2), pp. 79–100.

1981–83: Editor Muriel St. Clare Byrne, 'The Lisle Letters', 6 volumes. Byrne copied, transcribed, annotated and edited, producing a convincing non-original, which University of Chicago Press then abridged & published on 1 August 1983 as 'The Lisle Letters – Abridged'.

1981: Pauline Gregg, King Charles I, Dent, London, p. 445.

1983: Alan Richardson & John Bowden, The Westminster Dictionary of Christian Theology, pp. 285–86.

1984: Editors Eric Hobsbawm & Terence Ranger, 'The Invention of Tradition, Past and Present Publications', Cambridge University Press.

1986–2016: David Starkey, the "rudest man in Britain" wrote 8 books on Henry VIII.

1990: Arthur J. Slavin, The History Teacher, Vol. 23, No. 4, August 1990, pp. 405–31, Society for History Education.

1991: G. R. Elton: On Reformation and Revolution, p. 142, citing Arthur J. Slavin in 1990.

1991: Retha Warnicke, 'The Rise & Fall of Anne Boleyn: Family Politics at the Court of Henry VIII',

Cambridge University Press.

1991: Alison Weir, 'The Six Wives of Henry VIII', Grove Press, New York, p. 481.

1992: Antonia Fraser, 'The Wives of Henry VIII', Knopf, New York, p. 133.

1998: Michael Robson, 'St Francis of Assisi: The Legend and the Life', p. 104.

1999: Graham Edwards, The Last Days of Charles I, Sutton Publishing, Stroud, pp. 173, 183, 188–89.

1999: Ed. Laurence Keen, 'Studies in the Early History of Shaftesbury Abbey', published by Dorset County Council, Dorchester.

1999: Alister E. McGrath, 'Christian spirituality: an introduction', pp. 84–87.

1999: Maria Perry, 'The Word of a Prince: A Life of Elizabeth I from Contemporary Documents', Boydell Press.

2000: Retha M. Warnicke, 'The Marrying of Anne of Cleves: Royal Protocol in Early Modern England', Cambridge University Press, Cambridge, p. 252.

2004: Phyllis G. Jestice, 'Holy People of the World: a Cross-Cultural Encyclopedia', Vol. 3, pp. 393–94.

2004: Margaret Ruth Miles, 'The Word made Flesh: a History of Christian Thought', pp. 160–61.

2004: Patrick Riley, 'Character and Conversion in Autobiography: Augustine, Montaigne, Descartes, Rousseau, and Sartre', p. 43.

2005: Geoffrey Robertson, 'The Tyrannicide Brief', Chatto & Windus, London, pp. 201, 333.

2006: David Loades, 'Elizabeth I: A Life', Continuum International Publishing Group.

2007: Richard A. Burridge, 'Imitating Jesus: an inclusive approach to New Testament ethics', pp. 142–45.

2007: Orlando O. Espín, James B. Nickoloff, 'An Introductory Dictionary of Theology and Religious Studies', p. 609.

2008: David C. Alexander, 'Augustine's Early Theology of the Church; Emergence and Implications', p. 218.

2010: Elizabeth Norton, 'Anne of Cleves: Henry VIII's Discarded Bride', Amberley, Stroud, p. 108.

2011: Elizabeth Norton, 'Anne Boleyn, In Her Own Words & the Words of Those Who Knew Her', AbeBooks.co.uk.

2014: Joseph Gregory Hallett and Francisco Manoel, 'The Hidden King of England – Arma Christi – Unveiling the Rose', pp. 385, 1056.

2018: Nicola Clark, 'Gender, Family, and Politics: The Howard Women, 1485–1558', Oxford University Press, Oxford, p. 145.

2019: Heather Darsie, 'Anna, Duchess of Cleves: The King's Beloved Sister', Amberley Publ., pp. 17–20.

Artists & Paintings

1539: Hans Holbein, 3rd Duke of Norfolk Thomas Howard.

1884: Henry William Brewer (1836–1903) etched Westminster Old Palace in the time of Henry VIII, as an informed reconstruction, published in 'The Builder' magazine.

British History Online, Calendar of State Papers

1533, 29 May, Thursday: Anne Boleyn; 25 Hen. VIII. Add. MS. 6,113.

1533, 31 May: MS. L. f. 1. Coll. of Arms. 563. Queen Anne Boleyn, p. 6. of an early copy.

1533, 31 May: R. MS. 18, A. LXIV. B. M. 564. Queen Anne Boleyn. Versis and dities made at the coronation of Quene Anne, Latin and English, p. 29.

1533, 1–5 June: Vesp. C. XIV. 124. B. M. 583. Coronation Of Anne Boleyn, Henry VIII, pp. 262–75, www.british-history.ac.uk/ letters-papers-hen8/vol6/pp. 262–275.

1533, June: Harl. MS. 543, f. 119. B. M. 4, 'The noble tryumphant coronacyon of quene Anne, wyfe unto the most noble kynge Henry the VIII', printed by Wynkyn de Worde, for John Gough, p. 12.

P. R. O. 602. Queen Anne Boleyn.

Summa Theologica 2.2.186.5; 3.65.2.

Henry VIII: June 1533, 6–10, in Letters and Papers, Foreign and Domestic, Henry VIII, Volume 6, 1533, Editor James Gairdner, London, 1882, pp. 275–84.

www.british-history.ac.uk/letters-papers-hen8/vol6/pp275-284.

Harl. MS. 543, f. 119. B. M. 4, 'The noble tryumphant coronacyon of quene Anne, wyfe unto the most noble kynge Henry the VIII', printed by Wynkyn de Worde, for John Gough, p. 12.

Page: Notes and Queries – Series 11 – Volume 12.djvu/389, n s. xii. NOV. is, 1915, Notes and Queries, 381, en.wikisource.org/wiki/ Page:Notes_and_Queries_-_Series_11_-_Volume_12.djvu/389.

1910–98, G. E. Cokayne, The Complete Peerage of England, Scotland, Ireland, Great Britain

Volume V, App. H. "Marquis" ~ "Marchioness" ~ "Marchionissa Penbrochiæ, nunc vero Regina".

Volume 10, n.s., p.406, note f.

Statement of Claim of Joseph Gregory Hallett leading to Proclamations from 9 July 2020

2019, 1/17 Nov.: Joseph Gregory Hallett declares Patent Ambiguity QEII's Royal Style and Titles.

2019, 31 December: Joseph Gregory Hallett declares Queen Anne Boleyn's Royal Lineage OTH / 19 / 54733, pp. 1–2, 9, 28–31, 34, 42, 67: Addendum One, Smerwick – lands in Ireland, p. 34; Queen Elizabeth and Raleigh chat up a storm, p. 42.

2020, 26 January: Statement of Claim in support of Joseph Gregory Hallett declares the Mashiach–Christ–Messiah is the King of England OTH / 20 / 57374:

Addendum Eight ... Christ confirms his Birthplace by marking the next Birthplace, p. 33;

Addendum Twelve ... Definitions from the Bible, p. 69.

2020, 5 March: Confirmation of Joseph Gregory Hallett's Declaration of Queen Anne Boleyn's Royal Lineage, OTH / 20 / 64528, pp. 27–28, point xx, 5 March 2020.

2020, 5 March: Confirmation of Joseph Gregory Hallett's Declaration of Mashiach–Christ–Messiah is the King of England OTH / 20 / 64535.

2020, 31 March: Certified Declaration of Queen Anne Boleyn's Royal Lineage in Joseph Gregory Hallett, OTH / 20 / 70901.

2020, 31 March: Certified Declaration of Queen Anne Boleyn's Royal Lineage in Joseph Gregory Hallett, SRA3, OTH / 20 / 70907.

2020, 31 March: Certified Declaration Joseph Gregory Hallett is the Mashiach–Christ–Messiah & King of England OTH / 20 / 70911 & OTH / 20 / 70915 (SRA3).

These Statements of Claim, Confirmations, Declarations and Proclamations have all been accepted by Queen Elizabeth II, Prince Philip, British Royal family, head of Freemasonry, Archbishop of Canterbury, Prime Minister of UK, Prime Minister of Israel, President of Russia and President of the United States.

Television
2022, 13 January: BBC News, Prince Andrew's titles.

Newspapers
1983: Ed. Elizabeth Devine, The Annual Obituary – Muriel St Clare Byrne, St James Press, pp. 573–75.

2018, 23 July: Ian Cobain, The Guardian, 'Subversive civil servants secretly blacklisted under Thatcher', Prime Minister 1979–90.

The Encyclopædia Britannica, A Dictionary of Arts, Sciences, Literature and General Information
1910–11: Editor Hugh Chisholm, Eleventh Edition, Volume VIII, 21, Cambridge University Press:
"Pembroke, Earls of", pp. 78–80;
"Eucharist".

Catholic encyclopedia & Church Archives: "Imitation of Christ"; Eucharist, citing Luke 22:20.;
2021, 21 May: "The Church and Town of Sir Walter Raleigh", United Diocese of Cork, Cloyne and Ross.

Oxford English Dictionary, OED
"Incontynent" is 'To prove to be valid or true; to demonstrate the truth, to substantiate a charge, to enforce one's assertion by combat, or to inflict blows for the cause'.

Oxford Dictionary of National Biography, ODNB
1986: R. S. Thomas, "Jasper Tudor, Jasper of Hatfield, Duke of Bedford", Oxford Dictionary of National Biography; Ed. Ralph A. Griffiths & James Sherborwe, 'Kings and Nobles in the Later Middle Ages', St. Martin's Press, New York, p. 19.

The English Historical Review
2002: David Potter, "Sir John Gage, Tudor Courtier and Soldier (1479–1556)", 117 (474): 1109–46, 2002, p. 1129.

The History of Parliament: the House of Commons 1509–1558

1982: J. Pound, 'Thomas Rush (1487–1537) of Sudbourne, Suffolk, in Editor S.T. Bindoff, from Boydell and Brewer.

Reference

2009, October: Roland H. Hui, The Tudor Society. Martin Spies supplied original coronation text. "This page is old! We are a Museum & an unsorted Archive. www.oocities.org/coronation_book/1.htm.

2012: 'The Norton Anthology of English Literature: Sixteenth/Early Seventeenth Century, Volume B', p. 661.

1996: Hans Biedermann, 'The Wordsworth Dictionary of Symbolism', "Flower", p. 135.

Web & Wikipedia

1386: The worlds oldest surviving working clock at Salisbury Cathedral, Wiltshire.

1521–37: Lord John Hussey, Chief Butler of England.

1533:'Countess of Kent' was a mystery name

1983–89: Blackadder, BBC One, a pseudo-historical sitcom series.

2011: kimberlyevemusings.blogspot.com/2011/06/coronation-of-anne-boleyn-1-june-1533.html.

10/06/2017 Vila Giralda, Estoril, Portugal, Gtres News.

2017, 14 November: The Anne Boleyn Files, '14 November 1532 – Did they or didn't they?'

Early English Sonnets, www.sonnets.org/early.htm.

www.theanneboleynfiles.com/14-november-1532-didnt/, 2017.

www.theanneboleynfiles.com/anne-boleyns-remains-the-exhumation-of-anne-boleyn.

www.camelotintl.com, "Camelot International: Britain's Heritage and History".

www.camelotintl.com, reign of Queen Victoria, Anne's grave now identified on marble floor.

'The history of the county palatine and city of Chester', Vol. III, p. 51. "Brereton and Holt of Brereton"; Family Group Sheet, Notes for Sir Ranulphus I De Brereton, sites.rootsweb.com/~mwgrogan/data/nti18422.html.

Masonicdictionary.com.

www.mi5.gov.uk, "MI5 At The National Archives | MI5 – The Security Service".

'The real history of the Pearly Kings and Queens', Roman Road London, Megan Agnew, 11 August 2020, romanroadlondon.com/history-pearly-kings-queens/.

www.tudorplace.com.ar/Bios/AnthonyDenny(Sir).htm.

The Shakespearean Sonnet, shakespeare-navigators.com/romeo/Sonnet.html.

Anne Boleyn; Durham House; Marquis of Pembroke; Raleigh; Volta (dance) with Clive Owen as Raleigh, Abbie Cornish as Bess, and Cate Blanchett as Elizabeth I.

Lady Frances Brandon (1517–59).

"Caparisoned" is a horse in rich decorative coverings.

"Cope" is a long cloak, worn over a long white linen robe (alb) or white gown with wide sleeves (surplice) worn over an ankle-length garment with close-fitting waist and sleeves (cassock).

"Courser" is a swift or spirited horse.

Château Culleyn, Our Lady Church in Culleyn / Bulleyn.

Château de Chantilly has a straight garden road extending 1 & 3 miles either side, 25 miles north of Paris, and is immersed in a 10 acre flooded moat.

Comfits or Comfettes: Dried fruits, nuts, seeds or spices coated, sugared almonds.

'Countess of Kent' may be held by a female in her own right.

Edward II of England.

Edward Courtenay, 1st Earl of Devon (1527–18 September 1556+).

Eucharist, citing Luke 22:20.

Robert Fitzwalter.

Adrian Gilbert was alchemy lab assistant & 'great favourite' of Mary, Countess of Pembroke.

Henry Grey KB (16) 1st Duke of Suffolk, 3rd Marquess of Dorset (1517–54).

Lady Jane Grey (1537–54) the 'Nine Days' Queen'.

Henry VI of England.

Lord John Hussey ~ Husey ~ Hussie ~ Hosey ~ Huse (1465/6–29 June 1537).

Hypocras ~ Ypocras: Wine mixed with sugar, spices, cinnamon, heated ~ mulled wine.

Countess of Kent.

Marques of Dorset.

Marquess of Pembroke.

Oliver Cromwell, The Protectorate, 1653–58.

Dean of Salisbury.

"Surcoat" is a loose sleeveless outer robe of rich material worn as part of the insignia of an order of knighthood.

Tower Green.

Peter Vannes (c.1495–1563) Ambassador to the Republic of Venice (August 1550–September 1556).

Joseph Gregory Hallett's Website is:
kingjohnthethird.uk/

For Prophecies fulfilled:
kingjohnthethird.uk/videos/documentaries/

Joseph Gregory Hallett's Lawful Documents can be found here at:
kingjohnthethird.uk/lawful-documents/documents/

The Author's ebooks are available at:
kingjohnthethird.uk/product-category/ebooks/
Note: The print books are more up to date.

Joseph Gregory Hallett's videos can be found at:
www.youtube.com/@KingofUK/videos

Support the Author through the Patreon Community:
https://www.patreon.com/gregandcarrie

Joseph Gregory Hallett can be contacted
through his website or Youtube

Joseph Gregory Hallett has published 25 books
with seven translated into German and seven into Japanese.
Here is the 'British Frauds on England's History' series:

Queen Anne Boleyn's Great Escape and Legacy

Queen Anne Boleyn's grandson Sir Walter Raleigh ~ William
Shakespeare ~ Marquess of Pembroke ~ Prince King of England

Queen Anne Boleyn's Two Grandsons
Sir Walter Raleigh versus Francis Bacon

Queen Elizabeth gives Walter Raleigh America Forever
The "Lost Colony" was a Super Capable Military Force

Alligator versus Crocodile – How they Colonised North America

King James "the Shit" by the Dozen – The Golden Clown

Magna Carta Frauds King John didn't know

Magna Carta Frauds of the 1600s

Magna Carta Frauds of the 1700s

Magna Carta Frauds – King John's Concession to the Pope, Charter
of Liberties & Magna Carta Explained & Disclaimed

Bayeux Tapestry ~ The Big Lie ~ Not 1066 but 1719~27

Bayeux Tapestry ~ Patterns of The Big Lie

How to Become the Pope and Own the World

Made in United States
Troutdale, OR
02/23/2024

17929125R00206